Astonishing
Century

ᴊATE DUE

HH

A Rapid Reference Guide To the
Events and People We Remember.
Perfect for Creating
Your Personal Memoirs
or Family History.

ASTONISHING CENTURY

Edited by
Robert D. Joyce

Hawthorne House
Santa Ana, California

Hawthorne House books are published by
Pygmalion Press
1509C S. Raitt Street
Santa Ana, California 92704
(714) 545-5435
(800) 44WRITE
HAWTHORNEH@aol.com

Kate Hawthorne, Hank Hawthorne,
Irene English and William "Bill" Goodpage,
of the Hawthorne House "Staff,"
are fictitious, but represent the fine qualities
of professional family history preservationists
world-wide.

Any similarity to you or anyone you know,
is intended as a compliment but is
still purely coincidental.

Robert D. Joyce
September 1999

Cover design and the
Hawthorne House "staff" members
were created by artist

Michael Diebner
Garden Grove, California

Kate Hawthorne

"A big hello and welcome to our latest Hawthorne House publication, *Astonishing Century*. With so much material available on the 20th Century, why, *Astonishing Century*?

"One look inside tells the story. *Astonishing Century* is incredibly easy to use as a reference source. Each year jumps out at you on facing pages so there's no fumbling around with continuing information. Each year is subdivided into logical and comprehensive categories of information with most entries needing no more than one line—truly a rapid reference guide to the century.

"This format will have broad appeal to busy teachers, students and journalists and just about anyone who has an interest in 20th Century history—people who need a concise piece of information, right now!

"Astonishing Century will also be particularly valuable for people who are writing or taping their personal memoirs or doing histories of their families. It is a series of snapshots on what was happening and when—both the big world and national picture as well as the trivial everyday happenings that also affected our lives.

"Our book is not designed to teach history but rather for us 'ordinary folks' to recall, understand, interpret and appreciate the last hundred years as they impacted us as individuals, our families, friends and our community.

"But, I'm getting ahead of myself. I started and operate a small company called Hawthorne House, which assists people in preserving and publishing their stories for their friends, children and grandchildren. My coworkers are three wonderful professionals who will introduce this book and we will be your guides through the hundred years that are the subject of this *Astonishing Century*.

"I'm Kate. My background is in journalism; free lance magazine writing, specializing in family and home issues. In 1992 I sensed a growing interest in personal and family preservation, started Hawthorne House, and have been active in this exciting new field since that time. Our staff also includes my husband, Henry 'Hank' Hawthorne, Irene English and William 'Bill' Goodpage.

"Let me introduce them to you."

"Henry "Hank" Hawthorne

"This is my 'hubby,' Hank Hawthorne. We've been married a whole bunch of years and raised three children who are now off on their own.

"Hank is an engineer by training and spent most of his career as a Project Manager for several large aerospace companies. As Hawthorne House began to prosper, Hank agreed to join our staff as the business manager and marketing director."

Irene "Miss Picky" English

"Irene is a former teacher in the local community college system with an emphasis in history and literature. What a delight it was when she agreed to join our small group!

"She is our resident editor and proofreader who organizes manuscripts and makes the text so readable. Irene also has an uncanny sense of how to get the grammar and punctuation straight—which has led to her nickname of **Miss Picky**. We tease her about perfection but simply don't know how we'd manage without her."

William "Bill" Goodpage

"Bill Goodpage is our wonderful production manager. He's primarily responsible for taking finished manuscripts and converting them into beautiful family heritage books.

"Bill brings to us many years of experience in the graphic arts and printing fields. He is also a master bookbinder and has taught this unique craft in both university and industry workshop settings.

"His personal interest in and knowledge of 20th Century history, is also invaluable."

Ways You Can Use This Book

Adding Specific Facts or Details to Your Story

Say you got married in 1950 and are writing about what was happening in your life at the time. You check out that year for information about the Korean Conflict as that event loomed so strongly in your life at the time.

Adding Incidentals You'd Otherwise Forget

You have written about several events that happened to you in 1953. Before you finish, you flip open to 1953 and find that Joseph Stalin has died, Chevy has introduced the Corvette, and *Playboy* began publication. You decide to add information about the Corvette, because you were so excited about the car even though you couldn't afford it.

Bill Goodpage

As a Memory Jogger

Your husband was in service and you were working at a defense plant in 1944. Other than worrying about him, your life seemed rather boring. In fact, you're having trouble remembering much of what happened to you at the time. You check out 1944 and find that *I'll Walk Alone* and *Long Ago and Far Away* were popular songs. You begin to hum them and, suddenly, the memories begin to crowd your mind…"Oh yes, I remember."

To Better Sense the Mood of the Times

Astonishing Century attempts to capture the mood of the public in any particular year. **LIFESTYLE** tells you what we were thinking or doing. **INCIDENTALS AND TRIVIA** reminds you of the little stuff that seemed like such a big deal at the time, and **COMMENTARY** offers snapshots of contemporary life.

Just for Fun

Read through any series of years that hold particular interest for you or your family, and just enjoy the fun of "reliving" those good and not-so-good old days. From the very outset we have tried to make *Astonishing Century* the most enjoyable history book available—with touches of humor and whimsy sprinkled here and there among the more serious events. We certainly hope you agree.

Editorial Choices and Decisions

What We Chose to Include

We have included world and national events where they impacted the public. Some science and business was also included. However, we chose to place our emphasis on the simpler aspects of life like popular songs, the price of a quart of milk, and the latest fad.

What We Chose to Omit

A particular legislative tariff or immigration bill may have had significant impact on the nation as a whole, but it was omitted if it had little day-to-day relevance. Most political posturing was also omitted, unless it led to major events such as Prohibition or War. These have been very difficult editorial choices that will not satisfy everyone.

Hank Hawthorne

Irene Answers Some Frequently Asked Questions

Why haven't you included the scores of World Series and All Star Games? Or other major sporting events?

We seriously considered it, but soon found that SPORTS was overpowering other categories, simply because there are so many, each with special events.

I notice that movie stars in many cases are mentioned more frequently than other people who may have made a greater contribution to society. Your reasoning?

Our focus is on personal and family history rather than the great moments of history. People often remember their own lives more through movies, radio, and television than they do through many other historical events.

Do you feel that you have presented a fair and balanced view of the century?

"Miss Picky"

Irene English

Probably not. Our primary market is people who are preserving personal and family histories so we have included much ordinary life information that would be considered trivial for a traditional history book.

Clarification

A century consists of 100 consecutive calendar years. The 1st Century was years 1-100. The 20th Century consisted of the years 1901-2000.

The third millennium dawns on January 1, 2001. The reason is that since there was no year zero, every century begins with a 1. Most of us, no doubt, will celebrate the coming of the new century a year early.

Astonishing Century uses 1900-1999.

Possible Errors

We have been very diligent in cross referencing all major events to verify accuracy. Some data we found, particularly numbers, varied even from supposedly reliable sources. Names of places and people sometimes also had different spellings. We used numbers that were most generally agreed upon and spelled names the way most people remember them.
In the end, some errors are inevitable in a book of this type. We hope they are minimal.

This book is dedicated to
my father,

Robert James Joyce,

a 20th Century man
whose life was far too short.

Oh, how he would be astonished
if he could turn the pages of this book
with me today.

Special thanks to
Marge Malone
who so patiently and diligently
edited, corrected and refined the text

The
Astonishing Adventure
Begins Here

1900 *As the New Age Opens*

WORLD

The Boer War Continues in South Africa
V. I. Lenin Returns to Russia from a Three Year Siberian Exile
Troops Free Civilians Trapped in Beijing During the Boxer Rebellion

NATION

William McKinley Defeats William Jennings Bryan for President.
US Population Now 76 Million (40% Urban, 60% Rural) Per Capita National Debt is $16.60 ·
Hawaii Organized as a US Territory. American Samoa Acquired
The Gold Dollar Established as a Monetary Standard

ENVIRONMENT, SAFETY AND HEALTH

Native American Population Down to One Million. Only 30 Head of Bison Remain Alive
Contaminated Milk Is Still a Major Source of Food-Borne Diseases
Tuberculosis Is the Leading Disease Cause of Death
One Farmer Now Produces Food for Seven People
Less Than 150 Miles of US Roads Are Hard Surfaced

DISASTER

Galveston, Texas, Hurricane Kills 7,000; Worst Natural US Disaster
Bubonic Plague Epidemic Spread by Rats Strikes Honolulu. Fire Burns Most of the City

LIFESTYLE

Life Expectancy in US Now 47 Years. 4.1% Are over 65 Years (see 1999)
Workers Earn $2.50 to $10.00 Per Week. Working Women Mostly Farm Hands or Domestics
8,000 Automobiles Are Registered Throughout the Country. Trolleys Are Common
One Home in Thirteen Has a Telephone; One in Seven Has a Bathtub

SCIENCE AND TECHNOLOGY

Yellow Fever Virus Is Proved to Be Carried by a Mosquito.
Rayon, First Called Artificial Silk, Appears
Diesel Power Begins to Replace Steam for Tugboats
The US Navy Acquires Its First Submarine

BUSINESS AND INDUSTRY

Firestone Tire & Rubber Company Is Formed in Akron, Ohio
F.W. Woolworth Stores Adopt Bright Red Storefronts with Gold Lettering

CONSUMER PRODUCTS AND SERVICES

Hills Bros. Packs Ground Roast Coffee in Vacuum Tins
Kodak- Sells an Easy-to-Use Brownie Box Camera
Franklin, Auburn and Packard Motor Cars Are Introduced
Uneeda Biscuits Are the Top Seller (10 Million Packages Per Month)
Hershey Milk Chocolate Bar Goes on Sale
Infant Cereal Pablum Sold Through Doctor Recommendation
Wesson Oil (Pure Cottonseed Oil) Now Available
Campbell's Pork & Beans Are Marketed

America Is Mostly Rural

PRICES

Sugar	$ .04 per pound
Eggs	.14 per dozen
Butter	.25 per pound
Lean Beef	.07 per pound
Brownie Box Camera	$1.00

SPORTS

First International Auto Race (Paris to Lyons). Winner Averages 38 mph
Second Modern Olympic Games Are Held in Paris
Charles Comiskey Brings His Chicago White Sox into the American League
Baseball Cards Given Away with Cigarette Packs
Dribbling Starts in Basketball
Baseball Now Uses a Five Sided Home Plate

ARTS AND MEDIA

STAGE	*Fiddle-dee-dee*	
	Tosca	Giacomo Puccini
BOOK	*The Interpretation of Dreams*	Sigmund Freud
	The Tale of Peter Rabbit	Beatrix Potter
	Lord Jim	Joseph Conrad
	The Great Boer War	Conan Doyle (Knighted in 1902)
	Sister Carrie	Theodore Dreiser

MUSIC

The Cakewalk is a Ballroom Craze—First Black Influenced Social Dance
The Mandolin and Banjo Are Popular Instruments

Finlandia	Jean Sibelius	*A Bird in a Gilded Cage*
Rosie, You Are My Posie		*Good-Bye Dolly Gray*

PEOPLE

Ferdinand von Zeppelin Launches the First Rigid Airship
Carrie Nation, Anti-Saloon Crusader, Raids and Marches with a Hatchet
Gregor Mendel's Genetic Laws (1865) Finally Receive Broad Acceptance
Orville and Wilbur Wright Test a Glider at Kittyhawk, North Carolina
President McKinley Is the First US President to Ride in a Car
Theodore Roosevelt Has Little to Do as Vice President Elect

QUOTES

"Everything that can be invented has been invented."
Charles H. Duell, Commissioner of Patents, 1899

INCIDENTALS AND TRIVIA

The Ground Beef Hamburger Is Born in New Haven, Connecticut
Dueling Is Now Almost Universally Prohibited by Law
William McKinley Is the Last Civil War Veteran to be Elected President

1901 *A New Century Begins*

WORLD

The Boxer Rebellion Ends. China to Pay Indemnities to World Powers
The Boer War Continues in South Africa
The Commonwealth of Australia Is Formed
Queen Victoria Dies at 81. She Ruled England for 64 Years
First Nobel Prizes Awarded from Fund Established by Alfred B. Nobel
Armed Revolt Against the US Is Crushed in the Philippines.
The Platt Amendment Makes Cuba a US Protectorate

NATION

Alabama Adopts Literacy Tests That Greatly Disenfranchise Blacks
US Obtains Sole Rights to Build a Trans-Isthmian Canal
President McKinley Is Shot at Pan American Exposition on September 6
McKinley Dies on September 14 from Infected Wounds. Roosevelt (42) Becomes President
The Secret Service Is Assigned to Protect Roosevelt and Future Presidents
Rural Free Delivery of Mail Now Serves 185,000 (see 1924)
The US Army Nurse Corps and US Army Dental Corps Are Established

ENVIRONMENT, SAFETY AND HEALTH

The Critical Importance of Not Mixing Blood Types in Transfusions Is Uncovered.
Incompatible Blood Groups A, B, and O Are Discovered

LIFESTYLE

5.7 Million Live on US Farms or 42% of Population (see 1970, 1980)
Nine Million Immigrants Will Enter the US During This Decade
New York City Streetcars and Elevators Converted to Electric Power
Life Expectancy: White Males 48.2 Years, White Females 51.1 Years
Illiteracy in US Is Down to a Low of 10.7%

SCIENCE AND TECHNOLOGY

Obesity and Heart Disease Are Observed to Have a Strong Correlation
Mosquito Controls Rid Havana of Yellow Fever
Guglielmo Marconi Receives the First Transatlantic Wireless Message
Chromosomes Believed to Carry Building Blocks of Heredity
Adrenaline Is Isolated
White Blood Cells Are Shown to Fight Disease

BUSINESS AND INDUSTRY

Nordstrom's Retail Chain Starts as a Seattle Shoe Store
Johns Manville Company Founded. It Will Import Canadian Asbestos
United States Steel Co. Is Created by Financier, J.P. Morgan

CONSUMER PRODUCTS AND SERVICES

The Multigraph Machine Prints from a Typed or Handwritten Image
The First Soluble Instant Coffee Is Demonstrated
King C. Gillette Starts a Safety Razor Company
A Philadelphia Department Store Installs an Escalator
The Electric Typewriter Appears

A New President Takes the Helm   1901

PRICES

Women's Shoes	$ 1.50 per pair
Men's Shoes	2.50 per pair
Men's Pajamas	1.45
Women's skirt (tailored)	4.95
Men's Suit	16.00

SPORTS

Baseball's American League Is Founded.
The Foul Ball Is Now a Strike in Baseball's National League (except after two)
Boxing Becomes Legal in England
Connie Mack Is Named Manager of the Philadelphia Athletics.

ARTS AND MEDIA

STAGE

The Three Sisters	Anton Chekhov
The Wizard of Oz	Lyman Frank Baum
If I Were King	Justin McCarthy

BOOK

Up From Slavery	Booker T. Washington
Mrs. Wiggs of the Cabbage Patch	Alice Hegan Race
Kim	Rudyard Kipling
Monsieur Beaucaire	Booth Tarkington

MUSIC

I Love You Truly
Mighty Lak' A Rose
Boola Boola

PEOPLE

W. C. Roentgen Receives Nobel Prize in Physics for X-Ray Discovery
Artist Pablo Picasso Begins Painting his Blue Period Style
Who Is Richer, J.P. Morgan or Andrew Carnegie? Who Knows? Carnegie Earns
    $23 Million This Year with No Income Tax. He Sells Carnegie Steel to Morgan and
    Will Give Away 350 Million Dollars. (see 1909,1999)
Theodore Roosevelt Dines with Black Educator, Booker T. Washington, and the Following
    Uproar Shows the Prevalence of Racism

QUOTES

"Speak softly, but carry a big stick."
Theodore Roosevelt

INCIDENTALS AND TRIVIA

Mercedes Motorcar Named for Daughter of Distributor Who Buys Entire First Year Run of
    36 Cars on Condition of Naming the Vehicle.
US Library of Congress Prints its Catalog Entries in a Standardized Format on Small Cards
    and Distributes Them to Libraries.
Theodore Roosevelt, at 42, Is the Youngest US President (see 1960)
The Year 1901 Is the First Official Year of the Twentieth Century

1902 *Marie Curie Discovers Radium*

WORLD

Cuba Declares Its Independence from Spain. US Troops Withdraw
Boers Accept British Sovereignty in South Africa as War Ends
Thousands of Russians Die in Riots Against the Czarist Government
France's Panama Canal Company Offers to Sell Its Interests to the US
Australia Gives Women the Right to Vote (New Zealand First in 1893)

NATION

Roosevelt Declares the Philippine Insurrection to Be Over
Philippine Island Inhabitants Are Declared Territorial Citizens
Roosevelt Institutes Antitrust Action Against Many US Corporations
The Isthmian Canal Commission Recommends the Panama Route
The Census Bureau Is Established
Oregon Experiments with "Progressive" Politics (Women's Suffrage, Minimum Wage),
        Opening Government to Common People
Oliver Wendell Holmes Named Associate Justice of the Supreme Court
Months Long Miners' Strike Finally Brings About Reforms After Roosevelt Has the Army
        Run the Mines in the Public Interest.

ENVIRONMENT, SAFETY AND HEALTH

Reclamation Act Allows US Government to Set Aside Park Land. Roosevelt Will Add
        150 Million Acres to the Government Reserve
Congress Creates Crater Lake National Park in Oregon
Malnutrition, Causing Hookworm Disease, Is Serious in the Southern US

LIFESTYLE

The First Theater Designed for the Exclusive Showing of Movies, Opens in Los Angeles
Selected Population Figures:

New York City	3.4 Million
Chicago	1.7 Million
Los Angeles	103,000
Houston	45,000
Dallas	43,000

SCIENCE AND TECHNOLOGY

Rayon Is Patented by US Chemist A.D. Little
A Non-Caustic Antiseptic Helps Prevent Blindness in Newborn Infants
The Triangular "Flatiron Building" is New York's First Skyscraper
Marie Curie Discovers Radium
Synthetic Gemstones Are Produced in France
The Name Hormone (Rouse to Activity) Is Coined

BUSINESS AND INDUSTRY

The Dayton Company (department store) Is Founded in Minneapolis
The American Automobile Association (AAA) Debuts
Luxury Trains, Broadway Limited & 20th Century Limited Compete
Cyrus McCormick Jr. Founds the International Harvester Company
James D. Dole Creates the Hawaiian Pineapple Company
Merchant James Cash Penney Opens His First Store in Wyoming

White House Gets Indoor Plumbing 1902

CONSUMER PRODUCTS AND SERVICES

The Spark Plug Is Invented
The Brassiere Is Invented by a French Fashion Designer (see 1913)
Willis Haviland Carrier Develops the Air Conditioner
Phillip Morris Cigarettes Are Marketed
Pepsi Cola Company Is Founded by a North Carolina Pharmacist
Binney & Smith Company Markets Crayola Brand Crayons
The Teddy Bear (Named for the President) Is an Instant Success

SPORTS

Barney Oldfield Covers 5 mi. in 5 min., 20 sec. in a Henry Ford Racer
John J. McGraw Becomes Manager of the New York Giants

ARTS AND MEDIA

STAGE
Twirly Whirly — Lillian Russell
The Girls of Vienna — Franz Lehar
The Wild Rose — Eddie Foy
Mrs. Warren's Profession — George Bernard Shaw

MOVIE
A Trip to the Moon (short) — Georges Melies
A Trip to Mars (short) — Thomas Edison

BOOK
The Tailor of Glouster — Beatrix Potter
The Hound of the Baskervilles — Sir Arthur Conan Doyle
The Wings of the Dove — Henry James
The Story of My Life — Helen Keller
To Build a Fire — Jack London
Heart of Darkness — Joseph Conrad
The Virginian — Owen Wister

MUSIC

Symphony #2 Jean Sibelius
Symphony #3 Gustav Mahler
In the Good Old Summertime
Bill Bailey, Won't You Please Come Home?

In the Sweet Bye and Bye
On a Sunday Afternoon
Tell Me Pretty Maiden

PEOPLE

Enrico Caruso Makes His First Phonograph Recordings
Sheriff Bat Masterson Retires to Become a New York Sportswriter
Cecil John Rhodes Establishes the Rhodes Scholarships
Albert Einstein Secures a Position in the Swiss Patent Office
Frederick Remington Completes a Bronze Statue Titled, *Comin' Through the Rye*
Ida Tarbell Writes an Expose of the Oil Monopoly: *The History of Standard Oil Company*

INCIDENTALS AND TRIVIA

Buster Brown Comic Strip Appears
The First "Automat" Restaurant Opens in Philadelphia
Harry Burt Jr., Inventor of the Good Humor Bar, Makes Automobile Deliveries of Ice Cream
The White House Gets Indoor Plumbing

1903 Two Brothers Prove Manned Flight

WORLD

Czar Nicholas II Offers Domestic Reforms But Resentment Mounts in Russia
Panama Declares Its Independence From Colombia
Panama Canal Treaty Signed. US Recognizes the Independent Panama
V.I. Lenin & Bolshevik Extremists Split from Moderates at London Meeting
Turks Kill Thousands of Bulgarians in Continuing Balkan Turmoil

NATION

US Department of Commerce and Labor Is Established
Congress Centralizes the Military; Creates General Staff of the Army
Wisconsin Becomes the First State to Adopt Direct Primary Elections
US Supreme Court Declares Federal Police Power Greater Than States.
Massachusetts Is the First State to Issue Automobile License Plates

ENVIRONMENT, SAFETY AND HEALTH

Roosevelt Creates the Fish and Wildlife Reserve System
Food Handler Mary Mallon (Typhoid Mary), Is Linked to New York Epidemic
602 Die in Rush to Exits in Chicago's Iroquois Theater Fire (Will Speed Code Reforms)
Conventional Wisdom Says the Auto Is Too Small and Unreliable to Replace a Horse

LIFESTYLE

Not everything in this 'modern' age was wonderful as one historian notes:

"...working people were tied to long hours of work at inadequate wages; farmers knew many more bad years than good; only a few women escaped the daily drudgery of domestic work or exploitation on the job; whites demanded institutionalized deference from the blacks. Even some of the successful could not survey the scene without a shudder."

Richard C. Wade (Almanac of American History)

SCIENCE AND TECHNOLOGY

X-rays Found to Inhibit Cancerous Growths
Typhus Found to Be Transmitted Only by the Bite of a Body Louse
The Pacific Cable Links San Francisco with Manila
A Message Is Relayed Around the World in 12 Minutes
Marconi Sends a Wireless Greeting from Roosevelt to King Edward VII of England
Growing Use of Electricity Has Created a Shortage of Copper Wire
Wright Brothers First Gasoline Powered Manned Flight (59 sec.) at Kittyhawk, North Carolina

BUSINESS AND INDUSTRY

Buick Motor Car Company and the Ford Motor Company Are Incorporated
The Texas Company (Texaco) Brings in its First Well in Sour Lake
New Canning Methods by Van Kamp Will Make Tuna a Staple Rather Than a Delicacy
The 15 Story Wannamaker Department Store in New York Covers a Square City Block

CONSUMER PRODUCTS AND SERVICES

Sanka Coffee Introduced
Harley Davidson Markets Its First Production Model Motorcycle
Margarine, Formed By Hardening Vegetable Oils, Is a Low-Cost Substitute for Butter
Marijuana Is Used as a Pleasure Inducing Drug

But Will the Auto Ever "Fly"?   1903

SPORTS

New York Giants' Pitcher Christy Matheson Wins 30 Games
A Packard Automobile, First to Cross America (San Francisco-New York), Takes 52 Days
Ransom E. Olds Drives a Measured Mile in 1 Minute, 6 Seconds

ARTS AND MEDIA

STAGE	*Babes in Toyland*	Victor Herbert
	Man and Superman	George Bernard Shaw
MOVIE	*The Great Train Robbery*	(First Film to Tell a Story)
BOOK	*The Souls of Black Folk*	W.E.B. Du Bois
	The Call of the Wild	Jack London
	The Ambassadors	Henry James
	Typhoon	Joseph Conrad
	The Land of Little Rain	Mary Austin

MUSIC

Ida, Sweet as Apple Cider
Dear Old Girl
Sweet Adeline
Waltzing Matilda

PEOPLE

John Barrymore (21) Makes His Stage Debut; Siblings Lionel and Ethel Are Established Actors
Joseph Pulitzer Endows Fund for Various Prizes or Scholarships
John D. Rockefeller Contributes $7 Million to Fight Tuberculosis

QUOTES

"Between lovers a little confession is a dangerous thing."
Helen Rowland, *Reflections of a Bachelor Girl,* 1903

COMMENTARY

"Two self educated American brothers, bicycle builders by trade, Orville and Wilbur Wright, stunned the world and flabbergasted the experts by making four short heavier-than-air flights in an airplane of their own design and construction in December 1903. The experts had said it couldn't be done but the Wrights, like other visionaries of the time, believed that anything was possible.

"The Wrights went on to found a new industry in which they remained designers, builders and promoters. This was truly going to be an exciting century and the airplane would change civilization in ways no one could possibly imagine that December."

Kate Hawthorne

1904 Small Nations Have Passed Away

WORLD

Japan and Russia Clash over Claims to Korea and the Russo-Japanese War Begins.
Revolts Continue in Russia for Civil Liberties to Be Granted
Traditional Enemies, Britain and France, Ally to Hinder Germany's Imperialistic Ambitions

NATION

Theodore Roosevelt Wins Reelection, Defeating Democrat Alton B. Parker
Roosevelt Corollary to the Monroe Doctrine: US Can Intervene in Affairs of Western Nations
Eugene V. Debs of Indiana Is Again the Socialist Candidate for President
The Prohibition Party Offers Candidates for President and Vice President
Big Brothers Inc., Is Formed in New York
The National Tuberculosis Association Is Formed to Promote Research
Roosevelt Establishes Himself as a "Trustbuster"
Chicago's Million Dollar Orchestra Hall Opens: Designed by Architect Daniel Burnham

ENVIRONMENT, SAFETY AND HEALTH

The *Ladies' Home Journal* Launches an Expose on the Patent Medicine Business
National Child Labor Committee Now Protects Children From Harsh Working Conditions

DISASTER

Fire Destroys 75 Blocks of Downtown Baltimore
Fire on Hudson River Excursion Boat, S.S. General Slocum, Kills 1,030

LIFESTYLE

Immigrants to US Now Exceed One Million Per Year
Women's Hemlines "Sweep the Street" and Dresses Have Layers of Undergarments

SCIENCE AND TECHNOLOGY

Electron Radio Tube (John Ambrose Fleming) Allows for Transmission of Speech and Music
Scientist, Ivan Pavlov, Receives Nobel Prize for His Work on Conditioned Reflexes in Dogs
Rudolf Diesel's Engine Is Demonstrated at the St. Louis Fair
The First Section of the Subway System Is Completed in New York

BUSINESS AND INDUSTRY

Charles Stewart Rolls and Engineer Henry Royce Team Up to Create Rolls-Royce
The American Tobacco Company Is Formed Through Mergers
Bethlehem Steel Corporation Is Founded in New Jersey
Steamship Companies Cut Steerage Rates for Atlantic Crossing to Ten Dollars.

CONSUMER PRODUCTS AND SERVICES

Montgomery Ward and Sears Roebuck & Company Are Now Actively Pushing Catalog Sales
Tea Bags Are Introduced
George F. French Develops a Milder, Creamy Mustard
Postum Company Brings Out Post Toasties Corn Flakes
Columbia Introduces Flat Records, Playable on Both Sides
The Maxwell Motor Car Quickly Gains in Popularity
The Gillette Razor Blade Is Patented and Sales Soar

The Day of Empires Has Come

SPORTS

St. Louis: First Olympic Games Held in the United States
Denton T. "Cy" Young Pitches the First Perfect Baseball Game
The Reigning Heavyweight Champ Is James J. Jeffries

ARTS AND MEDIA

STAGE

The Cherry Orchard	Anton Chekhov
The Napoleon of Notting Hill	G.K. Chesterton
Sunday	Ethyl Barrymore
Mrs. Wiggs of the Cabbage Patch	Anne Crawford Flexner
Little Johnny Jones	George M. Cohan
Peter Pan (London)	J.M. Barrie

BOOK

The Shame of the Cities	Lincoln Steffens
The Golden Bowl	Henry James
The Crossing	Winston Churchill
The Deliverance	Ellen Glasgow
Cabbages and Kings	O. Henry
The Sea Wolf	Jack London
Poverty	Robert Hunter

MUSIC

Madame Butterfly	G. Puccini
Symphony #5	Gustav Mahler
Give My Regards To Broadway	

Yankee Doodle Boy
Frankie and Johnnie

PEOPLE

Dancer Isadora Duncan Receives Rave Reviews by Critics on Russian Tour
Blind and Deaf Helen Keller Graduates Magna Cum Laude from Radcliff
Rube Goldberg Begins His Career as a Cartoonist
William C. Gorgas Is Sent to Panama to Eliminate the Dreaded Yellow Fever

QUOTES

"The day of small nations has long passed away. The day of empires has come."
Joseph Chamberlain, British Politician 1904

COMMENTARY

"Funny how traditions start. On December 31, 1904, the New York Times moved to its new 25 story headquarters at the corner of 42nd and Broadway, renamed Times Square. To celebrate, there were festivities and fireworks in the evening. The tradition continued and New Year's Eve and the gigantic Times Square celebrations have become as much of an American tradition as Fourth of July picnics and parades."

Hank Hawthorne

1905 *The Oldsmobile Is Merry*

WORLD

Sun Yat-Sen Founds the Reform Movement in China to Overthrow the Manchu Dynasty
In Ireland, Sinn Fein, a Nationalist Political Party Is Born
Russian Troops Fire on Workers in St. Petersburg: "Bloody Sunday"
Japanese Naval Forces Defeat the Russians; a Peace Treaty Is Mediated
Norway Gains Independence from Sweden

NATION

Industrial Workers of the World (IWW) Is Founded in Chicago
First Rotary Club Is Founded
The Asiatic Exclusion League Seeks to Stop Japanese Immigration

ENVIRONMENT, SAFETY AND HEALTH

The US Forest Service Is Founded
The National Audubon Society Is Founded
Oil Strike in Oklahoma Near Tulsey Town (Tulsa)
Colorado River Water Diverted by California Forms the Salton Sea
The Population Density of Some New York Slums Exceed That of Bombay
Yellow Fever Epidemic Grips New Orleans and Results in 400 Deaths

LIFESTYLE

Brooklyn's Coney Island Is the World's Premier Amusement Park
Women Are Beginning to Work in Offices, Taking Some Jobs from Men

SCIENCE AND TECHNOLOGY

Swiss Physicist, Albert Einstein (26), Formulates His Theory of Relativity
First Successful Blood Transfusion
Alfred Binet, French Psychologist, Develops First Intelligence Tests
Female XX and Male XY Chromosomes Identified
First Artificial Joint Helps Hip Movement and Relief From Arthritis Pain
Novocaine Is Synthesized and Iodine Compounds Are Used to Treat Goiter.

BUSINESS AND INDUSTRY

The Caterpillar Tractor Is Developed
US Auto Production Reaches 25,000
L.C. Smith and Brothers Sells Its First Typewriter

CONSUMER PRODUCTS AND SERVICES

Vicks VapoRub and Palmolive Soap Are Marketed
Automobiles Now Have Bumpers and Shatterproof Windows
Neon Signs Begin to Appear. Alfred Fuller Begins Selling Brushes
The Spiegel Catalog Offers Merchandise Terms of $.75 Down and $.50/Month

PRICES

One-Cylinder Cadillac Sells for $800. Most New Cars Sell for Less Than $1,400, But Are Still
Too Expensive for the Average American Family

But Who Can Afford It? 1905

SPORTS

Tyrus "Ty" Cobb Begins His 24 Year Baseball Career
Jim Jeffries Retires as the Heavyweight Boxing Champion
Greyhound Dog Racing Starts in South Dakota Using a Circular Track and Fake Rabbit
American, May G. Sutton, Is the First Foreigner to Win the Wimbledon Singles
Billiard Player, Willie Hoppe (18), Wins World Championship

ARTS AND MEDIA

STAGE
The Merry Widow — Franz Lehar
Salome — Richard Straus
The Girl of the Golden West — Giacomo Puccini
Major Barbara — George Bernard Shaw

BOOK
The Clansman — Thomas Dixon Jr. (see *Birth* 1915)
The Game — Jack London
The House of a Thousand Candles — Meredith Nicholson
The House of Mirth — Edith Wharton
Sandy — Alice Hegan Rice
Where Angels Fear to Tread — E.M. Forster
The Scarlet Pimpernel — Baroness Orczy
A Modern Utopia — H.G. Wells

MUSIC

Liebesfreud (Love's Joy) Fritz Kreisler
Clair de Lune Claude Debussey
Symphony #5 Gustav Mahler
Parade of the Wooden Soldiers

Wait Till The Sun Shines Nellie
My Gal Sal
In My Merry Oldsmobile
In the Shade of the Old Apple Tree

PEOPLE

Alfred Stiglitz' Gallery Begins to Establish Photography as an Art Form
William Edward Burghardt (W.E.B.) DuBois, Black Atlanta University Professor, Leads a Movement to Abolish All Racial Discrimination in the United States
Henri Matisse (35) and Others Pioneer Painting's Impressionism Movement

QUOTES

"Sensible and responsible women do not want to vote."
Grover Cleveland (quoted in the *Ladies Home Journal*)
"Those who cannot remember the past are condemned to repeat it."
George Santayana 1905

REFLECTION

Author Robert Hunter in His Book, **Poverty**, Has Estimated That More Than 10 Million Americans Are Underfed, Under Clothed and Poorly Housed. Working Conditions for Women and Children Are Atrocious. For Now, Politicians Remain Largely Blind to These Issues

INCIDENTALS AND TRIVIA

The Term "Nickelodeon" Means Small Theaters Specifically Designed to Show Films
Roscoe "Fatty" Arbuckle and Other Movie Stars Do Cigarette Testimonials
Britain's Scotland Yard Makes Its First Conviction with the Help of a Fingerprint File

1906 *The Panama Canal Begins*

WORLD

England Forces the Ottoman Turks to Cede the Sinai Peninsula to Egypt
US Troops Take over Cuba by Request for 13 Days to Settle Election Disputes
Zuider Zee Drainage Reclaims Much Land in the Netherlands
Construction of the Panama Canal Begins. It Is Estimated to Take Eight Years to Complete

NATION

Roosevelt Makes the First Presidential Trip Outside the US to the Canal Zone
The Federated Boys' Clubs (later Boys' Clubs of America) Is Organized
Oscar S. Straus of New York Is Appointed Secretary of Commerce and Labor, Becoming
the First Jew to Hold a Cabinet Level Position

ENVIRONMENT, SAFETY AND HEALTH

Devil's Tower in Wyoming Is Dedicated as First National Monument
Nitrogen Enriched Fertilizers Increase Crop Yields
The Pure Food and Drug Act Passes
The Meat Inspection Act Passes
Pennsylvania Railroad Announces That It Will Use Only Steel Coaches as
Wooden Ones Are Fire Hazards and Telescope in Accidents

DISASTER

Earthquake Strikes San Francisco on April 18 and Fires Sweep the City for
3 Days. 452 Killed; 25,000 Buildings Destroyed; 250,000 Left Homeless
Atlanta Is Placed Under Martial Law in Race Riots That Kill 21

SCIENCE AND TECHNOLOGY

A Successful Transatlantic Wireless Transmission Is Made from New York
to Lee De Forest in Ireland
August von Wasserman Develops a Blood Test for Syphilis
The Whooping Cough Bacterium Is Isolated
Richard Oldham Establishes the Existence of the Earth's Core

LIFESTYLE

Use of Cigars and Chewing Tobacco Is Common Among Men. Public Spitting
and Use of Cuspidors Is Considered a Right

CONSUMER PRODUCTS AND SERVICES

Light Bulbs Now Use Tungsten Filaments
The Thermos Bottle Appears
Lever Bros. Introduces Lux Flakes for Delicate Fabrics
The Jukebox Begins Service
Children's Book Series, *Bobbsey Twins* and *Hardy Boys* Are Launched
The Victrola Is Born: Horn Enclosed in the Machine and Tone Arm Is Covered by a Lid

PRICES

Sirloin Steak	$.25 per pound
Lamb, Ham, Pork	.20 per pound

San Francisco Begins Again

SPORTS

First French Grand Prix Auto Race
Football Now Uses the Forward Pass
A Stanley Steamer Sets an Incredible Auto Speed Record of 127 mph.

ARTS AND MEDIA

STAGE

Barbara's Millions	Lillian Russell
The Great Divide	Henry Miller,
Forty Five Minutes from Broadway	George M. Cohan

BOOK

The Quest of the Historical Jesus	Albert Schweitzer
The Forsythe Saga (first volume)	John Galsworthy
The Jungle	Upton Sinclair
The Gift of the Magi (short story)	William Porter (O. Henry)
The Spirit of the Border	Zane Grey
The Spoilers	Rex Beach
What Is Man?	Mark Twain

MUSIC

The King Porter Stomp
("Jelly Roll" Morton)
China Town

School Days
Anchors Aweigh

PEOPLE

President Roosevelt Receives the First Nobel Peace Prize for Helping End the Russo-Japanese War
Sarah Bernhardt's Tour of 226 Performances Grosses a Million Dollars
Ruth St. Denis Charms New York Audiences with Her Modern Dances

QUOTES

"Historian: A broad-gauge gossip."
"Saint: A dead sinner, revised and edited."
Ambrose Bierge

COMMENTARY

Kate Hawthorne

"In a effort to quell growing revolutionary threats, parliamentarian elections are held in Russia, but to little avail. The Duma now has so many members demanding social reforms, that the Czar dissolves the elected body.

"The country had earlier been eager to go to war with Japan in order to focus the people on a common enemy and to minimize the growing social and economic problems at home. The war turned out to be a disaster and intensified domestic problems to a flashpoint.

"Revolution now appears inevitable because of Russia's population mixture, the repressive and unpopular autocratic government, and the great disparity between the wealthy and the poor."

INCIDENTALS AND TRIVIA

Roosevelt Uses the Term "Muckracker," Meaning Good But Sensational, to
Describe Expose Authors Such as Ida Tarbell and Upton Sinclair

1907 *America Flexes Its Muscles*

WORLD

US Marines Land in Honduras to Protect US Lives and Property
America's Fleet of 16 Battleships Steams to Key World Ports to Demonstrate US Might
Britain, France and Russia Forget Traditional Rivalries and Form an Alliance Against
    German Expansion. The Germans Are Outraged

NATION

Oklahoma Becomes the 46th State
Mother's Day Is Proclaimed
1907 Immigration Act Allows the President to Restrict Immigration of Japanese Laborers
Corporations Are Forbidden from Contributing to National Office Election Campaigns
House Speaker, and Veep Now Earn $12,000. Senators and Congressmen Receive $7,500

ENVIRONMENT, SAFETY AND HEALTH

Christmas Seals Go on Sale to Fight Tuberculosis
Conservation: The US Forest Service Begins to Use the Word
Pellagra Is Found in Mississippi Where Corn Meal Is a Staple Food

DISASTER

Bubonic Plague Kills 1.3 Million in India
US Coal Mine Explosions Kill Hundreds

LIFESTYLE

1.29 Million Immigrants Enter the US, an All-Time High

SCIENCE AND TECHNOLOGY

The First Seaplane Is Flown
Radioactive Uranium Decay Is Used to Determine Geologic Age
Bacteria Are Suspected as Causes of Malaria and Sleeping Sickness
The Theoretical Possibility of Black Holes in Space Is Considered
Wireless Telegraphy Service Starts Between the United States and Ireland

BUSINESS AND INDUSTRY

Ringling Brothers Circus Buys the Barnum and Bailey Circus for $410,000
The DeForest Radio Telephone Company Broadcasts in New York
Cunard's Luxurious Mauretania and Lusitania Liners Begin Atlantic Service
US Automobile Production Reaches 43,000
Bell and Howell Is Founded to Improve Motion Picture Equipment
Neiman-Marcus Opens in Dallas and Bullock's in Los Angeles

CONSUMER PRODUCTS AND SERVICES

First Daily Comic Strip: *A. Mutt* (later Mutt & Jeff) by Bud Fisher
Printed Movie Film Titles Replace Theater Commentator Explanations
R.J. Reynolds Introduces Prince Albert Tobacco
Thor Washing Machine Is the First Completely Self Contained Washer
Metered Taxicabs, Imported from Paris, Appear in New York
Hershey Makes a Candy "Kiss"

PRICES

Brush Automobile	$500
Cadillac Automobile	800
Horse	200

SPORTS

Joe Tinker (shortstop), Johnny Evers (second) and Frank Chance (first) of the
Chicago Cubs Turn the Double Play into an Art Form
Walter Perry Johnson (19) Begins His Baseball Career
Cooperstown NY Is Considered to Be the Birthplace of Baseball

ARTS AND MEDIA

STAGE   *Ziegfield Follies of 1907 (the First)*   Florenz Ziegfield
              The Merry Widow   Franz Lehar
              The Talk of the Town   George M. Cohan

MOVIE   *Rescued from an Eagle's Nest*

BOOK   *The Mother (supporting revolution)*   Maxim Gorki
             Pragmatism   William James
             Heart of the West   O Henry
             Songs of a Sourdough   Robert Service
             The Secret Agent   Joseph Conrad
             What It Means to be Colored   Mary C. Terrell

MUSIC

It's Delightful To Be Married   *Glow Worm*
Dark Eyes   *On the Road to Mandalay*

PEOPLE

Florence Nightingale Receives the British Order of Merit
Maria Montessori Opens the First Daycare Center in Rome
Teenage Dancer Vaslav Nijinski Debuts in St. Petersburg
Florence Lawrence Becomes the Biograph Girl (first movie celebrity)
David Wark (D.W.) Griffith Enters the Movie Industry as an Actor/Writer
Architect Frank Lloyd Wright Designs the First of His Horizontal Line "Prairie Houses"
Annette Kellerman, Australian Swimmer, Is Arrested for Indecent Exposure
    at Boston's Sunset Beach for Wearing a One Piece Suit with No Skirt

QUOTES

"Practical politics consists in ignoring facts."
            Henry B. Adams   (1907)

INCIDENTALS AND TRIVIA

Children Generally Play on Their Own without Adult Supervision, Except for the Rich
The Terms "Radio" and "It" for Sex Appeal Are Coined
Maytag Reluctantly Enters the Washer Market as a Way to Deal with Seasonal Slumps
    in the Farm Implement Business

1908 *An Airplane Crashes*

WORLD

The Belgian Parliament Confiscates the Congo from the Personal Ownership of the King
and Makes It Property of the State
Two Cent Postage Established Between US and Britain
Transatlantic Steerage Rate from Genoa, Italy to New York Is $12.00

NATION

Roosevelt Decides Not To Run for a Second Term and Endorses Taft
William Howard Taft Defeats William Jennings Bryan for President; Ohio, Normally
Republican, Goes Democratic and Dry
Industry-Wide Boycott of Labor Is Held to be Restraint of Trade
The Federal Bureau of Investigation (FBI) Is Created
The US Navy Establishes a Nurse Corps

ENVIRONMENT, SAFETY AND HEALTH

States Can Now Establish Maximum Working Hours for Women

DISASTER

Massive Earthquake and Tidal Waves in Southern Italy, Sicily Kill 75,000
Pennsylvania Mine Explosion and Cave-In Entombs Over 100 Miners

LIFESTYLE

Huge Merry Widow Hats with Dotted Veils Are Popular with Women

SCIENCE AND TECHNOLOGY

The Gyroscopic Compass Is Developed
Silencer for Guns Is Developed
The Gas Helium Is Liquefied for the First Time
New Barium X-Ray Technique Allows Photos of Soft Body Tissue
Ammonia Is Synthesized from Nitrogen, Forming the Basis for Synthetic Fertilizers
Sunspots Believed to be a Magnetic Phenomenon
The New Geiger Counter Can Measure Levels of Radioactivity

BUSINESS AND INDUSTRY

General Motors Corporation Formed by Merger of Buick and Oldsmobile
Henry Ford Introduces the First Model T.
Wurlitzer Puts "Automated Musical Instruments" with Money Slots in Hotels and
Restaurants

CONSUMER PRODUCTS AND SERVICES

Paper Cups
Cellophane
Coffee Filters
Stereopticon Slides Illustrate Popular Songs Sung in Movie Theaters and Vaudeville Houses
Pathe News Offers the First Regular Weekly Newsreel Concept

An Automobile Takes Off 1908

PRICES

First Model T Ford Sells for $850. Price Will Later Drop (see 1924)

SPORTS

Baseball Outlaws the Spitball
Basketball Introduces the Five Foul Rule to Reduce Rough Play
US Wins 15 of 28 Track & Field Gold Medals at London Olympics
Jack Johnson Beats Tommy Burns for Heavyweight Boxing Crown, Becoming the First Black
    Boxing Champion. Many Americans Are Resentful

ARTS AND MEDIA

STAGE   *Ziegfield Follies*

MOVIE   *The Adventures of Dolly*   D.W. Griffith's First Directed Film
            The Fatal Hour

BOOK   *A Room With a View*   E.M. Forster
           Anne of the Green Gables   Lucy Maud Montgomery
           The Wind in the Willows   Kenneth Grahame
           The Trail of the Lonesome Pine John Fox Jr.
           The Circular Staircase   Mary Roberts Rinehart

MUSIC

Symphony #1   Sir Edward Elgar
The Book of the Hanging Gardens Arnold Schoenberg
Shine On Harvest Moon
Take Me Out to the Ball Game

PEOPLE

Wilbur Wright Creates a Sensation Flying an Airplane in Paris
Julia Ward Howe Is the First Female Member of the American Academy of Arts and Letters
Dancer Isadora Duncan Is a Huge Success in Her Second American Tour

QUOTES

**"There is no subject on which more dangerous nonsense is talked or thought about
than marriage."**
           George Bernard Shaw (1908)

REFLECTION

New Technology Is Never Error Free or Danger Proof. Orville Wright Loses a Propeller on a
Demonstration Flight at a Virginia Army Base. The Plane Falls 75 Feet, Badly Injuring
Wright. His Passenger, an Army Lieutenant, Is the First Aircraft Fatality. His Death Does
Not Affect the Growing Enthusiasm for Powered Flight.

INCIDENTALS AND TRIVIA

Major Stage Actors and Actresses Are in Films, But Screen Credits Are Still Rare
Thomas Edison Wants Movies Limited to One Reel Since He Believes Movie Goers Have
    Only a Ten-Minute Attention Span

1909 Taft Continues Roosevelt's Policies

WORLD

South Africa Gains Dominion Status from Britain with Boers and English Having Equal
    Rights But Not Equality for Blacks or Coloreds
Britain and Germany Are Deadlocked in a Race to Build More of the New
    Dreadnought Class Battleships

NATION

The 16th Amendment to Authorize an Income Tax Is Passed
First US Credit Union Started in New Hampshire
National Association / Advancement of Colored People (NAACP) Is Founded.
The Immigration Act Is Revised to Prohibit Criminals, Anarchists, and Diseased
    Persons from Entering the US. Some Countries Are Emptying Their Prisons
The Bureau of Mines Is Created to Improve Safety and Health Conditions
The Lincoln Penny Replaces the Indian Head Penny

ENVIRONMENT, SAFETY AND HEALTH

President Sets Aside 3 Million Acres of Public Land for Conservation

SCIENCE AND TECHNOLOGY

Haley's Comet Is Observed
Bakelite, the First Successful Plastic, Is Invented by Leo Baekeland
Gene Is a Word Now Used to Describe a Factor in Heredity
French Aviator, Louis Bleriot, Crosses the English Channel in a Monoplane
The SOS Distress Signal Is First Used by the American Ship, Arapahoe
German Bacteriologist, Paul Erlich, Develops Salvarsan, an Arsenic
    Compound Effective in Treating the Dreaded Venereal Disease, Syphilis

BUSINESS AND INDUSTRY

Orville and Wilbur Wright Create the Wright Company
Herring-Curtis Company Produces the First Commercial Airplane
The Bell and Howell Company Produces a "Flicker Free" Motion Picture Camera
General Motors Acquires the Cadillac Brand from Henry Leland

CONSUMER PRODUCTS AND SERVICES

The Public Loves Ford's New Model T. It Offers Affordable and Reliable Transportation
Electric Toasters Appear
Billboard, the Entertainment Trade Newspaper, Publishes Sheet Music of Popular Songs
Shock Absorbers Appear on Cars, Making Driving Much More Comfortable

SPORTS

Tristam "Tris" Speaker Begins His 19 Year Baseball Career
Football's Field Goal Is Reduced to Three Points, Down from Four in 1904
Clay Tennis Courts Are Introduced, But Most Tennis Is Still Played on Grass

ARTS AND MEDIA

French Painter Henri Matisse Produces *The Dance*

STAGE		
	The Fortune Hunter	John Barrymore
	Ziegfield Follies	Fanny Brice, Sophie Tucker
	Get-Rich-Quick-Wallingford	George M. Cohan
	Strife	John Galsworthy

MOVIE		
	The Curtain Pole	Mack Sennett
	A Corner in Wheat	D.W. Griffith
	The Lonely Villa	D.W. Griffith
	The Gibson Goddess	Mary Pickford
	Ranch Life in the Great Southwest	Tom Mix
	Gertie the Dinosaur (animated cartoon)	
	First Newsreels Are Produced and Shown	

BOOK		
	Ann Veronica	H.G. Wells
	Three Lives	Gertrude Stein

MUSIC

Electra	Richard Straus
Le Coq d'Or	Nikolai Rimski-Korsakov

When Irish Eyes Are Smiling   *I Wonder Who's Kissing Her Now*
Mother Machree   *Put on Your Old Grey Bonnet*
By the Light of the Silvery Moon   *On Wisconsin*
Oh Promise Me

PEOPLE

US Adm. Robert E. Peary Claims He Reached the North Pole April 6, 1909. Dr. Frederick Cooke
          Later Claims He Reached the Pole a Year Earlier. Peary Is Ultimately Given Credit
John D. Rockefeller Is the First US Billionaire (see 1901,1999)
Sigmund Freud Lectures in the United States
Mary Pickford (16) Hires on at Biograph for $10 a Day
Lee DeForest Broadcasts Enrico Caruso from Backstage of the Metropolitan Opera House.
          It Is Heard Only by Local Ham Radio Operators

REFLECTION

"...life at the end of the opening decade of the twentieth century seemed far less secure for the privileged classes of Europe than it had seemed at the beginning. It was just as clear that they would not give up their privileges without a fight. Everywhere the future of Europe suddenly seemed very uncertain."

          Elizabeth Campling
          Portrait of a Decade 1900-09

INCIDENTALS AND TRIVIA

At over 330 Pounds, William Howard Taft Is Our Largest President
Jigsaw Puzzles Are Very Popular
So Is Gin Rummy

1910 *Scientific Management Is Born*

WORLD

Edward VII Dies. George V Is King of England
Japan Annexes Korea
The Union of South Africa Is Created
Revolution Breaks Out in Mexico

NATION

US Population Now 92 Million
Mann Act Prohibits Interstate Transport of Women for Immoral Purposes
Boy Scouts of America Is Founded
First Father's Day Is Celebrated in Spokane, Washington
The Christian Endeavor Society Seeks to Ban All Motion Pictures Depicting Kissing
       Between People Who Are Not Related
Congress Establishes the Postal Banking System
Congress Requires Radio Equipment Be Installed on All US Passenger Ships

ENVIRONMENT, SAFETY AND HEALTH

Mining Accidents Killing Hundreds of Miners Continue to Haunt the Nation

LIFESTYLE

4% of US Adults Have College Degrees
Slightly Less than Half of US Adults Have a Grade School Education
6.4 Million US Farms (35% of Population)
US Population Is Now 92 Million. 4.3% Over Age 65
8.7 Million Immigrants Have Entered the US Since 1900
Weekends off from Work Are Becoming More Common
Some Consider V Neck Garments to be Unhealthy and Immoral

SCIENCE AND TECHNOLOGY

Lung Disease Now Diagnosed With Aid of X-rays
Marie Curie Isolates Pure Radium Metal (Later Cancer Treatment)
First Launch of an Airplane from the US Cruiser Birmingham

BUSINESS AND INDUSTRY

F.W. Woolworth Now Has Over 200 Stores Nationwide
Steel Begins to Replace Wood in Automobile Bodies

CONSUMER PRODUCTS AND SERVICES

Bathroom Scales
Electric Cooking Ranges
Electric Toasters Are a Status Symbol
First Automatic Transmissions Appear in Autos

PRICES

Canned Soup	$ .10
Canned Tomatoes	.06
Canned Corn	.09

But Working Is Still Dangerous *1910*

SPORTS

President Taft Throws a Baseball Out on Opening Day: Presidential First
Barney Oldfield Reaches 133 mph at the Daytona Racetrack

ARTS AND MEDIA

STAGE

Naughty Marietta	Victor Herbert
The Girl of the Golden West	Giacomo Puccini
The Firebird	Igor Stravinsky
Misalliance	George Bernard Shaw

MOVIE

Her Terrible Ordeal	
A Tale of Two Cities	Norma Talmadge
Life of Moses	
Uncle Tom's Cabin	
The House With Closed Shutters	
Ramona	D.W. Griffith, Mary Pickford

BOOK

The Spirit of Romance	Ezra Pound
The Finer Grain	Henry James
Burning Daylight	Jack London
The Rosary	Florence Barclay
A Modern Chronicle	Winston Churchill

MUSIC

Ah, Sweet Mystery of Life	*Come Josephine in My Flying Machine*
I'm Falling in Love with Someone	*Down by the Old Mill Stream*
Put Your Arms Around Me Honey	*Let Me Call You Sweetheart*

PEOPLE

Frederick W. Taylor Champions the Scientific Management Movement
British Comedian, Charles Chaplin, Appears in a New York Vaudeville Skit
Enrico Caruso Sings in an Experimental Radio Broadcast
Glenn H. Curtiss Breaks Several Air Speed Records at the First American Aviation Meet
Andrew Carnegie Establishes the Carnegie Foundation for International Peace with $10,000,000

QUOTES

"If men knew how women pass the time when they are alone, they'd never marry."
William S. Porter (O Henry)
(1862-1910)

"The right word may be effective, but no word was ever as effective as a rightly timed pause."
Samuel Clemens (Mark Twain)
(1835-1910)

INCIDENTALS AND TRIVIA

Although They Are Increasingly Common, When Electric Lights Are Installed in Hotels
And Public Places, Notices Remind People Not To Light Them With a Match
The Tango Craze Sweeps the Country

1911 *Revolution Is Bringing Change*

WORLD

Revolutionaries Overthrow China's Manchu Dynasty
Sun Yat-sen Is Elected as the First President of China
Famine Causes the Starvation of 30 Million Russians
US Troops Guard the Border as the Mexican Revolution Brings Down Its Government
Italy Declares War on the Ottoman Turks.

NATION

California Women Gain Suffrage Through Constitutional Amendment
US Supreme Court Orders Standard Oil & American Tobacco Corporation Breakups
The National Progressive Republican League Is Formed to Enact Progressive Legislation

ENVIRONMENT, SAFETY AND HEALTH

US, Japan, Britain and Russia Sign a Treaty to Ban Seal Hunting
The Society of Automotive Engineers Sets Standards for Auto Parts Production

DISASTER

Factory Fire Kills 146, Mostly Young Women, in New York City. Reforms Are Demanded

LIFESTYLE

US Population Now at Least 25% Foreign Born in All Parts of the Country Except the South

SCIENCE AND TECHNOLOGY

Roald Amundsen Reaches the South Pole
Italy Uses the Airplane for Offensive Bombing in the Turkish-Italian Conflict
The Word "Vitamin" Enters Our Vocabulary
Atomic Nucleus Is Discovered
Superconductivity Is Discovered
First Cross Country Flight, Sheepshead Bay, N.Y. to Pasadena, Calif, (84 hours, 4 min.)

BUSINESS AND INDUSTRY

Race Driver Louis Chevrolet and Charles Durant Form Chevrolet
Movie Theaters Now Over 10,000 in the US. Films Are Often Two and Even Three Reels
The Computer Tabulating Recording Company is Formed (Later IBM)
Kraft (German for Strength) Packaging Paper Process Revolutionizes the Paper Industry

CONSUMER PRODUCTS AND SERVICES

Crisco Hydrogenated Vegetable Shortening Marketed by Proctor & Gamble
Cold Cream Is Marketed
Electric Frying Pans Are Available
The Rotary Eggbeater Appears
Invented by Charles F. Kettering, Electric Self-Starters Begin to Replace Cranks in Cars
Domino Brand Sugar Appears in Markets
Kellogg Offers 40% Bran Flakes

But America Hardly Notices

SPORTS

Pitching Legend, Cy Young, Retires. First Pitcher to Win 500 Games
The Cork-Center Ball Is Introduced in Baseball
Golfer Bobby Jones Wins His First Title at Age 9
Jim Thorpe & Carlisle Indian School Defeat Harvard in Football Victory
The First Indianapolis 500 Auto Race

ARTS AND MEDIA

Man with a Guitar	(painting)	Georges Braque

STAGE

Petrouchka	Igor Stravinski
Der Rosenkavalier	Richard Straus
Treemonisha	Scott Joplin
Beaucaire	Booth Tarkington
Kismet	Edward Knoblock

MOVIE

The Miser's Heart
A Terrible Discovery
The Last Drop of Water
The Battle
Vanity Fair
David Copperfield
Enoch Arden

BOOK

The Innocence of Father Brown	C.K. Chesterton
Ethan Frome	Edith Wharton
Principles of Scientific Management	Frederick Taylor
The Iron Woman	Margaret Deland
Dawn O'Hara	Edna Ferber
The Winning of Barbara Worth	Harold B. Wright

MUSIC

Alexander's Ragtime Band	Irving Berlin
Memphis Blues	W.C. Handy
Everybody's Doin' It	Irving Berlin
I Want a Girl, Just Like the Girl...	*Oh, You Beautiful Doll*
When I Was 21 and You Were Sweet 16	*My Melancholy Baby*
Goodnight, Ladies	

PEOPLE

Andrew Carnegie Creates the Carnegie Foundation to Further Education
Frank Lloyd Wright Completes Taliesin East at Spring Green, Wisconsin
Walter Gropius Designs a Steel Skeleton Building Whose Walls Are "Glass Curtain" Walls
Explorer Hiram Bingham Discovers the Inca City of Macchu-Pichu

CRIME AND PUNISHMENT

Mona Lisa, the Famous Painting by Leonardo Da Vinci, Is Stolen from the Louvre
      in Paris (Later Recovered Intact)

INCIDENTALS AND TRIVIA

Charles Pajean of Illinois Invents Tinkertoys. One Million Sets Sold the First Year

1912 *The Unsinkable Titanic Is Lost*

WORLD

Sun Yat-sen and Chiang Kai-shek Establish a Republic in China
Balkan Trouble: Montenegro Battles the Ottoman Empire
US Marines Land in Honduras, Cuba and Nicaragua to Protect American Interests

NATION

Woodrow Wilson Becomes the 28th President. Defeats William Howard Taft and New
        Progressive (Bull Moose Party) Teddy Roosevelt
New Mexico and Arizona Become the 47th and 48th States
Nine States Are Now Dry
Massachusetts Enacts the First Minimum Wage Law for Women and Children
Girl Guiding Is Established. Will Become Girl Scouts of America
US Chamber of Commerce Founded
Ham Radio Operators Must Now Secure a License to Broadcast
New Postal Regulation Requires Advertising in Media to Be Labeled "Advt."
New Homestead Act Reduces Residency from Five to Three Years

ENVIRONMENT, SAFETY AND HEALTH

The US Public Health Service Is Established

DISASTER

The Unsinkable Titanic Strikes an Iceberg on Her Maiden Voyage and Sinks. 1,500 Die

LIFESTYLE

Federal Workers Now Enjoy an 8-Hour Workday. Private Industry Jobs Are Still 10-12
        Hours Per Day, Six Days a Week
Stunt Flying Is the Rage at Fairs and Outdoor Events. Many Are Killed During Their Acts

SCIENCE AND TECHNOLOGY

Morse Code SOS Is Adopted as the International Distress Signal
A Decompression Device Is Developed for Underwater Divers
Gestalt Psychology Is Debated
The Theory of Continental Drift Is Proposed
Cosmic Radiation Discovered
Protons and Electrons Are Discovered Within the Atom
The Conversion of One Atomic Element into Another Is Demonstrated

BUSINESS AND INDUSTRY

A&P Stores Begin a Major Expansion. Cash and Carry Only
Columbia Discontinues Cylinder Records but Edison Holds Firm
Cadillac Claims the Slogan, *Standard of the World*

CONSUMER PRODUCTS AND SERVICES

Movies Go to Five Reels (Reel = 10 min.) as the Public Demands Longer, Complex Stories
Hamilton Beach Electrifies the Home Sewing Machine
A German Firm Develops an Electric Iron
The Oreo Sandwich Cookie, LifeSavers Candy and Hellmann's Mayonnaise Are Introduced

A Professor Becomes President

SPORTS

International Lawn Tennis Association Established
The Open Net Is Introduced to Basketball. No Stopping to Retrieve Ball
Harriet Quimby Is the First Woman to Swim the English Channel
Jim Thorpe Wins the Olympic Pentathlon and Decathlon
Football Gets a Fourth Down and a Touchdown Value of Six Points, Up from Five

ARTS AND MEDIA

STAGE   *Hokey Pokey*   Lillian Russell
              Androcles and the Lion   George Bernard Shaw

MOVIE   *The Keystone Cops (Series Begins)*   Mack Sennett
              An Unseen Enemy   Lillian and Dorothy Gish
              Cleopatra

BOOK   *Riders of the Purple Sage*   Zane Grey
              Death in Venice   Horace Mann
              The Theory of Psychoanalysis   Carl G. Yung

MUSIC

Daphne and Chloe   Maurice Ravel
Symphony Number 9 in D   Gustav Mahler
Peg O' My Heart
Waiting for the Robert E. Lee   *Moonlight Bay*
That Old Gal of Mine   *The Sweetheart of Sigma Chi*

PEOPLE

Charlie Chaplin Contracts with the Keystone Company for $150/Week
Henry Ford, a Prohibitionist, Establishes Rules of Off-The-Job Behavior For Workers
Clarence Birdseye in Labrador, Discovers that Fish, Quickly Frozen, Can Be Defrosted
      Months Later, Still Fresh
Robert F. Scott's Party of Five Reaches the South Pole One-Month After Roald Amundsen.
      Exhausted and Beset by Blizzards, They All Perish on Their Return Trip
Robert Sarnoff, of Wireless Marconi Company, Wins Recognition for His Coverage of the
      Titanic Disaster

QUOTES

"A man who has a million dollars is as well off as if he were rich."
                John Jacob Astor
                (1864-1912)

"I am just going outside and I may be some time."
                Lawrence Oates (1880-1912)*
          * Scott Antarctic Party Member Walking Out into a Blizzard

INCIDENTALS AND TRIVIA

A Driver Is Jailed for Speeding
Minsky's Burlesque Theater Has an Audience Runway on which 80 Chorus Girls Strut
Current Slang: **Beat It!**, **Peeved**, **Sure!** and **It's a Cinch**

1913 *America Gets an Income Tax*

WORLD

The Second Balkan War Begins as Bulgaria Attacks Greeks and Serbs

NATION

The 16th Amendment Creates the Federal Income Tax
The 17th Amendment Brings About Direct Election of US Senators
The Federal Reserve System Is Created
Thousands of Civil War Veterans at Gettysburg Reunion, Celebrate the 50th Anniversary

ENVIRONMENT, SAFETY AND HEALTH

Steamships Are Ordered to Carry Enough Lifeboats for All Passengers
The Los Angeles Owens River Aqueduct Completion Will Make Los Angeles a Boom Town

DISASTER

The Dayton Flood in the Miami River Valley of Ohio Kills More Than 400

LIFESTYLE

Ragtime Is Everybody's Favorite. A Dance Variation of the Two-Step Becomes the Foxtrot.
    The Tango, Hesitation Waltz and Turkey Trot Are Also Popular
New York's Palace Theater Opens During the Glory Days of Burlesque and Quickly Becomes
    the Premier Place for Acts to Perform
The Term, *Airplane*, Begins to Replace *Aeroplane*

SCIENCE AND TECHNOLOGY

Physicist Niels Bohr Offers a Theory of Atomic Structure
Vitamins A and B Are Isolated
Mammograms Now Possible
Formica Is Created
The First Artificial Kidney Is Used

BUSINESS AND INDUSTRY

Ford Establishes the Modern Assembly Line
World's Tallest: Woolworth Building in New York at 60 Stories
The Movie Studios Move West to Hollywood from New York and New Jersey
American Messenger Company Becomes Merchant's Parcel Delivery Through Merger (See 1925)

CONSUMER PRODUCTS AND SERVICES

R J. Reynolds Company Introduces Camel Brand Cigarettes
The First Truly Modern Brassiere Is Introduced by Mary Phelps Jacob Who Sells Her Patent
Brillo Pads Appear
Home Refrigerators Are Available but Very Expensive (see 1916)
Newspaper Crossword Puzzles Appear
The Talon Slide Fastener Replaces the Buttonhook (see 1923)

Europe Becomes a Time Bomb

SPORTS

Walter Johnson of the Washington Senators, Pitches 56 Scoreless Innings
College Football Players Begin Wearing Identifying Numbers

ARTS AND MEDIA

STAGE   *The Rite of Spring*   Igor Stravinsky
                The Sunshine Girl   Vernon and Irene Castle

MOVIE   *The Squaw Man*   *(full length movie)*   Cecil B. DeMille
                The Battle of Elderbush Gulch   Lillian Gish, Mae Marsh

BOOK   *O Pioneers*   Willa Cather
                A Boy's Will *(first poetry collection)*   Robert Frost
                Sons and Lovers   D.H. Lawrence
                Totem and Taboo   Sigmund Freud
                Pollyanna   Eleanor H. Porter
                Trees *(poetry)*   A. Joyce Kilmer

MUSIC

Soda Fountain Rag   Duke Ellington
Peg O' My Heart   *Now Is the Hour*
You Made Me Do It   *If I Had My Way*
Ballin' the Jack

PEOPLE

Vernon and Irene Castle, Dance Team, Lead the Dancing Craze
Anti-Saloon League's Wayne Wheeler, Argues That Prohibition Should Be a National Issue
John D. Rockefeller Donates $100 Million to Start the Rockefeller Foundation
Coco Chanel Introduces V-Neck Shirts and Berets to Replace Huge Hats and Feathers

QUOTES

"You can have it in any color as long as it's black."
                         Henry Ford (about his 1913 Model T)
     Earlier T's were available in other colors, but assembly line simplicity
     and rapid drying time forced the single color.

REFLECTION

The first income tax levied 1% on net income up to $20,000 and slightly graduated above
that. If married, the tax on $20,000 was only $160. The average worker paid no tax. The tax
yielded little national income but was considered fair by a nation in the mood for reform.

INCIDENTALS AND TRIVIA

Woodrow Wilson (Ph.D. Political Science) Will Be the Most Highly Educated President
       of the Century
Actress Mabel Normand Ad Libs by Throwing a Pie (Crew Dessert) at Ben Turpin During the
       Filming of a Keystone Comedy. Pie Throwing Soon Becomes a Movie Comedy Staple
Teddy Roosevelt Coins the Term, *Lunatic Fringe,* After Viewing a Modernist Art Exhibit. His
       Comments Are Not at the Art, But the Conservative Critics Who Condemn Its Nudity

1914 *The European War Erupts*

WORLD

Austrian Archduke Francis Ferdinand and His Wife Are Assassinated at Sarajevo
Austria-Hungary Goes to War with Serbia
Prior Assistance Treaties Widen the Conflict: Britain, France and Russia (Allies) Oppose
    Germany, Turkey and Austria-Hungary
The European Conflict Begins to Settle in as Trench Warfare, Where Lines Hardly Move
Several US Marines Are Arrested in Tampico, Mexico. Failing to Get a Proper Apology, US
    Forces Temporarily Occupy Vera Cruz

NATION

Wilson Issues a Proclamation of Neutrality Aimed at Keeping US Out of the European War
The Panama Canal Opens (see 1906), Linking the Atlantic and Pacific Oceans
The Federal Trade Commission Is Established
The American Society of Composers, Authors and Publishers (ASCAP)
    Is Formed to Protect Musical Copyrights
The Clayton Antitrust Act Becomes Law
Coxey's Army of Unemployed Workers, Marches on Washington, DC
Suffragettes March on Washington, DC to Demand Voting Rights for Women
The Navy Establishes an Oil Reserve in Teapot Dome, Wyoming

ENVIRONMENT, SAFETY AND HEALTH

George Washington Carver Develops a Soil-Replenishment Program
The Passenger Pigeon and Carolina Parakeet Are Declared Extinct

LIFESTYLE

Harrison Narcotics Act Prohibits Use of Free-Traffic Cocaine, Popular in Patent Medicines
A Knee-Length Skirt on a One-Piece Costume Is an Acceptable Women's Bathing Garment
US Farmhands Now Migrate North From Texas to Canada, Picking Crops as They Ripen

SCIENCE AND TECHNOLOGY

Robert Goddard Experiments with Liquid Fuel Rockets
Clouds of Gas and Dust Observed: The Space Between Stars Is Apparently Not Empty

BUSINESS AND INDUSTRY

Cadillac Develops the V8 Engine
Ford Offers $5/Day for Workers and Is Crushed with Applicants.
The Teletype Machine Is Invented
The New Republic Magazine Begins Production
White Star Line Launches Brittanic, Sister Ship to the Sunken Titanic
Brothers Horace and John Dodge Are Successful with Their All-Steel Bodied Cars
Cunard's SS Aquatania Makes Its Maiden Atlantic Voyage to New York

CONSUMER PRODUCTS AND SERVICES

US Fashion Shows Now Use Live Models
Pyrex Glassware
Wrigley Introduces Doublemint Gum
The Stutz Bearcat Auto Is Introduced

SPORTS

Jack Dempsey Starts Boxing as Kid Blackey
Golfer Walter Hagen Wins the US Open at Age 21

ARTS AND MEDIA

STAGE	*Pygmalion*	George Bernard Shaw
	Watch Your Step	Vernon and Irene Castle
MOVIE	*Kid Auto Races at Venice (tramp outfit)*	Charlie Chaplin
	Tillie's Punctured Romance	Charlie Chaplin, Marie Dressler, Mabel Normand
	Neptune's Daughter	
	The Wrath of the Gods	
	The Avenging Conscience	
	The Spoilers	
	The Perils of Pauline	Pearl White (does her own stunts)
BOOK	*Penrod*	Booth Tarkington
	A Portrait of the Artist as a Young Man	James Joyce
	The Congo and Other Poems	Vachel Lindsay
	Tarzan of the Apes	Edgar Rice Burroughs

MUSIC

A London Symphony   Ralph Vaughan Williams
St. Louis Blues   W.C. Handy
That's an Irish Lullaby
They Didn't Believe Me   *Play a Simple Melody*
It's a Long Way to Tipperary   *Keep the Home Fires Burning*
You're the Only Girl for Me   *The Missouri Waltz*
      By the Beautiful Sea

PEOPLE

Mary Pickford's Income Breaks $100,000 Per Year as Movie Star Salaries Begin to Escalate
Cecille B. DeMille and William S. Hart Are New Movie Celebrities
Margaret Higgins Sanger Discusses Birth Control in Her Book, *The Woman Rebel.*
Thomas Lipton Expands His Grocery Retailing Empire to Over 500 Shops

COMMENTARY

"It is an odd time in Washington. The US does not want to take sides in Europe but stands ready to flex its muscles in the Caribbean. We routinely send in the Marines for peacekeeping missions when we have any notion that a country is unstable or that it might ask a European friend to intervene in its internal affairs. It is called the Roosevelt Corollary to the old Monroe Doctrine. It got us the rights to build the Panama Canal and Americans believe that we have the responsibility to monitor and police Latin America."

"Miss Picky"
Irene English

INCIDENTALS AND TRIVIA

Cleveland Employs the First Red and Green Signals for Traffic Control

1915 *The European War Continues*

WORLD

First Use of Poison Gas at the Second Battle of Ypres
Excessive Propaganda by All Parties Makes War Evaluation Difficult for the Public
Czar Nicholas II Takes Personal Control of the Russian Army
Haiti Becomes a US Protectorate

NATION

The US Coast Guard Is Established
Supreme Court Says Employers Can't Deny Employment to Union Members
The Ku Klux Klan Reappears in Georgia
Nevada Establishes a Quick Divorce Law
Margaret Sanger Founds the National Birth Control League But Is Arrested
        and Jailed on Obscenity Charges for Her Book, *Family Limitation*
The Kiwanis Club Is Founded in Detroit

ENVIRONMENT, SAFETY AND HEALTH

Rocky Mountain National Park Is Created

DISASTER

Cunard's Lusitania Is Torpedoed by a German Submarine; 1,195 Die. America Is Outraged.
        After Several Notes, Germany Promises Safe Travel for Clearly Marked Neutral Ships
Excursion Steamer, Eastland, Capsizes at Her Chicago Pier, Killing 852

LIFESTYLE

Taxicabs Are Now Common in Major Cities
Death Certificates Come into General Use in the US

SCIENCE AND TECHNOLOGY

Albert Einstein Completes His Theory of Relativity. Physics and Astronomy Are Now Viewed
        Dramatically Different than Before
Cross Country Phone Call: Alexander G. Bell in New York, Thomas Watson in San Francisco
Pellagra Found to be Caused by a Niacin Deficiency
A Dysentery Causing Bacteria Is Found

BUSINESS AND INDUSTRY

August Fruehauf Invents the Semi-Trailer
Hollywood Becomes the Capitol of the Motion Picture Industry

CONSUMER PRODUCTS AND SERVICES

The 78 rpm Record Appears
Victor Talking Machine Company Markets Its Victrola (The Name Will Become Generic)
Ford Produces the Millionth Model T. The Price Is Now $440
Aspirin Is Now Available Without a Prescription

SPORTS

Jess Willard Knocks Out Jack Johnson (26th Round) for Heavyweight Boxing Championship

ARTS AND MEDIA

STAGE	*The Princess Pat*	Victor Herbert
	Stop! Look! Listen!	Irving Berlin
MOVIE	*Birth of a Nation*	D.W. Griffith, Lillian Gish, Mae Marsh
	The Tramp	Charlie Chaplin
	The Lamb	Douglas Fairbanks
	Just Nuts	Harold Lloyd
BOOK	*Of Human Bondage*	Somerset Maugham
	The Metamorphosis	Franz Kafka
	The Song of the Lark	Willa Cather
	Spoon River Anthology	Edgar Lee Masters
	Bib Ballads	Ring Lardner

MUSIC

Hello Frisco, Hello (See Science)   *M-O-T-H-E-R*
I Didn't Raise My Boy to Be a Soldier   *Nola*
Pack Up Your Troubles in Your Old...

PEOPLE

New Movie Personalities Include Hal Roach, Harold Lloyd, and Douglas Fairbanks
David Sarnoff Proposes Manufacture of "Radio Music Boxes" to American Marconi but the
    Company Rejects the Idea

QUOTES

"**M** is for the million things you gave me,
O means only that she's growing old,
T is for the tears she shed to save me,
H is for her heart of purest gold,
E is for her eyes, with love-light shining,
R means right, and right she'll always be,
Put them all together, they spell **MOTHER**,
A word that means the world to me."
                     Howard Johnson 1915

COMMENTARY

"D.W. Griffith's *Birth of a Nation* broke new cinematic ground in so many ways plus its vast scope and three-hour length set the stage for an entirely new way of making motion pictures. Following two families, it traced their lives from before, through and after the Civil War.

"Over the years, however, for many the film has been difficult to view objectively, because of the strong southern orientation of *The Clansman* book (see 1905), the basis for the film. Blacks, although not treated with hostility, are portrayed with condescension. The role of the Ku Klux Klan is upsetting to many when viewed with knowledge of later Klan bigotry.

"Yet, overall, *Birth of a Nation* must be considered a masterpiece and a major cultural contribution to the 20th Century."

Bill Goodpage

1916 *Millions Die in European Hell*

WORLD

Most of Europe Is Drawn into the War Where the Front Only Moves Yards at a Time
The Battle of Verdun Claims 350,000 French Troops and Nearly as Many Germans
Pancho Villa Raids New Mexico, Then Retreats to Mexico. Gen. John J. Pershing and US
       Troops Pursue Him Across the Border
Rasputin, the "Mad Monk" Is Assassinated in Russia

NATION

Woodrow Wilson Narrowly Defeats Charles Evans Hughes for President
Denmark Sells the Virgin Islands to the US for 25 Million
Many Temperance Congressmen Elected. It Is Now Politically Smart to Stand for Prohibition
The President Emphasizes "Preparedness" as Sentiment Against Neutrality Increases

ENVIRONMENT, SAFETY AND HEALTH

The National Park Service Is Established
Colorado Springs Dentist Frederick Motley, Discovers That His Patients Have Fewer
       Cavities Because of Natural Fluoride Salts in the City's Drinking Water Supply
US Supreme Court Rules that Users and Sellers of Opium Are Liable for Prosecution

DISASTER

Poliomyelitis Epidemic Kills over 6,000 in US and Leaves Thousands More Crippled

LIFESTYLE

24 States Are Now "Dry." This Year Added Michigan, Montana, South Dakota and Nebraska
Coco Chanel Uses Undergarment Fabric Jersey For Outerwear. A Hit.
Women Have Still Not Been Granted Suffrage in Most States

SCIENCE AND TECHNOLOGY

Vitamins A and B Are Claimed to be Important for Growth
First Tanks Enter as Weapons in the Battle of the Somme
Tanks and Machine Guns Will Define the Character of This War

BUSINESS AND INDUSTRY

Annual Auto Production Exceeds One Million Units for the First Time
Dodge Introduces the First All Steel Automobile Body
Nash Motors Is Founded
Sinclair Oil and Refining Is Founded
Piggly Wiggly, a "Super" Market Opens in Memphis
Pacific Aero Products (Later Boeing) Is Founded in Seattle by William Boeing

CONSUMER PRODUCTS AND SERVICES

American Tobacco Company Introduces Lucky Strike Cigarettes
Electric Clocks
Liquid Nail Polish
First Supermarket With Self Service and Checkout Opens in Tennessee
Auto Windshield Wipers Begin to Appear
Double Shell Enameled Bathtubs Begins Replacing the Cast Iron, Claw Foot Tubs
Hudson Motors Introduces the Pricey, Hudson Super Six Sedan

Our President Preaches Preparedness 1916

PRICES

Mechanical Home Refrigerator	$900
Ford Model T	350

SPORTS

Grover Cleveland Alexander Pitches 15 Shutouts for the Phillies
The Rose Bowl Tradition Begins. Washington State Beats Brown 14-0
The Professional Golfers' Association (PGA) Is Founded

ARTS AND MEDIA

STAGE	*Our Mrs. McChesney*	Edna Ferber
	The Pearl Fishers	George Bizet
	Robinson Crusoe, Jr.	Sigmund Romberg, Al Jolson
	Ziegfield Follies	Fanny Brice, W.C. Fields
MOVIE	*Intolerance*	Lillian Gish, Mae Marsh
	Hell's Hinges	William S. Hart
BOOK	*Chicago Poems*	Carl Sandburg
	The Spirit of Judaism	Martin Buber
	Democracy and Education	John Dewey
	A Heap O' Livin'	Edgar Guest

MUSIC

I Ain't Got Nobody
La Cucaracha
You Belong to Me
Ireland Must be Heaven for My Mother Came from There

PEOPLE

Jeannette Rankin of Montana Becomes Our First US Congresswoman
Louis D. Brandeis Becomes First Jewish American on the Supreme Court
Margaret Sanger Opens a Public Birth Control Clinic in Brooklyn and Adds the Term,
      "Birth Control" to Our Vocabulary
Norman Rockwell Begins Painting Covers for Saturday Evening Post
Charlie Chaplin's Salary Spirals to an Unbelievable $675,000 Per Year
Frank Lloyd Wright Completes Tokyo's Ornate Imperial Hotel

QUOTES

"Money is a horrid thing to follow, but a charming thing to meet."
      Henry James (1843-1916)

"Poverty keeps together more homes than it breaks up."
      H.H. Munro (Saki) 1870-1916

INCIDENTALS AND TRIVIA

The Submachine Gun, Invented by Brig. Gen. John Thompson Is Known as the Tommy Gun
Engineers Predict That the World's Petroleum Resources Will Be Exhausted in 30 Years
Brewers Split From Hard Liquor Allies. Believe Beer Will Be Exempt from a Prohibition Act

1917   "And We Won't Be Back...

WORLD

Vladimir Lenin Returns to Russia After Years of Exile
Czar Nicholas II Abdicates as Revolution Spreads Through Russia
A.F. Karensky Heads a Short-Lived Provisional Government and Troops Pull Back
Bolsheviks V.I. Lenin and Leon Trotsky Assume Leadership
Serbia, Slovenia, Montenegro & Croatia Agree to Form Yugoslavia
US Troops Pulled From Mexico after Four Years of Searching for Pancho Villa
First Troops of the American Expeditionary Force Arrive in France
Arab Forces Led By T.E. Lawrence Capture Port of Aqaba from Turks
German U-boats Sink 10 Million Tons of Shipping, But Their Effectiveness Is Declining

NATION

US Severs Diplomatic Relations and Declares War on Germany
Congress Passes Selective Service, Plus War Revenue and Espionage Acts
Puerto Rico Becomes a US Territory and its People Become US Citizens
Liberty Bonds Are Sold to the Public to Raise Money for the War
Herbert Hoover, Director of the Food Administration, Urges Americans to Observe "Meatless
     Mondays" and " Wheatless Wednesdays."
Supreme Court Upholds Eight-Hour Workday for Railroads
Immigration Act, Passed Over the President's Veto, Bars Most Asiatic Laborers

DISASTER

Typhus Sweeps Russia, Compounding Defeats and Revolution. Three Million Will Die
Race Riots in East St. Louis Kill 39 People

LIFESTYLE

New York State Grants Women Equal Voting Rights
First Class Postage Is Now Three Cents

SCIENCE AND TECHNOLOGY

British Use Massed Tanks for the First Time in Battle of Cambrai
Vitamin D Is Produced from Cod Liver Oil
Mount Wilson, California, Is Home to a New 100 Inch Telescope
Technology Permits Firing Airplane Machine Gun Forward Without Hitting the Propeller
Major Edwin H. Armstrong Develops a Radio Circuit That Standardizes A.M. Radios
Helium Is Produced in Quantity for Observation Balloons in France

BUSINESS AND INDUSTRY

Union Carbide Founded
Paramount Acquires the Popular Fatty Arbuckle and Young Acrobat, Buster Keaton
Grain Shortage Further Hurts the Distilling Industry
Newspaper Editorials and Advertisements Tend to Portray US Breweries of German
     Heritage as "Tools of the Hun." German Names Are Generally Unpopular

CONSUMER PRODUCTS AND SERVICES

First Commercial Frozen Food Created by Clarence Birdseye
Keds Markets First Tennis Footwear

"Till It's Over, Over There!" 1917

SPORTS

First Sunday Baseball Game Played at NY's Polo Grounds. Violates Existing "Blue Law."
National Hockey League Formed
Chicago and Cincinnati Play the First Double No Hit Game in Baseball. Reds Win in the 10th.

ARTS AND MEDIA

STAGE	*Maytime*	Sigmund Romberg
	Over There	George M. Cohan
	Why Marry?	Jesse Lynch Williams
MOVIE	*Cleopatra*	Theda Bara
	Wild and Wooley	
	Poor Little Rich Girl	
BOOK	*The Innocents*	Sinclair Lewis
	King Coal	Upton Sinclair

MUSIC

Classical Symphony   Sergei Prokofiev
Over There   *Oh Johnny, Oh Johnny, Oh*
You're in the Army Now   *The Bells of St. Mary's*
Hail, Hail, The Gang's All Here   *Till the Clouds Roll By*
For Me and My Gal   *Goodbye Broadway, Hello France*

PEOPLE

Leopold Stokowski Makes First Recordings With the Philadelphia Orchestra
Jascha Heifitz (16), Violinist, Makes His American Debut in New York
Franklin Roosevelt Is Assistant Secretary of the Navy

CRIME AND PUNISHMENT

Dutch Dancer, Mata Hari, Guilty of Spying for Germany, Is Executed by Allies

QUOTES

"The world must be made safe for democracy."
Woodrow Wilson

COMMENTARY

"Patriotism, optimism and enthusiasm ran high. It was the correct and moral obligation for this young and increasingly powerful nation to aid the Allies and bring a quick conclusion to this 'war to end all wars.'

"We really no longer remembered war. It was over 50 years since the Civil War ended. The Spanish American War really didn't count. It was short and decisive with fewer than 400 actual battle casualties. Plus the newspapers fed the public grossly incorrect stories of American exploits and valor. It was almost fun.

"This new war would be quite different as our young men were about to find out."

"Miss Picky"
Irene English

1918   *What Is Truly More Obscene?*

WORLD

US and Austrian Expeditionary Forces Fail to Rout Bolsheviks from the Ukraine
Gen. Pershing's September Offensive Breaks a Long Stalemate. 15,000 Germans Captured
Kaiser Wilhelm of Germany Abdicates
War Ends as the Armistice Is Signed on November 11 in Paris
Hungary Declares Independence from Austria
Czechoslovakia Becomes a Separate Nation
Estonia, Latvia, and Lithuania Declare Independence from Russia
Former Czar Nicholas II and Family Secretly Executed by Bolsheviks
Lenin Moves the Capitol from St. Petersburg to Moscow

NATION

The Sedition Act Provides Penalties for Those Who Hinder the War Effort
Wilson Outlines a 14 Point Plan for World Peace
First Airmail Stamps Are Issued. An Upside Down Plane on Some Become Collector's Items

ENVIRONMENT, SAFETY AND HEALTH

The Enormous Acreage in Oats to Feed Horses and Mules Will Rapidly Decline

DISASTER

500,000 Die in US from Influenza Epidemic (25 million worldwide)

LIFESTYLE

Daylight Savings Time Is Introduced. Farmers Dislike Milking in the Dark
46% of Fractures Result in Permanent Disability, Mostly Amputation; 12% Are Fatal

SCIENCE AND TECHNOLOGY

Cod Liver Oil Is Proven to Cure Rickets. Had Been a Common North Sea Remedy for Years
New York to Washington and New York to Chicago Air Mail Debuts
US Is Officially Divided into Four Time Zones
Astronomer, Harlow Shapley Calculates Our Solar System Is at the Outer End of our Galaxy
Radios Now Have Been Standardized and Extensively Used for Military Communication

BUSINESS AND INDUSTRY

General Motors Acquires Detroit's Fisher Body Company
Hershey Chocolate Company Is Donated to the Milton Hershey School for Orphan Boys
Warner Bros. Movie Studio Is Founded

CONSUMER PRODUCTS AND SERVICES

Kotex Sanitary Napkins Are Introduced
The Pop Up Toaster Is a Novel Idea
Lever Bros. Markets Rinso, a Granulated Laundry Powder

SPORTS

Knute Rockne Becomes Head Football Coach at Notre Dame
30-1 Long Shot, Exterminator, Wins the Kentucky Derby. Will Go on to Win 34 Major Stakes

An Irish Novel? Or a War? 1918

ARTS AND MEDIA

STAGE	Ziegfield Follies	Will Rogers, Eddie Cantor, Marilyn Miller
	The Passing Show of 1918	Fred and Adele Astaire
MOVIE	Tarzan of the Apes	Emo Lincoln, Enid Markey
	Thirty a Week	Tallulah Bankhead
BOOK	Raggedy Ann Stories	Johnny Gruelle
	My Antonia	Willa Cather
	The Magnificent Ambersons	Booth Tarkington
	The Cornhuskers	Carl Sandburg

MUSIC

Swanee

Rock-a-Bye Baby

Oh! How I Hate to Get Up in the
   Morning

The Caissons Go Rolling Along

Till We Meet Again

K-K-K-Katy

After You've Gone

Somebody Stole My Gal

Beautiful Ohio

PEOPLE

Captain Eddie Rickenbacker Hailed as a Dogfight "Ace" with 26 Kills

US Sgt. Alvin York Single-Handedly Captures 132 German Soldiers

Robert L. Ripley Creates His Newspaper Feature, *Believe It Or Not!*

QUOTES

"What passing-bells for those who die like cattle?
Only the monstrous anger of the guns."

Wilfred Owen (1893-1918)

"A teacher affects eternity; he can never tell where his influence stops."

Henry Adams (1838-1918)

COMMENTARY

"Our boys came home, now men aged far beyond their years. They had lived with death and pain and mutilation. They knew hunger, loneliness, sadness and deprivation. For many who spent much time at the front it all seemed like such an enormous waste of humanity.

"Yet, particularly among the officers on both sides, there remained a quaint notion of nobility about it all. Manfred von Richtofen (The Red Baron) downs 80 planes and is, himself, killed. The Allies bury him with full military honors. Yes, there is still glory in war and it will return to haunt us."

"Miss Picky"

Irene English

INCIDENTALS AND TRIVIA

US Post Office Burns Copies of *Little Review* Magazine for Carrying Pre-Publication Installments of James Joyce's book, *Ulysses*, Considered Obscene

1919   *We Return to Normalcy*

WORLD

The Versailles Peace Treaty Is Signed
The League of Nations Is Created. President Wilson Takes Active Role
Wilson Receives the Nobel Peace Prize for Settlement of the War and the League of Nations
The Weimar Republic Is Established in Germany. Inflation Is Rampant
Benito Mussolini Founds the Fascist Party in Italy
Turks Exterminate 1.5 Million Armenians
There Is Widespread Famine in Germany and Much of Europe
The Third International Comintern Meets in Moscow to Plan World-Wide Revolution

NATION

US Senate Isolationists Refuse to Endorse the Wilson Backed Treaty
The American Communist Party Is Formed
Congress Passes Legislation to Enforce the 18th Amendment on Prohibition. Bans
     Manufacture and Sale of Any Drink of More Than 0.5% Alcohol.
The 19th Amendment Granting Women Suffrage Passes. Needs Ratification by the States
The American Legion Is Created by an Act of Congress
President Wilson Suffers a Stroke in October That Leaves Him Partially Paralyzed

ENVIRONMENT, SAFETY AND HEALTH

Congress Creates Grand Canyon National Park and Zion National Park in Utah

LIFESTYLE

Summer Chautauquas, Travelling Entertainment Programs, Are Very Popular, Particularly
     in Smaller Towns Across the Country
Labor Unrest Hits the US. Four Million Workers Are Either on Strike or Locked Out

SCIENCE AND TECHNOLOGY

Karl von Frisch Discovers That Bees Communicate to Find Nectar
First Transatlantic Flight From Newfoundland to Ireland

BUSINESS AND INDUSTRY

Charlie Chaplin, Mary Pickford, Douglas Fairbanks and D.W. Griffith Form United Artists
Radio Corporation of America (RCA) Is Formed
Hollywood Agrees to Censor Movies
The First Municipal Airport Opens Near Tucson, Arizona

CONSUMER PRODUCTS AND SERVICES

Odo-Ro-No Deodorant Cream Uses the Term B.O. in Advertising
Kellogg's All Bran Cereal Is Marketed
Fleishmann Company Ads Urge Women to Buy Bakery Bread Instead of Home Baking
The Pogo Stick Is Patented

PRICES

Milk	$.15 per quart
Eggs	.62 per dozen
Sirloin Steak	.61 per pound

As A New Era Begins

SPORTS

"Jack" Dempsey (the Manassa Mauler) Defeats Jess Willard for World Heavyweight Boxing Title
The Cincinnati Reds (NL) Defeat the Chicago White Sox (AL) 5 Games to 3 in Best of Nine

ARTS AND MEDIA

STAGE	*Up In Mabel's Room*	Helen Hayes, Alfred Lunt
	George White Scandals	George White, Ann Pennington
	Saint Joan	George Bernard Shaw
MOVIE	*The Cabinet of Dr. Caligari*	(German)
	Broken Blossoms	Lillian Gish, Richard Barthelmess
	Male and Female	Gloria Swanson
BOOK	*The American Language*	H.L. Mencken
	Ten Days That Shook the World	John Reed
	Winesberg, Ohio	Sherwood Anderson
	Collected Poems	Thomas Hardy

MUSIC

The World Is Waiting for the Sunrise
How Ya Gonna Keep Them Down on the Farm?
A Pretty Girl Is Like a Melody

Rose of Washington Square
Let the Rest of the World Go By
Beautiful Heaven
Oh, What a Pal Was Mary

PEOPLE

Mohandas K. Ghandi Initiates Passive Resistance in India
Dancer, Walter Winchell, Begins a Newspaper Column in *Billboard*
Paul Whiteman Forms an Orchestra to Specialize in "Symphonic Jazz"
Pianist, Jan Paderewski, Becomes First Premier of the Republic of Poland
Arthur Murray Starts His Dance Instruction Business
Father Devine (George Baker) Sets Up "Heavens" for His "Angels" in Harlem

QUOTES

"The man who dies rich thus dies disgraced."
Andrew Carnegie
1835-1919

COMMENTARY

"Our President travels to Europe to personally push the Treaty of Versailles and create the League of Nations. However, a now isolationist Congress, tired of war and wanting to avoid future European involvement, refuses to ratify the Treaty. The League will be born, but without American support it will exercise little world power.
"His stroke makes it obvious, but Wilson is a broken president."

Kate Hawthorne

INCIDENTALS AND TRIVIA

Oregon Is the First State to Tax Gasoline

1920 *A Scandal Stains Baseball*

WORLD

World Economies Struggle in the Wake of the Devastating Great War
Returning Soldiers Find Few Employment Opportunities
Unemployment Grows as Does Inflation
Russia Suffers a Disastrous Drought
The League of Nations Meets But It Lacks Participation by the US and the Soviet Union

NATION

The 18th Amendment on Prohibition of Alcohol (Volstead Act) Becomes Law.
The 19th Amendment, Woman Suffrage, Becomes Law in August
The League of Women Voters Is Founded in Chicago by Carrie C. Catt
Republicans Nominate Warren G. Harding and Calvin Coolidge
Democrats Nominate James M. Cox and Franklin D. Roosevelt
Cox Supports the League of Nations While Harding Plays It Down
America Wants to Forget the War. Voting Women Go Republican
Warren G. Harding Handily Defeats Democrat James M. Cox for President
Ruling Declares the Communist Labor Party Is Outside the Scope of US Deportation Laws
The American Civil Liberties Union (ACLU) Is Formed by Noted Social Reformers

ENVIRONMENT, SAFETY AND HEALTH

Local Overfishing Closes the Last San Francisco Salmon Cannery
Canning Industry Promises Higher Safety Standards as Numerous Botulism Cases Appear

LIFESTYLE

6.4 Million US Farms (30% of Population)
Rural vs. Urban America Is About 50-50
US Population Is Now 108 Million. 4.7% Over Age 65

SCIENCE AND TECHNOLOGY

There Are About 5,000 Radio Receivers in the US, Mostly Experimenters (see 1925)
A Radio Transmitter Is Built Atop the Westinghouse Building in East Pittsburgh

BUSINESS AND INDUSTRY

An Industry Is Born. Station KDKA, Pittsburgh, Broadcasts the Presidential Election Results
Air Mail Planes Cross the Country. It's Still Slow and Very Dangerous
US Wells Supply Two Thirds of the World's Petroleum
David Sarnoff Proposes Building $75 Radio Music Boxes. He Believes a Million Can Be Sold
Prohibition Forces California Vineyards to Diversify into Table Grapes and Raisins (Sunkist)
Aircraft Designer, Donald Douglas (28), Starts Douglas Aircraft Company
Sugar Prices Drop to Three Cents Per Pound. Wages Fall Drastically in Puerto Rico
The First Miss America Contest Is Held in Atlantic City

CONSUMER PRODUCTS AND SERVICES

Baby Ruth Candy Bars
Chanel Nº 5 Perfume Is Introduced
Trojan Brand Condoms Are Manufactured
Winnie Winkle, the Breadwinner, Newspaper Cartoon Appears
Breeder, Rudolph Boysen, Creates the Boysenberry, a Cross of Three Berries

Is a Washington Scandal Next? 1920

SPORTS

The New York Yankees Acquire Babe Ruth from the Boston Red Sox for Payment of $125,000
Judge Kenesaw Mountain Landis Is Elected Commissioner of Baseball's Major Leagues
Chestnut Colt, Man o' War Is Retired After Winning 20 of 21 Major Races
Eight Chicago White Sox Players Are Tried and Acquitted of Throwing the 1919 World Series

ARTS AND MEDIA

	Reclining Nude	Amadeo Modigliani
STAGE	*Heartbreak House*	George Bernard Shaw
	Beyond the Horizon	Eugene O'Neill
	The Emperor Jones	Eugene O'Neill
	The Tragedy of Richard III	John Barrymore
MOVIE	*Way Down East*	Lillian Gish, Richard Barthelmess
	The Kid	Charlie Chaplin, Jackie Coogan
	Dr. Jekyll and Mr. Hyde	John Barrymore
	Madam X	Pauline Frederick
BOOK	*Main Street*	Sinclair Lewis
	This Side of Paradise	F. Scott Fitzgerald
	The Age of Innocence	Edith Wharton
	The Sheik	Edith W. Hull
	Three Soldiers	John Dos Passos
	The Brimming Cup	Dorothy Canfield
	Outline of History	H.G. Wells

MUSIC

When My Baby Smiles at Me
Left All Alone Again Blues
Wild Rose
Mah Lindy Lou
Look For The Silver Lining
Blue Moon

If You Would Care for Me
Kitten of the Keys
Down in Chinatown
Japanese Sandman
Margie
Whispering

PEOPLE

Charles Ponzi Fleeces 1,000's of Their Savings with a Postal Coupon Scheme
Henry Cabot Lodge Leads the Senate to Reject Joining the League of Nations
Arturo Toscanini Records for the Victor Talking Machine Company
Fabled Joan of Arc Is Canonized in Rome

COMMENTARY

"Sports fans are stunned as eight Chicago White Sox players, including the illiterate but revered "Shoeless" Joe Jackson, are accused of taking bribes to throw the 1919 World Series so that gangsters could make a killing.

"The players are found innocent but are banned from baseball forever and the team sadly carries the nickname, Black Sox, for many years."

Bill Goodpage

1921 *Alcohol Sales Are Prohibited*

WORLD

US Refuses to Recognize Russia's Communist Government, Now Near Collapse
Southern Ireland Gains Dominion Status. Six Protestant Northern Counties Do Not

NATION

Congress Imposes National Immigration Quotas (Emergency Quota Act)
Junior Achievement Is Created to Develop Business Skills in Young People
President Harding Names Former President William Howard Taft as US Chief Justice
Harding Dedicates the Tomb of the Unknown Soldier in Arlington National Cemetery
Armistice Day Becomes a National Holiday
The Russian Famine Relief Act Authorizes 20 Million in Seed, Grain and Preserved Milk

ENVIRONMENT

More Than a Million Trucks Move Goods on Nation's Highways Up from 100,000 in 1909
Boll Weevil Infestations Cut Cotton Production in Half in Georgia and South Carolina
The Federal Highway Act Standardizes US Road Building Practice

LIFESTYLE

Although Illegal to Manufacture, Transport, or Sell Beverages with More Than 0.5% Alcohol,
    Buying and Consuming Alcohol Is Legal. Sacramental Wine Sales Boom!
Ten Million Prescriptions for Alcohol Will Be Written Each Year During Prohibition
Speakeasies, Private Closed Bars and Clubs Proliferate, and Women Drink Alongside Men
Cigarette Consumption Up to 43 Billion Per Year from 10 Billion Ten Years Ago

SCIENCE AND TECHNOLOGY

Insulin Is Extracted from a Pancreas for the First Time
Table Salt Is Now Iodized with Potassium Iodide to Prevent Goiter, But Is Not Mandatory
The Rorschach, Reaction to Ink Blots Test Is Tested
The Navy Creates the USS Langley, the First Aircraft Carrier Through a Ship Conversion

BUSINESS AND INDUSTRY

RCA, Begins Production of "Radio Music Boxes"
General Mills Creates the Betty Crocker Name for Homemaker Letters and Recipe Requests
Generators Are Now Standard Equipment on Model T Autos
Corning Glass Can Now Produce 30,000 Light Bulbs Per Hour

CONSUMER PRODUCTS AND SERVICES

White Castle Hamburgers ($.05 each) Begins Business in Wichita, Kansas
I Scream Bar (Later, Eskimo Pie) Is Created in Onawa, Iowa
Readers Digest Using Condensed Magazine Articles Is Founded
The Cartoons, *Smitty*, and *Tillie the Toiler* Appear
Mounds Candy Bars and Band-Aid Adhesive Bandages Are Available
Drano Sink Plumbing Cleaner Crystals Makes Its Appearance
Arrow Shirts for Men Have the Collar Attached

SPORTS

First Radio Coverage of a World Series Using Broadcast Bulletins

But I Have a Doctor's Prescription   1921

ARTS AND MEDIA

STAGE	*The Perfect Fool*	Ed Wynn
	Blossom Time	Sigmund Romberg
	Shuffle Along	Eubie Blake (First Broadway Musical Written, Acted and Produced by Blacks)
	Bill of Divorcement	Katharine Cornell
	Anna Christie	Eugene O'Neill
MOVIE	*The Sheik*	Rudolph Valentino, Adolph Menjou
	The Mark of Zorro	Douglas Fairbanks, Noah Beery
	Camille	Rudolph Valentino
	The Four Horsemen of the Apocalypse	Rudolph Valentino
	Disraeli	George Arliss
BOOK	*Mysterious Rider*	Zane Grey

MUSIC

Second Hand Rose
April Showers
Ain't We Got Fun

Baby Face
I'm Just Wild About Harry
Ma, He's Makin' Eyes at Me

PEOPLE

Captain Billy Mitchell Shockingly Demonstrates That a Bomber Can Sink a Battleship
Franklin Roosevelt (39) Is Stricken with Polio
At Age 71, Samuel Gompers is Elected President of the A.F. of L. for the 40th Time
"Weary Willy," Emmett Kelly's (22) Sad Face Clown Makes His 50 Year Debut

REFLECTION

A New York Times Editorial States That Robert Goddard's Rockets Cannot Possibly Work Because There Is Nothing in Space for the Rocket's Exhaust to Push Against.

COMMENTARY

"Prohibition started before the turn of the century in the plains of rural Kansas. Temperate, God fearing, farmers saw towns grow and were disgusted by the sinful behavior that typically accompanied growth. They believed that alcohol was at the root.

"Immigrants—and there were so many of them—didn't help. They loved their beer as a part of daily life. Temperates believed it was time to raise our moral and spiritual values—strike down devil alcohol and give men back to their families. We had won the war and now it was time to free the nation from crime, poverty, and depravity.

"The great moral experiment was beginning with a glorious solution."

Hank Hawthorne

INCIDENTALS AND TRIVIA

Warren G. Harding Is the First US President Born After the Civil War
and the First President to Ride in a Car for His Inauguration
Knee-Length Skirts for Women Become Popular But Raise Much Public Comment

WORLD

The Permanent Court of International Justice Opens at the Hague
War Debts Are a Complex Issue
Fascist, Benito Mussolini, Takes Control of the Italian Government
Vladimir I. Lenin Proclaims the Union of Soviet Socialist Republics (USSR)
Entrance to King Tutankhamen's Tomb Discovered in Egypt
A Naval Limitation Treaty Is Signed by France, Italy and Japan
Germany's Stock Market Collapses. The Mark Plummets in Value

NATION

The Lincoln Memorial Is Completed in Washington D.C.
Women Now Have Citizenship Independent of Their Spouses
The Teapot Dome Oil Lands Are Brewing a Scandal That May Affect the President

LIFESTYLE

The Word "Obey" Is Removed From the Marriage Service by the US Protestant
      Episcopal Church
More Americans Now Live in Cities Than on Farms and Small Towns

SCIENCE AND TECHNOLOGY

Hoyt Taylor and Leo Young Conduct US Radar Research
Alexis Carrel Discovers White Corpuscles, Blood Agents that Prevent the Spread of Infection

BUSINESS AND INDUSTRY

New York City Installs the First Mechanical Switchboard. Exchange Is Called Pennsylvania
Technicolor Film Is Developed But Is Little Used
Hollywood Establishes a Regulation Code to Ward Off Government Censorship
Campbell Soup Company Is Established
Ford Motor Company Buys Lincoln Motor Company from Henry Leland

CONSUMER PRODUCTS AND SERVICES

Maytag Demonstrates an Electric Dishwasher
A Thom McAn Shoe Store Opens
Hudson Produces the First Enclosed Steel Auto
Mah Jongg Is Introduced and the US Goes Crazy For It
True Confessions Magazine Is Born

PRICES

Bootleg Scotch	$25.00 per fifth
Bootleg Champagne	25.00 per fifth
Men's Shoes	4.00 per pair

SPORTS

Gene Sarazen (21) Wins Golf's US Open Tournament

While the US Is Getting Healthy   1922

ARTS AND MEDIA

STAGE

The Hairy Ape	Eugene O'Neill
Abie's Irish Rose	Anne Nichols
Rain	Somerset Maugham
Hamlet	John Barrymore, Tyrone Power

MOVIE

Orphans of the Storm	D.W. Griffith, Lillian and Dorothy Gish,
Oliver Twist	Lon Chaney, Jackie Coogan
Blood and Sand	Rudolph Valentino, Lila Lee
Our Gang (short)	Hal Roach, Jackie Cooper
Nanook of the North	Robert Flaherty
Robin Hood	Douglas Fairbanks
Tess of the Storm Country	Mary Pickford

RADIO

The Fred Waring Show
Will Rogers
The Happiness Boys

BOOK

Tales of the Jazz Age	F. Scott Fitzgerald
Babbitt	Sinclair Lewis
Julia	Booth Tarkington
If Winter Comes	A.S.M. Hutchinson
The Wasteland	T.S. Eliot
The Enormous Room	e.e. cummings

MUSIC

Chicago	*Song of Love*
Carolina in the Morning	*April Showers*
Toot Toot Tootsie Good-bye	*Say It With Music*
Wish I Could Shimmy Like Sister Kate	*Rose of the Rio Grande*

PEOPLE

President Harding Is the First President Heard Over Radio
Life Magazine Drama Critic, Robert Benchley, Begins a Second Career as a Humorist
Lt. James H. Doolittle (26) Flies Across the Country in One Day (21½ hours)
Charles Atlas Wins the *Most Perfectly Developed Man* Contest
Mary "Texas" Guinan, Begins Her Career as a Nightclub Hostess in Classy Speakeasies

QUOTES

"Every new invention that is practical and economical...will be brought to (your) notice. The time spent on housework can be enormously reduced in every home, without any loss to its comfort, and often with a great increase to its well-being."
    The Reason for Good Housekeeping
    Good Housekeeping Magazine March 1922

"Hello Sucker!"

    "Texas" Guinan

INCIDENTALS AND TRIVIA

US Post Office Officials Destroy 500 Copies of James Joyce's *Ulysses*
Films Require Bedroom Scenes with Twin Beds and They Become Quite Fashionable
The Word "Commercial" Is Coined for the First Paid Radio Announcement

1923 *President Warren Harding Dies*

WORLD

US Occupation Forces in Germany Return Home
German Inflation Soars Out of Control
Russia Makes a Dramatic Recovery From Famine Levels Two Years Prior
Lenin Creates the First of Many Forced-Labor Camps

NATION

President Harding Dies of Natural Causes in San Francisco While on a Western Tour
Calvin Coolidge Is Sworn in as the 30th US President by His Father, a Notary Public.
New York State Withdraws from Prohibition Enforcement and Hands It Back to the US
Treasury Department Runs the Bureau of Prohibition. Its 1,500 Agents Make Little Impact
Lacking Any Organization, Farmers Overproduce Basic Crops Like Wheat

DISASTER

A Massive Earthquake Claims 150,000 Lives in Tokyo and Yokohama Frank Lloyd Wright's
    Imperial Hotel Survives Intact

LIFESTYLE

14 Million Automobiles Are Registered in the US. There Are 108 Auto Manufacturers
Cops and Judges Look the Other Way or Are "On the Take." Only an Estimated 1% of Liquor
    Is Being Stopped Through Enforcement

SCIENCE AND TECHNOLOGY

A Tetanus Vaccine Is Now Available
In a Public Demonstration of Mechanical Television, a Still Picture of President Harding
    Is Transmitted Wirelessly
Lee De Forest Develops a Method of Recording Sound Directly on Film

BUSINESS AND INDUSTRY

Metro and Sam Goldwyn Studios Combine as MGM
Pet Milk Company Is Formed
United States Steel Reduces Its Standard Workday from 12 to 8 Hours
Birdseye Seafoods Opens but the Public Is Wary of Frozen Foods
Ethyl Corp. Adds Tetraethyl Lead as a Gasoline Additive to Reduce Pre-Ignition (pinging)
The Hertz Drive-Ur-Self System Begins Operations
Major Auto Producers Start Annual Model Changes to Obsolete Older Cars and
    Drive Smaller Competitors Out of Business

CONSUMER PRODUCTS AND SERVICES

Maidenform Brassieres (with a little uplift) Are Marketed
Col. Jacob Schick Patents an Electric Shaver
A&W Root Beer Stands Appear
Time, A Slick News Magazine, Begins Publication
The Butterfinger Candy Bar Is Born
B.F. Goodrich Galoshes Use the Term, ZIPPER, for Their Slide Fastener (See 1913)
Coco Chanel Markets a Synthetic Odor Perfume Called Chanel #5
Moon Mullins (with his Kid Brother, Kayo) Comic Strip Appears

Calvin Coolidge Is Sworn In 1923

SPORTS

Yankee Stadium Opens in New York City
Amateur, Robert "Bobby" Jones Wins the US Open Golf Tournament
Luis Angel Firpo Knocks Jack Dempsey Out of the Ring but Dempsey Retains the Title

ARTS AND MEDIA

STAGE

Artists and Models	Frank Fay (Bare Breasts Set off a Censorship Drive)
Ziegfield Follies	Fanny Brice
Poppy	W.C. Fields
Icebound	Owen Davis

MOVIE

The Ten Commandments	C.B. DeMille Theodore Roberts, Estelle Taylor
Our Hospitality	Buster Keaton, Natalie Talmadge
The Hunchback of Notre Dame	Lon Chaney,
The Covered Wagon	Alan Hale,
Anna Christie	Blanche Sweet
Down to the Sea in Ships	William Walcott, Clara Bow

RADIO

The Eveready Hour (variety)
A&P Gypsies
Dr. Walter Damrosch and His Orchestra
Ed Wynn

BOOK

Lost Lady	Willa Cather
Etiquette	Emily Post
Through the Wheat	Thomas Boyd

MUSIC

Barney Google	*I Love Life*
Charleston	*Sonny Boy*
That Old Gang of Mine	*Linger Awhile*
Yes, We Have No Bananas	

PEOPLE

Juan Terry Trippe Founds Pan American World Airways
Wilhelm Messerschmitt (27) Opens an Aircraft Manufacturing Plant
Preacher, Aimee Semple McPherson, Dedicates Her Huge Angelus Temple in Los Angeles
A.C. Nielson (26) Starts a Data Collection and Market Research Company
Walter P. Chrysler Becomes President of Maxwell Motor Cars

QUOTES

"I believe that television, which is the technical name for seeing as well as hearing by radio, will come to pass in due course."
David Sarnoff

INCIDENTALS AND TRIVIA

Calvin Coolidge Is the Only US President Born on the Nation's Birthday (Born July 4, 1872)
Coolidge Lights the First White House Christmas Tree, a Tradition That Will Endure
Good Humor Adds Bobsled Bells to the White Refrigerated Delivery Trucks. White-Uniformed
"Chauffeurs" Jingle Around Youngstown, OH

1924 *Radio Is Really Catching On*

WORLD

Turkey's New President Abolishes the Caliphate, the Veil and Establishes Western Ways
A Power Struggle Begins Between Josef Stalin and Leon Trotsky After Lenin Dies

NATION

Calvin Coolidge Easily Defeats Democrat John W. Davis for President
J. Edgar Hoover Becomes Director of the Federal Bureau of Investigation
Congress Grants US Citizenship to All American Indians
Toastmasters International Is Founded in Santa Ana, California
Rural Free Delivery of Mail Now Reaches 6.5 Million (see 1901)
The Soldier's Bonus Bill Offers Paid-Up 20 Year Annuities for Most Veterans
The Dawes Plan Will Reorganize German War Debt Payments and Stabilize Their Economy
First Macy's Thanksgiving Day Parade in New York City

ENVIRONMENT, SAFETY AND HEALTH

The First Effective Chemical Pesticides Are Introduced

LIFESTYLE

The Rivoli Theater on Broadway Installs Refrigeration for Cooling
There Are Now 2.5 Million Radios in the US (See 1920) Most Are Crystal Sets with Earphones
70% of All Bread Is Now "Store Bought," Up from 30% in 1910

SCIENCE AND TECHNOLOGY

Astronomer Edwin Hubble Shows that Galaxies Are "Island Universes"
Raymond Dart Identifies a Fossil of a Close Relative of Early Humans
The US Navy Purchases a German Dirigible and Renames It the *Los Angeles*
Two Douglas Aircraft Plywood, Spruce and Canvas *World Cruisers* Complete an
       Around the World Flight

BUSINESS AND INDUSTRY

IBM Corporation Is Formed by Thomas Watson
First Chrysler Automobile Is Sold by Maxwell Motors. Features 4 Wheel Hydraulic Brakes
General Motors Introduces the Pontiac
The First US Diesel Electric Locomotive Goes into Service

CONSUMER PRODUCTS AND SERVICES

Radio Sales Rise Dramatically from $60 Million Last Year to $350 Million
Little Orphan Annie Comic Strip by Harold Gray, Debuts
Betty Crocker Gets a Voice on the *Cooking School of the Air*
Wheaties Breakfast Cereal Goes on the Market
Kimberly Clark Introduces Celluwipes (later Kleenex), a Disposable Handkerchief

SPORTS

The Boston Bruins Become the First American Team in the National Hockey League
Harold "Red" Grange and Others Are Making Football a Very Popular Sport

Do I Hear a Rhapsody?

ARTS AND MEDIA

STAGE	All God's Chillun Got Wings	Eugene O'Neil, Paul Robeson, Mary Blair
	The Student Prince	Sigmund Romberg
	Desire Under the Elms	Eugene O'Neill, Walter Huston
	What Price Glory	Maxwell Anderson
	Rose Marie	Rudolph Friml
MOVIE	The Navigator	Buster Keaton, Kathryn McGuire
	Greed	ZaSu Pitts, Jean Hersholt
	Jubilo Jr.	Hal Roach, Our Gang Children's Group
RADIO	Ipana Troubadors	
	Schrafft's Tearoom Orchestra	
BOOK	So Big	Edna Ferber
	In Our Time	Ernest Hemingway

MUSIC

California, Here I Come
Indian Love Call
Rose Marie
I Wonder What's Become of Sally
The Man I Love

Oh, Lady Be Good
Tea for Two
Lady Be Good
Fascinating Rhythm

PEOPLE

Serge Koussevitsky Begins His 25-Year Career as Conductor of the Boston Symphony Orchestra
Nathan Leopold & Richard Loeb Sentenced to Life Imprisonment for the Killing of Bobby Franks

QUOTES

"Words, as is well known, are the great foes of reality."
                Joseph Conrad (1857-1924)

"While the State exists, there can be no freedom; when there is freedom, there will be no State."   V.I. Lenin (1870-1924)

"When I give a man an office, I watch him carefully to seen whether he is swelling or growing."   Woodrow Wilson (1856-1924)

COMMENTARY

"Loving history as I do, there are many past moments that I wish I could have personally observed. Certainly one that I would have cherished would to have been in the audience at New York's Aeolian Hall on February 2, 1924. Paul Whiteman's Palais Royal Orchestra, already well known for broadening American musical tastes to classical and classical jazz, that night played an all American music concert.

The main selection was Rhapsody in Blue, just completed by George Gershwin, with the composer at the piano. It marked Gershwin as a serious composer for the first time and Rhapsody was so popular that Whiteman's first recording sold over a million copies!"

Kate Hawthorne

1925 *The Klan Boldly Marches*

WORLD

World Powers Agree to Ban Poison Gas in Any Future Wars
France Begins Construction of a Heavily Fortified Maginot Line Facing Germany
Reza Shah Pahlevi Assumes Power in Persia
Popular Field Marshall Paul von Hindenburg Is Elected President of Germany

NATION

Teacher, John T. Scopes, Is Arrested for Teaching Darwin's Theories of Evolution. Prosecuted
    by William Jennings Bryan and Defended by Clarence Darrow, He Is Convicted and
    Fined $100 in What Becomes Known as the "Scopes Monkey Trial"
The Ku Klux Klan Parades 40,000 Strong in Washington D.C.; It Has 5 Million US Members
Henry Ford Inaugurates Commercial Air Service Between Chicago and Detroit
Gen. William "Billy" Mitchell Goes Before a Court-Martial for His Public Remarks About Air
    Over Naval Superiority and Military Incompetence. He Is Convicted and Resigns
A System of Standardized Route Numbers Greatly Simplify Road Directions

DISASTER

Worst Tornado in US History Kills 689 People in Missouri, Illinois and Indiana
US Army Dirigible, Shenandoah, Is Wrecked in Ohio, Killing Fourteen

LIFESTYLE

The Term, MOTEL Is Coined by a California Innkeeper
The Night Club Business Is Booming
The Florida Land Boom Reaches Its Peak. Land Values Implode as Many Investors Find
    That the "Lots" They Purchased Are under Water
The Charleston Dance Craze Goes Well With Short Skirts and Short Hair. Some Dancers
    Add Metal Taps to Shoes and Soon Taps Are Common
Starched Collars for Men Are Still Part of "Sunday Best" Dress

SCIENCE AND TECHNOLOGY

An Antitoxin for Scarlet Fever Is Developed

BUSINESS AND INDUSTRY

Merchants Parcel Delivery Becomes United Parcel Service (UPS)
Chrysler Corporation Is Created from a Reorganization of Maxwell Motors
AT&T Organizes Bell Laboratories to Consolidate Its Research Activities

CONSUMER PRODUCTS AND SERVICES

General Electric Introduces the Round Monitor Top Refrigerator
Craftsman Brand Hand Tools Appear in Sears' Winter 1925/26 Catalog
The *New Yorker* Magazine Debuts
Lorillard Introduces Old Gold Cigarettes with "Not a Cough in a Carload."
The Brunswick Panatrope Is an All-Electric Record Player with a Loudspeaker"

SPORTS

Henry "Lou" Gehrig Begins a 14-Year, 2,130 Consecutive Game Career with the N.Y. Yankees
Robert "Lefty" Groves Begins His 17-Year Career with the Philadelphia Athletics

ARTS AND MEDIA

STAGE	*No No Nanette*	Otto Harbach, Vincent Youmans
	The Coconuts	Groucho, Chico, Harpo, Zeppo Marx, Margaret Dumont
MOVIE	*The Gold Rush*	Charlie Chaplin, Georgia Hale
	The Big Parade	King Vidor, John Gilbert
	The Phantom of the Opera	Lon Chaney, Mary Philbin
RADIO	*The Smith Family*	Jim and Marian Jordan
	Grand Old Opry	Roy Acuff, Hank Williams, Ernest Tubbs, many others
BOOK	*An American Tragedy*	Theodore Dreiser
	The Great Gatsby	F. Scott Fitzgerald
	Manhattan Transfer	John Dos Passos
	Arrowsmith	Sinclair Lewis
	Porgy	Du Bose Heyward

MUSIC

Sweet Georgia Brown
Don't Bring Lulu
A Cup of Coffee, a Sandwich and You
Tea for Two

I Want to Be Happy
Show Me the Way to Go Home
Collegiate
Thanks for the Buggy Ride

PEOPLE

Mrs. William B. Ross of Wyoming Becomes the First Woman Governor
Publisher, William Randolph Hearst, Opens His "Castle" at San Simeon, California
Al Capone Takes over as Boss of Chicago Bootlegging

QUOTES

"The business of America is business."
          Calvin Coolidge (1925)

"Blow some my way."

          Woman to man lighting a cigarette in a Chesterfield
          advertisement, suggesting that women should smoke

COMMENTARY

          "The Ku Klux Klan is reborn. The original Klan formed to
fight Reconstruction by harassing blacks after the Civil War, lasted
only a few years. This new Klan, which also started in the South, has
also been very active in the North and Midwest. Intolerant of black
people, their bigotry also now seems to be anti-Semitic and anti-
Catholic as well.
          "Clothed in robes, masks and odd looking caps to maintain
secrecy, they march and strut, threaten, burn crosses and carry out
random lynchings. Clearly they want to draw power to themselves
through their militancy and their ability to create fear, as they
pursue their apparent quest for a pure, white America."

"Miss Picky"
Irene English

WORLD

Josef Stalin Assumes Total Control in the Soviet Union. Leo Trotsky Is Expelled
Benito Mussolini and His Fascist Party Assume Total Control in Italy
Chiang Kai-shek Assumes Party Control in China After the Death of Sun Yat-sen
US Marines Temporarily Occupy Nicaragua to Quell an Uprising

NATION

Congress Establishes the US Army Air Corps
Negro History Week, 2nd Week in February, Organized by Carter Woodson.

ENVIRONMENT, SAFETY AND HEALTH

Safety Glass Windshields Are Now Standard Equipment on Expensive Autos Like the Stutz

LIFESTYLE

Civilian Labor Force Unemployment Rate Is 1.8 %
Attitudes Toward Prohibition Are Changing:
    18.9% Are Satisfied with the Law
    49.8% Want the Law Modified
    31.3% Want a Complete Repeal
Movies Are America's Favorite Form of Entertainment

SCIENCE AND TECHNOLOGY

Lt. Commander Richard E. Byrd and Pilot, Floyd Bennett Fly Across the North Pole
Airship Dirigible *Norge* Crosses the Pole within Days of Byrd and Bennett
The B Vitamin Is Proven to Be More Than One Vitamin
X-rays Are Found to Produce Mutations. Their Extensive Use Will Be Scaled Back

BUSINESS AND INDUSTRY

RCA Creates the National Broadcasting Company (NBC), Which Begins Radio Broadcasting.
    Initial Program Reaches Two Million
Film Studios Actively Working on Sound. Warner Promotes Vitaphone and Fox-Case
    Counters with Movietone
Ford Introduces a 40-Hour Work Week
The All-Metal Ford Pullman Monoplane Looks Strikingly Modern
Greyhound Corporation Is Formed to Create Bus Competition for Railroads
B.F. Goodrich Company Creates a Synthetic Rubber Compound

CONSUMER PRODUCTS AND SERVICES

The Chrysler Imperial Competes with Cadillac, Lincoln, Packard and Pierce-Arrow
Ford Model T Production Ends (see Trivia)
A New Permanent Waving Method Makes the "Permanent" Very Fashionable
Minnesota Valley Canning Company of Minnesota Introduces the Jolly Green Giant
    Character for Their Canned Peas
The Book of the Month Club Is Formed
Union Carbide Offers Prestone, an Ethylene Glycol Anti-Freeze for Automobile Radiators
Frieda Carter of Tennessee, Invents Miniature Golf
Canned Ham by the Hormel Company Is an Instant Hit with the Public

Dictators Abroad Tighten Control 1926

SPORTS

Gertrude Ederle, Becomes the First American Woman to Swim the English Channel
James Joseph "Gene" Tunney Narrowly Defeats Jack Dempsey on Points to Become
        Heavyweight Boxing Champion
Baseball Now Uses Cushioned, Cork Center Baseballs

ARTS AND MEDIA

STAGE	*The Desert Song*	Sigmund Romberg
	Gentlemen Prefer Blondes	Anita Loos
	Sex	Mae West (Police Close the Play)
MOVIE	*Don Juan*	John Barrymore, Mary Astor, Myrna Loy, Hedda Hopper
	Tumbleweeds	William S. Hart, Barbara Bedford
	The Temptress	Greta Garbo, Lionel Barrymore
	Ben Hur	Ramon Navarro, Francis X. Bushman
	What Price Glory?	Victor McLaglen, Edmond Lowe, Dolores Del Rio
	Putting Pants on Phillip	Stan Laurel, Oliver Hardy
RADIO	*Father Coughlin*	
	The Smith Brothers (Trade and Mark)	
BOOK	*Abraham Lincoln, the Prairie Years*	Carl Sandberg
	The Sun Also Rises	Ernest Hemingway
	Topper	Thorne Smith
	The Private Life of Helen of Troy	John Erskine
	The Story of Philosophy	Will Durant
	Winnie the Pooh	A.A. Milne

MUSIC

The Desert Song	*Baby Face*
The Birth of the Blues	*Charmaine*
Bye Bye Blackbird	*Gimme A Little Kiss...*
Do-Do-Do	*When the Red, Red Robin...*
Someone to Watch Over Me	*Muskrat Ramble*

PEOPLE

Robert H. Goddard Launches a Liquid Propelled Rocket That, He Believes, Will Someday
        Take Men to the Moon
Evangelist Sister Aimee Semple McPherson Vanishes from a Beach and Is Believed to Be
        Drowned. She Returns a Month Later After an Apparent Tryst with Her Lover
Joseph P. Kennedy Takes Control of a Low Budget Studio Producing Westerns. Stars Include
        Tom Mix and Horse, Tony
Harvey Firestone Extends His Rubber Tree Plantation Empire to Liberia in Africa
Entertainer, Josephine Baker (20), Opens a Paris Night Club
Harry Houdini Remains Underwater 91 Minutes with Supposedly Only 6 Minutes of Air

INCIDENTALS AND TRIVIA

In 25 years, Ford Produced 15 Million Model T Automobiles; Approximately Half of All Cars
        in the United States.

1927 *Lindy Is America's Hero*

WORLD

London Severs Relations with the USSR, Which Retaliates by Executing 20 British "Spies"
Saudi Arabia Attains Its Independence
A Communist Uprising Is Crushed In China

NATION

Supreme Court Rules That Illegal Income Is Taxable. A New Tool Against Gangsters
Grauman's Chinese Theater Opens in Hollywood
Massachusetts Enacts the First Compulsory Automobile Insurance Law
The Academy of Motion Picture Arts and Sciences Is Created
Sculptor, Gutzon Borglum, Starts Carving Four Presidents in South Dakota's Black Hills

DISASTER

Entire Crew (40) of US Submarine S-4 Dies After Their Vessel Sinks off Massachusetts

LIFESTYLE

Vaudeville Is Seriously Hurt By Movies and Radio. Top Stars Sign on with the Networks
Millions of Sears Roebuck and Montgomery Ward Catalogs Are Issued. Most Rural Homes
        Have at Least One
280 Broadway Shows Open in 1927-28 Season—An All-Time Record

SCIENCE AND TECHNOLOGY

The First Iron Lung Is Employed
The Underwater Holland Tunnel Linking Manhattan with New Jersey Is Completed
Army Air Corps Pilots Fly from San Francisco to Honolulu

BUSINESS AND INDUSTRY

Ford Motor Company Unveils the Model A
DuPont Patents Cellophane, a Transparent, Moisture-Proof Packaging Material
Lenders Bagel Bakery Is Founded
J.C. Penney Opens Store 500
The Volvo Is Manufactured and Sold in Sweden to Combat Imports

CONSUMER PRODUCTS AND SERVICES

"Cyclone" Roller Coaster Opens at Brooklyn's Coney Island
Bill Marriott Creates the First of His Hot Shoppe Restaurants
Children's Wagon Builder, Antonio Passin, Introduces the Radio Flyer
The First Car Radios Are Introduced
Victor Markets a Phonograph with an Automatic Record Changer
Continental Baking Offers Hostess Cakes and Wonder Bread
Borden Introduces Homogenized Milk
Colgate Promotes "Super Suds" for Laundry and Kitchen
Daniel F. Gerber of Michigan Creates Gerber Foods for Babies

PRICES

Transatlantic Cable Telephone Calls Are Now Possible at $75 for Three Minutes

"Showboat" Is a Smash Hit 1927

SPORTS

Ty Cobb Passes the 4,000 Hit Level
Babe Ruth Hits a Season High 60 Home Runs and a New Major League Record
Tunney Again Defeats Dempsey to Retain Boxing Title. Dempsey Knocks Tunney Down But
    Not Out in Controversial Long Count by the Referee in the Seventh Round
Pitcher, Walter Johnson Ends His Career. He Pitched 113 Shutouts and Struck Out 3,503

ARTS AND MEDIA

STAGE	*Show Boat*	Jerome Kern, Oscar Hammerstein II
	Burlesque	Barbara Stanwyk
	The Barker	Walter Huston, Claudette Colbert
	Coquette	Helen Hayes
MOVIE	*The Jazz Singer*	Al Jolson, William Demarest (Partial Sound)
	Flesh and the Devil	John Gilbert, Greta Garbo
	Sunrise	George O'Brien, Janet Gaynor
	It	Clara Bow, Antonio Moreno

RADIO

The Collier Hour	*Roxy's Gang*
The Chesterfield Supper Club	*Palmolive Hour*
The Majestic Theater Hour	*Atwater Kent Hour*

BOOK	*Elmer Gantry*	Sinclair Lewis
	The Collected Poems of Ezra Pound	Ezra Pound
	The Magic Mountain	Thomas Mann
	The Bridge of San Luis Rey	Thornton Wilder

MUSIC

Blue Skies	*Thou Swell*
Let a Smile Be Your Umbrella	*Strike Up the Band*
I'm Looking Over a Four Leaf	*'S Wonderful*
* Clover*	*Old Man River*
Ain't She Sweet?	*Can't Help Lovin' That Man*
Me and My Shadow	* of Mine*
My Heart Stood Still	*Why Do I Love You?*

PEOPLE

Charles A. Lindbergh (25) Flies Solo Across the Atlantic from Long Island to Paris. Four
    Million People Turn Out for His Broadway Ticker Tape Parade Upon His Return
Franklin Roosevelt Founds the Georgia Warm Springs Foundation to Treat Polio Victims

CRIME AND PUNISHMENT

Nicola Sacco and Bartolomeo Vanzetti Are Executed for the 1920 Killing of a Factory Guard.
    Many Feel They Were Innocent and Railroaded for Their Radical Beliefs

QUOTES

"Who the hell wants to hear actors talk?"
    Harry M. Warner
    Warner Brothers 1927

1928 *Hoover Gets the White House*

WORLD

The Kellogg-Briand Peace Pact, Outlawing War, Is Signed by 21 Countries

Josef Stalin Orders Collectivization of Soviet Agriculture in the First Five Year Plan. Millions of Kulaks (Rich Peasants) Will Be Liquidated or Exiled to Siberia for Resisting

Chiang Kai-shek Takes Beijing and Is Elected President of China

NATION

Herbert Hoover Easily Defeats Democrat Alfred E. Smith for President. Attacks on Smith's Catholicism Are Vicious but Effective

The National Conference of Christians and Jews Is Founded to Fight Bigotry

The Civilian Labor Force Unemployment Rate Is 4.2 %

ENVIRONMENT, SAFETY AND HEALTH

Boulder Canyon (Dam) Project Is Approved for Irrigation, Flood Control and Electric Power in the Western States

A Flood Control Act Will Build Extensive Levees on the Lower Mississippi River

Congress Authorizes Brice Canyon National Park in Utah

Florida's Tamiami Trail through the Everglade Swamps Links Miami with Fort Myers

DISASTER

A Florida Hurricane Causes Lake Okeechobee to Overflow, Killing 1836

California's St. Francis Dam, 3 Years Old, Gives Way and Kills 45

SCIENCE AND TECHNOLOGY

Alexander Fleming Discovers Penicillin in Green Mold Culture

A Schenectady, NY, Station Broadcasts Test Patterns to a Few Hundred Local TVs

German Dirigible, Graf Zeppelin, Makes the First Commercial Flight Across the Atlantic

BUSINESS AND INDUSTRY

Willam Paley, Cigar-Company Fortune Heir, Buys CBS

Walter and Cordelia Knott Open a Tea House and Berry Market in Buena Park, CA

Minnesota Mining and Manufacturing Company Creates Cellophane Tape

Chrysler Introduces the Medium Priced DeSoto (see 1961)

Chrysler Claims Its Imperial 80 Is America's Most Powerful Automobile

Chrysler Offers the Plymouth as an Alternative to Ford and Chevrolet

John Northrop Quits Lockheed to Form His Own Company

CONSUMER PRODUCTS AND SERVICES

Edwin Shoemaker of Monroe, Michigan, Invents the La-Z-Boy Recliner

Fleer Chewing Gum Company in Philadelphia Introduces Pink Bubble Gum

Kelloggs Adds Rice Crispies to Its Cereal Lineup

Broccoli Is Imported from Italy and Grown in California

PRICES

NAB, a Peanut Butter Cracker Sandwich Pack, Sells for Five Cents

First Class Postage Is Reduced a Penny, Back to Two Cents

SPORTS

Gene Tunney Retires From Boxing as the World Champion.
Jimmy Foxx Starts His Baseball Career with the Philadelphia Athletics

ARTS AND MEDIA

STAGE		
	Animal Crackers	Marx Brothers
	Whoopie	Eddie Cantor
	Three Cheers	Will Rogers
	Strange Interlude	Lynn Fontanne
	Front Page	Charles MacArthur, Ben Hecht
	Diamond Lil	Mae West (She and the Cast are Hauled Off to Jail)
	Blackbirds of 1928	Bill Robinson, Adelaide Hall
MOVIE		
	The Lights of New York	(First All-Talking Movie)
	Wings	Clara Bow, Buddy Rogers, Richard Arlen
	Seventh Heaven	Frank Borzage, Janet Gaynor
	The Way of All Flesh	Emil Jannings
	The Singing Fool	Al Jolson, Betty Bronson
	Street Angel	Frank Borzage, Janet Gaynor, Charles Farrell
	Sadie Thompson	Gloria Swanson, Lionel Barrymore
	Plane Crazy (animated)	Mickey Mouse Makes His Silent Film Debut
RADIO		
	The Chase and Sanborn Hour	Maurice Chevalier, Eddie Cantor
	Amos 'n' Andy	Freeman Gosden (Amos,) Charles Correll (Andy)
	The Voice of Firestone	Hugh James, Howard Barlow Orchestra
BOOK		
	John Brown's Body	Stephen Vincent Benet
	Coming of Age in Samoa	Margaret Mead
	Lady Chatterley's Lover	D. H. Lawrence (Banned in US Until 1959)

MUSIC

Bolero   Maurice Ravel
Makin' Whoopie   *I'm Sitting On Top of the World*
Lover Come Back to Me   *There's a Rainbow 'Round My*
You Took Advantage of Me   *Shoulder*
I Wanna Be Loved By You   *Sonny Boy*
Let's Do It (Let's Fall in Love)   *I Can't Give You Anything But Love*
It All Depends On You   *Baby*

PEOPLE

The Highwire Wallendas Debut with the Ringling Brothers Circus
Lawrence Welk (24), Starts a Small Band in South Dakota
Rudy Vallee (27), Forms a Band in New York and Uses a Megaphone to Amplify His Voice

QUOTES

"Some folk like their luck buttered."
                    Thomas Hardy (1840-1928)

INCIDENTALS AND TRIVIA

A Moving Electric Sign Is Installed on the Times Square Building

1929 *Wall Street Collapses*

WORLD

Josef Stalin Expels Leon Trotsky from the USSR, Ending All Threats to His Rule
Vatican City Is Created as a Sovereign State in Rome
The Kingdom of Serbs, Croats and Slovenes Becomes the Kingdom of Yugoslavia (see 1991)

NATION

Prohibition Is Now Believed to be Unenforceable. The Public Is Opposed, Apathetic, or Profiting
US Gross National Product Is $103 Billion (see 1932,1940)
"Black Tuesday" Wall Street Crash on October 28
Banks Fail, Unemployment Soars, as the Great US Economy Suddenly Goes Sour

ENVIRONMENT, SAFETY AND HEALTH

The US and Canada Create a Joint Action to Preserve Niagara Falls
A Baltimore Study Shows That 60% of the Area Children Have Rickets

LIFESTYLE

Approximately 60% of All US Citizens Have Incomes of $2,000 or Less, Which Is Considered
        to Be the Minimum for the Basic Necessities of Life
Average Weekly Wage Is $28.00
Gang Murders Are Prevalent in Big Cities. Chicago's St. Valentines Day Massacre Stuns the Nation

SCIENCE AND TECHNOLOGY

Astronomer Edwin Hubble Determines that the Universe Is Expanding
Lt. James H. Dolittle Guides a Consolidated NY2 Biplane Over New York's Mitchell Field in
        the First All-Instrument Flight
Lt. Commander Richard E. Byrd Flies Over the South Pole
The Graf Zeppelin Completes the First Around the World Flight

BUSINESS AND INDUSTRY

General Motors Buys the German Opal Motors
Auburn Introduces a Front Wheel Drive Model Automobile
There Are Now Over 15,000 A&P Stores Nationwide
Coca Cola Adopts the Slogan, *The Pause That Refreshes*
Aviation Pioneer, Glenn Curtiss, Displays a Mobile Home Trailer
Grumman Aircraft Begins Operations

CONSUMER PRODUCTS AND SERVICES

Talking Pictures Have Now Virtually Ousted the Silent Films
Avon Personal Care Products Become Available
The Tom Thumb Miniature Golf Course Is Patented
Ford Builds a Boxy Wooden Body Around a Model A and Creates the First Station Wagon
Kodak Introduces 16mm Film and Home Cameras and Projectors
Nestle Colorinse Is a Home Use Hair Coloring Product
Popeye, The Sailor Man Cartoon

PRICES

A Three Ounce Letter Sent Air Mail for $.25 Will Cross the Country in Only 31 Hours

Banks Fail, Unemployment Soars 1929

ARTS AND MEDIA

Abstract Painter, Georgia O'Keefe, Paints *Black Flowers* and *Blue Larkspur*

STAGE	*A Wonderful Night*	Archie Leach (Later Cary Grant)
	Boom Boom	Archie Leach, Jeanette MacDonald
	Show Girl	Ruby Keeler
MOVIE	*Broadway Melody*	Bessie Love, Anita Page
	The Divine Lady	Frank Lloyd
	In Old Arizona	Warner Baxter
	Coquette	Mary Pickford
	The Iron Mask	Douglas Fairbanks, Belle Bennett
	The Coconuts	Groucho, Harpo, Chico, Zeppo Marx
	The Virginian	Gary Cooper, Richard Arlen, Walter Huston
	Bulldog Drummond	Ronald Coleman, Joan Bennett
	The Green Goddess	George Arliss, Alice Joyce
	Wild Orchids	Greta Garbo
	His Glorious Night	John Gilbert (Squeaky Voice Ends His Career)
RADIO	*The Fleischmann Hour*	Rudy Vallee
	The Goldbergs	Gertrude Berg
	First Nighter	Don Ameche
	The Hour of Charm	Phil Spitalny & All Girl Orchestra, Including Evelyn and Her Magic Violin
BOOK	*All Quiet on the Western Front*	Erich Maria Remarque
	Look Homeward Angel	Thomas Wolfe

MUSIC

Stardust
Am I Blue?
With a Song in My Heart
Tip Toe Thru the Tulips With Me

Can't We Be Friends?
You Do Something for Me
Just a Gigolo
Honeysuckle Rose

QUOTES

"A woman must have money and a room of her own if she is to write fiction."
Virginia Woolf (1929)

COMMENTARY

"Ten years have passed since the Volstead Act, but things just haven't worked out the way they were supposed to. Instead of ridding the country of poverty and crime by banning alcohol, it seems it has only gotten worse. Everyone's drinking but pretending we're not. Gangsters own the liquor and own a lot of local governments too.

"Some folks are saying that we should make liquor legal—take the money from the mobs and put the taxes back in the treasury. That makes sense to ordinary citizens.

"President Hoover wants Prohibition laws 'studied' but the Democrats want it repealed."

Bill Goodpage

1930 *Ain't Got Much Money*

WORLD

The Economic Depression Is Now Worldwide
In Turkey, Constantinople Becomes Istanbul; Angora Becomes Ankara
South African White Women Gain Suffrage. Blacks of Both Sexes Are Disenfranchised
Other Major Powers Raise Tariffs to Retaliate Against the US Hawley-Smoot Tariff Act

NATION

Due to the Depression US Emigration Exceeds Immigration for the First Time in History
Over 1,300 US Banks Close This Year
Congress Appropriates $300 Million for Road Construction
The Hawley-Smoot Tariff Act Raises Duties on Many Items to Protect US Jobs
Congress Creates the US Veterans Administration

ENVIRONMENT, SAFETY AND HEALTH

Congress Authorizes the Carlsbad Caverns National Park in New Mexico
Extreme Drought Extends over the South and Midwest

DISASTER

320 Prisoners at Ohio State Penitentiary Die in a Fire. Built for 1500, the Prison Houses 4300

LIFESTYLE

The US Population Is Now 123 Million. 5.5% Are Over Age 65. 25% Are on Farms
4.5 Million Are Estimated to be Unemployed, But One in Every Five Owns an Automobile
Illiteracy Is Down to 4.3% of the Population

SCIENCE AND TECHNOLOGY

Sir Frank Whittle Patents the Jet Engine
Philo T. Farnsworth Develops a New Electronic TV Scanning Device
Laura Ingalls Becomes the First Woman to Fly Across the US
A. Harold Bromley Becomes the First Person to Fly Across the Pacific
Astronomers at the Lowell Observatory in Arizona Discover the Planet Pluto
Vitamin D Is Isolated and Will Be Used to Fortify Foods

BUSINESS AND INDUSTRY

Newly Formed United Airlines Institutes Airline Stewardess Service
Pan American Airlines Begins Service to South America
TWA Is Formed Through a Merger
Dry Ice (Solid Carbon Dioxide) Is Available Commercially

CONSUMER PRODUCTS AND SERVICES

The Twinkie, a Banana Cream-Filled Cake, Is Born
Wonder Bread Is Now Available "Sliced"
Jiffy Biscuit Mix
Mars Distributes Snickers Candy Bars
King Cullen Supermarket on Long Island Is Open All Night
Sunbeam Offers the Mixmaster, a Kitchen Food Blender
The Toastmaster Automatic Toaster Is Marketed

SPORTS

Max Schmeling of Germany Is Awarded the Heavyweight Title over Jack Sharkey after
Sharkey Fouls Him in the Fourth Round
Hack Wilson of Chicago's Cubs Sets a Season Record of 191 Runs Batted In

ARTS AND MEDIA

STAGE

Girl Crazy	Ginger Rogers, Ethyl Merman
The Last Mile	Spencer Tracy
Once In A Lifetime	Moss Hart, George Kaufman
Flying High	Bert Lahr, Kate Smith
Tonight Or Never	Helen Gahagan, Melvyn Douglas
Grand Hotel	Greta Garbo, Joan Crawford

MOVIE

All Quiet on the Western Front	Lewis Milestone Lew Ayres
Disraeli	George Arliss, Joan Bennett
The Divorcee	Norma Shearer
Little Caesar	Edward G. Robinson, Glenda Farrell
Hell's Angels	Howard Hughes, Jean Harlow
Anna Christie	Marie Dressler, Greta Garbo

RADIO

Believe It or Not	Robert Ripley Vocalist: Harriet Hilliard
Easy Aces	Goodman and Jane Ace
Sherlock Holmes	Basil Rathbone, Tom Conway
The March of Time	Westbrook van Voorhis

BOOK

The Maltese Falcon	Dashiell Hammet
Cimarron	Edna Ferber
As I Lay Dying	William Faulkner
The Bridge	Hart Crane

MUSIC

I've Got Rhythm	*Can This Be Love?*
Bidin' My Time	*Dancing on the Ceiling*
Body and Soul	*Embraceable You*

PEOPLE

Charles Evans Hughes Is Named Chief Justice of the US Supreme Court
Vannevar Bush Invents the "Differential Analyzer," the First Analog Computer

QUOTES

"Time...marches on!"

Westbrook van Voorhees

Garbo Talks: **"Gif me a viskey, and don't be stingy, baby."**
Greta Garbo in *Anna Christie*

INCIDENTALS AND TRIVIA

Frozen Foods Do Not Sell Well. Few Consumers and Stores Have Freezers

1931 *People Are Smoking More*

WORLD

Japan Marches into Chinese Manchuria in Violation of the 1928 Kellogg-Briand Pact
China, Preoccupied with Rebel Communist Mao Zedong, Mounts Little Defense
Canada Raises Tariffs, Effectively Cutting Off Two Thirds of US Imports
The US Proposes a One-Year Moratorium on War Debts and Reparations. Many Nations
      Agree But It Has Little Long Term Economic Impact
Germany's Banking System Is Collapsing

NATION

Report Says 4-5 Million Are Unemployed and the Depression Worsens Daily
Presidential Commission Recommends Amending the Prohibition Act Instead of Repeal
The Star Spangled Banner Becomes the Official US National Anthem
Nevada Legalizes Gambling
US Produces a Record Wheat Crop But Prices Fall and Many Farmers Can't Cover Debts
Automobile Sales Collapse. Half of the 1929 Year Auto Workers Are Unemployed
Engineer, Henry J. Kaiser, Organizes Six Contractors to Build the Boulder Dam

LIFESTYLE

Americans Take Money Out of Banks and Hoard Gold. Another 2,300 Banks Close This Year
Hundreds of "Hunger Marchers" Descend on Washington but Are Turned Away
US Birth Rates Decline Due to Severe Economic Conditions

SCIENCE AND TECHNOLOGY

Physicist Harold Urey Discovers Heavy Hydrogen (Deuterium). Water Molecules with This
      Isotope Create "Heavy Water."
Wiley Post and Harold Getty Circle the Globe in Eight Days
Radio Waves Are Discovered Coming from Space
New York's 102 Story Empire State Building Is Completed. The Tallest Building in the World
The George Washington Bridge, Connecting New York and New Jersey Is Opened
Vitamin A Is Isolated

BUSINESS AND INDUSTRY

Movie Theaters Begin Showing Double Features to Boost Business
Mechanical Refrigeration Production Exceeds One Million a Year
Rolls Royce Acquires Bentley Motors. Will Sell a Rolls with a Different Grille as a Bentley
Freon Refrigerant Begins Replacing Ammonia and other Dangerous Gasses in Refrigerators

CONSUMER PRODUCTS AND SERVICES

Comic Strip, *Dick Tracy*, Penned by Chester Gould, Appears
Walt Disney's *Mickey Mouse* Cartoon Strip Also Begins Publication
Felix the Cat, Cartoon Also Appears. Maybe Cartoons Will Cheer Us Up
Lucky Strike Cigarettes Now Outsell Camels. Radio Advertising Promotes Smoking
General Mills Markets Bisquick

PRICES

Four Cylinder Plymouth	$570-$630
Ford Model A	$450-$550
Six Cylinder Chevrolet	$490-$600+

Chimneys Are Smoking Less

ARTS AND MEDIA

STAGE

Mourning Becomes Electra	Eugene O'Neill
Private Lives	Noel Coward, Gertrude Lawrence
Of Thee I Sing	George Gershwin, Victor Moore
Band Wagon	Fred and Adele Astaire
The Barretts of Wimpole Street	Katherine Cornell, Brian Aherne

MOVIE

Cimarron	Richard Dix, Irene Dunne
Skippy	Jackie Cooper
A Free Soul	Lionel Barrymore, Norma Shearer, Clark Gable
Min and Bill	Marie Dressler, Wallace Beery
Frankenstein	Colin Clive, Boris Karloff, Mae Clarke
Dracula	Bela Lugosi, Helen Chandler
The Public Enemy	James Cagney, Jean Harlow, Joan Blondell,

RADIO

Buck Rogers in the 25th Century
The Ed Sullivan Show
The Carnation Contented Hour
Little Orphan Annie
Lum and Abner
Kate Smith

BOOK

The Good Earth	Pearl Buck
Sanctuary	William Faulkner
The Glass Key	Dashiel Hammett
Only Yesterday	Frederick Lewis Allen
The Joy of Cooking	Irma Rombauer

MUSIC

Grand Canyon Suite   Ferde Grofe
You're My Everything
When Your Lover Has Gone   *I Found a Million Dollar Baby*
Of Thee I Sing   *Where the Blue of the Night Meets the Gold of the Day*

PEOPLE

Jane Addams, Social Reformer and Pacifist, Is the First American Woman to Receive the Nobel Peace Prize. She Shares It with Fellow American, Nicholas M. Butler
Al "Scarface" Capone Is Convicted of Tax Evasion and Sentenced to 11 Years in Prison

COMMENTARY

"The US Public Health Service issues a warning that excessive smoke from home chimneys and factories is becoming a serious health issue. However, most Americans are unconcerned. They would prefer to see the belching chimneys that are the hallmark of a prosperous economy."

INCIDENTALS AND TRIVIA

The Miniature Golf Craze That Swept the Nation Only Three Years Earlier, Now Finds Little Interest

Irene English "Miss Picky"

Intellectuals Want Communism

WORLD

Britain Has 2.8 Million Unemployed; Germany Has 6.5 Million Unemployed

Famine in the Ukraine and Caucasus Kills Millions of Kulaks Who Have Resisted Farm
　　　Collectivization. Stalin Purposely Keeps Food and Supplies Out of These Areas

US and Canada Agree to Develop the St. Lawrence Seaway

NATION

US Gross National Product at $41 Billion Is Less Than Half of Pre-Depression (see 1929,1940)

The 20th Amendment Calls for the New President to Be Sworn in on January 20, Earlier Than Before

Thousands of Veterans Camp Out in Washington, Demanding Cash for Their Bonus Certificates
　　　Their Action Fails to Spur Congress. Many Leave When Offered Travel Money Home and the
　　　Remainder Are Driven Out by US Troops Commanded by Douglas MacArthur

Many Prominent Intellectuals Back Communism as the Only Answer to the Nation's Problems

President Hoover Makes the Five Day Week Standard for Government Workers

Dem. Franklin D. Roosevelt Soundly Defeats Herbert Hoover for President on a Theme of
　　　"The Forgotten Man at the Bottom of the Economic Pyramid." John Garner Elected VP

The Tomb of the Unknown Soldier Is Dedicated in Arlington Cemetery

First Class Postage Is Increased to Three Cents

ENVIRONMENT, SAFETY AND HEALTH

Many States Now Require Safety Glass in Automobile Windshields

US Roue 66 Opens A Continuous Route Between Chicago and Los Angeles

LIFESTYLE

Civilian Labor Force Unemployment Rate Is Officially 23.6 % with 11Million Unemployed

More Americans Are Hungry or Ill-Fed Than at Any Time in the Nation's History

The Average Weekly Wage Falls to $17 and Bread and Soup Lines Feed Thousands in Cities

A Million Americans Return to Farms and Rural Areas; Others Hop Freight Trains Searching for
　　　a Better Life Someplace Else. Hobo Villages and "Hoovervilles" Are Commonplace

SCIENCE AND TECHNOLOGY

The First Sulfa Drugs Are Used

Vitamin C Is Isolated

Physicist, Ernest Lawrence, Builds a Cyclotron

Edwin Herbert Land (23) Invents Polaroid Film

BUSINESS AND INDUSTRY

The Dow Jones Industrial Average Falls to a Low of 41.22, Down from 381.17 in September 1929

Woolworth's Chain of "Five and Dime" Stores Starts Offering 20 Cent Items

Hudson Offers a Streamlined Styled Terraplane Model, But Hardly Anyone Is Buying

Ford Ends Model A Production and Prepares to Produce a Low Priced V8

CONSUMER PRODUCTS AND SERVICES

Walter Knott Creates the Boysenberry, a Cross Between the Red Raspberry,
　　　Blackberry and Loganberry

The Zippo Windproof Cigarette Lighter Is Born

Bank Nights Are Popular for Weeknight Movie Audiences as Prizes and Money Are Awarded

Mars, Inc. Sells *Three Musketeers* Candy Bar for a Nickel

The People Want Roosevelt

SPORTS

Jack Sharkey Takes a Fifteen Round Decision over Max Schmeling
Pitcher J.H. "Dizzy" Dean Starts His Career with the St. Louis Cardinals
Mildred "Babe" Didrikson (18) Wins the Javelin Throw and Hurdles at the Olympic Games

ARTS AND MEDIA

STAGE	*The Warrier's Husband*	Katherine Hepburn
	Chrysalis	Humphrey Bogart, Margaret Sullavan
	Good-Bye Again	James Stewart
MOVIE	*Dr. Jekyll and Mr. Hyde*	Fredric March, Miriam Hopkins
	The Sin of Madelon Claudet	Helen Hayes, Lewis Stone, Robert Young
	Scarface	Paul Muni, Ann Dvorak, George Raft
	Tarzan the Ape Man	Johnny Weismuller, Maureen O'Sullivan
RADIO	*The Fire Chief*	Ed Wynn
	The Fred Allen Show	Portland Hoffa, Kenny Delmar
	The Jack Benny Program	Mary Livingston, Dennis Day, Phil Harris, Eddie Anderson, Mel Blanc
	One Man's Family	(longest running radio soap)
BOOK	*Beyond Desire*	Sherwood Anderson
	Brave New World	Aldous Huxley
	Tobacco Road	Erskine Caldwell

MUSIC

Forty Second Street
April in Paris
Night and Day
Louisiana Hayride

Brother, Can You Spare a Dime?
You're Getting to Be a Habit With Me
Let's Have Another Cup of Coffee
Isn't It Romantic?

PEOPLE

Amelia Earhart, First Woman to Fly the Atlantic Solo and Across the US Nonstop
Gypsy Rose Lee Is Burlesque's Most Successful Stripper
Hattie Caraway of Arkansas Is the First Woman Elected to the US Senate

CRIME AND PUNISHMENT

Charles Lindbergh Jr., 20 Months, Is Kidnapped. Despite Paying $50,000 Ransom, the
Child's Body Is Found on the Estate Two Months Later

COMMENTARY

"Times are bad and seem to be getting worse. Franklin
Roosevelt promises a New Deal for all Americans and we'd all like
that. Some say his ideas are too radical, but he is always smiling,
very positive and instills confidence in people when he speaks.
"Clearly the country wants change but they want change in
more traditional ways than are being offered by the Socialist,
Norman Thomas and Communist Party Candidate, William Foster."

Kate Hawthorne

1933 *A Crippled President*

WORLD

The US Finally Recognizes the Government of the USSR
Adolph Hitler Becomes Chancellor of Germany
Nazis Stage Massive Public Book Burnings in Berlin and Boycott Jewish-Owned Businesses
All German Political Parties Except the Nazi Party Are Outlawed
Germany Withdraws from the League of Nations

NATION

A Special Session of Congress Begins 100 Days of New Deal Legislation
The 21st Amendment Passes, Repealing Prohibition (18th Amendment)
Frances Perkins Is Named Secretary of Labor. First Woman in the Cabinet
President Roosevelt Declares a Three Day Bank Holiday to Ease the Failure Crisis
Private Gold Holdings Must Be Exchanged for Currency or Coin
The President in Miami in an Open Touring Car, Is Shot at by a Would-Be Assassin. He is
        Unhurt, But Mayor Anton Cermak of Chicago Will Die of His Wounds
The National Industrial Recovery Act Becomes Law
Blue Eagle Posters in Stores and Factory Windows Show Cooperation with NRA Goals
The Century of Progress Exposition Opens in Chicago

ENVIRONMENT, SAFETY AND HEALTH

The Tennessee Valley Authority Is Created
The Civilian Conservation Corps (CCC) Is Created

DISASTER

Navy Dirigible, USS Akron, Crashes in the Atlantic off New Jersey, Killing 73 of 76

LIFESTYLE

President Roosevelt Delivers the First of His Radio "Fireside Chats."
A Drive-in Movie Theater Opens in Camden, New Jersey
Lynchings Spread Across the South as 42 Blacks Die at the Hands of Lynch Mobs

SCIENCE AND TECHNOLOGY

The Influenza Virus Is Isolated

CONSUMER PRODUCTS AND SERVICES

First Comic Book, *Funnies on Parade*, Appears. Features Mutt and Jeff
The First Mickey Mouse Watches Are Sold
The Postal Telegram Company of New York Offers a Singing Telegram
Phillip Morris Cigarettes Are Introduced
Campbell Markets Chicken Noodle and Cream of Mushroom Soups

PRICES

Butter	$.28 per pound	Milk	$.10 per quart
Eggs	.29 per dozen	Bread	.05 per loaf
Sirloin Steak	.29 per pound	Potatoes	.02 per pound

SPORTS

Primo Carnera Knocks Out Jack Sharkey for Heavyweight Title
The National League Wins Baseball's First All Star Game
Helen Jacobs Is the First Woman to Wear Shorts in Tennis Tournament Play

ARTS AND MEDIA

STAGE Half of New York's Theaters Are Dark Because of the Depression

Both Your Houses	Maxwell Anderson
Tobacco Road	Henry Hull, Dean Jagger
Roberta	Jerome Kern, George Murphy, Bob Hope
Ah, Wilderness!	Eugene O'Neill

MOVIE

King Kong	Fay Wray, Bruce Cabot, Robert Armstrong
Private Life of Henry VIII	Charles Laughton, Binnie Barnes
Forty-Second Street	Ruby Keeler, Dick Powell, Warner Baxter
The Three Little Pigs	*(animated short)* Disney

RADIO *Jack Armstrong, The All-American Boy*
The Lone Ranger
Ma Perkins (soap)
The Romance of Helen Trent (soap)

BOOK *Anthony Adverse*   Hervey Allen

MUSIC

We're In the Money	*Lazy Bones*
I Wanna Be Loved by You	*It's a Sin to Tell a Lie*
It's Only a Paper Moon	*Sophisticated Lady*
Smoke Gets In Your Eyes	*Keeps Raining All the Time*
Did You Ever See a Dream Walking?	*Carioca*

PEOPLE

Albert Einstein Arrives in the US as a Refugee from Nazi Germany
Court Decides That James Joyce's *Ulysses* Is Not Obscene. The "Dirty" Words Are in Context

QUOTES

"...the only thing we have to fear is fear itself."
Franklin Roosevelt
Inaugural Speech

"Roosevelt said: 'Once I spent two years in bed, trying to move my big toe. That was the hardest job I ever had to do. After that, anything else seems easy.' Now a crippled man was about to teach a crippled nation how to walk again."
Edward Robb Ellis
A Nation In Torment pg. 264

INCIDENTALS AND TRIVIA

On His Radio Program, Al Pearce Creates the Character of Elmer Blurt, a Shy Door-To-Door Salesman Who Knocks and Then Says, "Nobody home, I hope, I hope, I hope."

1934   *We'll Redistribute the Wealth*

WORLD

Adolph Hitler Assumes the Presidency as Germany's von Hinderberg Dies
Heinrich Himmler Becomes Head of German Concentration Camps

NATION

The Federal Communications Commission Is Established
A Vast New Number of Government Agencies Are Born to Fight the Depression. Government
     Expenses Rise by 20%
Bank Closures Are Down and Unemployment Has Stabilized
Republicans Claim the New Agencies Are Wasting Money But Democrats Increase Their
     Margins in Congress in This Off-Year Election
Welfare Redistribution Schemes Abound to Tempt and Confuse the Public (see People)
Advocates of Technocracy Suggest Management of Society by Technical Experts
A Federal Prison Opens on Alcatraz Island in San Francisco Bay (see 1963)

ENVIRONMENT, SAFETY AND HEALTH

Growing Western Dust Storms Are Blamed Largely on Past Bad Plowing Methods
Congress Creates the Great Smoky Mountains National Park

LIFESTYLE

Civilian Labor Force Unemployment Rate Is 21.7% 4.7 Million Families Are on Relief
"Oakies" and "Arkies" Begin a Mass Exodus West to California for a Better Life

SCIENCE AND TECHNOLOGY

Enrico Fermi Bombs Uranium with Neutrons

BUSINESS AND INDUSTRY

American Airlines Is Formed Through Mergers
North American Aviation Begins Production of a Military Training Plane
Chrysler Motors Introduces the Radically Designed Chrysler Airflow Model

CONSUMER PRODUCTS AND SERVICES

The Superman Character, by Siegel & Shuster, Appears in Detective Comics
Cartoonist Al Capp Introduces Us to "Li'l Abner" and His Friends
Milton Caniff Pens the Adult Comic Strip, *Terry and the Pirates*
Distiller's Corporation Introduces Seagrams 7 Crown Whiskey
A Launderette with Four Washing Machines Opens in Fort Worth

SPORTS

Max Baer Scores a TKO over Primo Carnera in 11 Rounds to Take the Heavyweight Title
The First Masters Golf Tournament Is Held in Augusta, Georgia

CRIME AND PUNISHMENT

Bank Robber, Charles "Pretty Boy" Floyd, Is Shot to Death by Federal Agents in Ohio
John Dillinger, Public Enemy #1, Is Shot Outside of a Movie Theater in Chicago
Bonnie Parker and Clyde Barrow Are Also Gunned Down

ARTS AND MEDIA

STAGE
Anything Goes   Cole Porter, Ethyl Merman
Life Begins At 8:40   Bert Lahr, Ray Bolger, Frances Williams

MOVIE
It Happened One Night   Clark Gable, Claudette Colbert
The Gay Divorcee   Fred Astaire, Ginger Rogers, Betty Grable
Cleopatra   Claudette Colbert, Henry Wilcoxin
The Thin Man   William Powell, Myrna Loy,
Stand Up and Cheer   Shirley Temple

RADIO
Gangbusters
Let's Pretend (children)
Major Bowes and the Original Amateur Hour

BOOK
Good-bye Mr. Chips   James Hilton
The Thin Man   Dashiell Hammett
Tender Is the Night   F. Scott Fitzgerald

MUSIC

Rhapsody on a Theme by Paganini Op. 34   Sergei Rachmaninoff
I Get a Kick Out of You   *Anything Goes*
You and the Night and the Music   *The Gypsy in Me*
You're the Top   *Beer Barrel Polka*
Autumn In New York   *I Only Have Eyes for You*

PEOPLE

The Dionne Quintuplets Are Born on the Family Farm in Callender, Ontario, Canada
Huey Long of Louisiana Offers Wealth Redistribution: "Every Man a King."
Candidate for Governor, Upton Sinclair, Offers End Poverty in California (EPIC)
Francis Townsend's Pension Plan Argues for $200 a Month for Anyone Unemployed Over 60

QUOTES

"Cream of wheat is so good to eat *Let's Pretend* Radio Program
Yes we have it every day ... "   Commercial Theme Song

"Good morning Mr. and Mrs. America and all the ships at sea."
                                        Walter Winchell

COMMENTARY

"Based partly on Economist Thorstein Veblen's theories, Technocracy reaches its peak following by 1934. It preaches a logical redistribution of wealth through credits that everyone would be given on some sort of a scientific 'needs' basis. It sounds logical and a little mystical and makes sense when people are desperate. It, along with other wealth distribution schemes will soon fade away, except for a few die-hard believers."

Hank Hawthorne

INCIDENTALS AND TRIVIA

Clark Gable Takes Off His Shirt in a Movie and Is Not Wearing an Undershirt

1935 *Storm Clouds over Europe*

WORLD

Hitler Creates the Luftwaffe to Be Run by Herman Goering
The Nuremberg Laws Deprive Jews of German Citizenship
Heinrich Himmler Starts a Breeding Program for an "Aryan Super Race"
The Swastika Becomes the Official Symbol of Nazi Germany
Jazz Music of Black or Jewish Origin Is Banned in Germany
Germany and Japan Withdraw from the League of Nations
Persia Is Renamed Iran by Reza Shah Pahlevi

NATION

The Work Progress Administration (WPA) Is Created
Membership in the US Communist Party Peaks at 75,000
Civilian Conservation Corps (CCC) Reaches 500,000 Participants
The US Army Air Corps Is Formed
The Wagner Act Is Passed. Collective Bargaining Is Now the Law of the Land
Federal Deposit Insurance Corp. (FDIC) Is Created to Protect Bank Deposits
The Neutrality Act Is Signed in an Attempt to Keep the US Out of European War
Roosevelt Signs an Act to Stop Arms Sales to Belligerents Word-wide
Alcoholics Anonymous Is Founded

ENVIRONMENT, SAFETY AND HEALTH

Dust Storms in Western States Turn Many Days into Nights
Colonial Williamsburg Is Restored with Help of a John D. Rockefeller Gift
Rural Electrification Administration (REA) Is Created (10% of Rural US Has Electricity)

DISASTER

Massive Hurricane Sweeps Florida Keys, Killing Over 400 People
USS Dirigible Macon, Crashes. The Military Loses Interest in Dirigibles (see 1933)

SCIENCE AND TECHNOLOGY

Vitamin B2 (Riboflaven) Synthesized. Vitamin E Isolated
Richter Scale Developed to Measure Earthquake Intensity
A Flight Across Antarctica Claims Large Land Tracts for the US
Nylon Created at E. I. duPont

BUSINESS AND INDUSTRY

Pan American Provides First In-Flight Hot Meals
Boeing Shows Off Its New B-17 Bomber to the Army
French Liner S. S. Normandie Begins Atlantic Passenger Service
Gallup Poll Founded and the Neilson Ratings Begin for Radio

CONSUMER PRODUCTS AND SERVICES

Canned Beer Appears—Kreuger Cream Ale of New Jersey (see 1962)
Adolph's Meat Tenderizer (Powdered) Appears
Eastman Kodak Introduces 16mm Film and Home Equipment
The *Monopoly* Board Game Is Introduced by Parker Brothers
Business Week Magazine Begins Publication

Lullabies Over Broadway

SPORTS

Samuel "Sammy" Snead (22) Becomes a Professional Golfer
James J. Braddock (29) Wins World Heavyweight Title from Max Baer
Jockey Eddie Arcaro Begins His 26 Year Career
Crosley Field in Cincinnati Hosts the First Night Baseball Game (see 1988)

ARTS AND MEDIA

STAGE		
	Porgy and Bess	George Gershwin
	Jubilee	Cole Porter
	Jumbo	Billy Rose, Jimmy Durante
	The Petrified Forest	Leslie Howard

SCREEN		
	The Bride of Frankenstein	Boris Karloff, Elsa Lanchester
	The Crusades, (C. B. DeMille)	Loretta Young, Henry Wilcoxin
	Mutiny on the Bounty	Charles Laughton, Clark Gable
	A Night at the Opera	Marx Brothers
	Captain Blood	Errol Flynn, Olivia de Havilland

RADIO		
	Your Hit Parade	Doris Day, Frank Sinatra, Dinah Shore
	Fibber McGee and Molly	Jim and Marian Jordan
	Flash Gordon	Gale Gordon

BOOK		
	Tortilla Flat	John Steinbeck
	Judgement Day	James T. Farell
	Of Time and the River	Thomas Wolfe

MUSIC

Cheek to Cheek	*I'm In the Mood for Love*
East of the Sun	*Moon Over Miami*
Red Sails in the Sunset	*It's Delovely*
You Are My Lucky Star	*Begin the Beguine*
Lullaby of Broadway	*Just One of Those Things*

PEOPLE

Humorist Will Rogers and Pilot Wiley Post Killed in Alaskan Air Crash
Benny Goodman Hailed as the "King of Swing"
Louisiana Governor Huey "Kingfish" Long is Assassinated
William "Count" Basie Band Is Formed in Kansas City
Amelia Earhart Flies From Hawaii to California
Kirsten Flagstad Acclaimed as the Greatest Living Wagnerian Soprano
Howard Hughes Breaks the Airplane Speed Record

QUOTES

"Everyone's ignorant, just on different subjects.."
Will Rogers (1879-1935)

INCIDENTALS AND TRIVIA

First Parking Meters Are Installed in Oklahoma City

1936 *Pennies from Heaven*

WORLD

USSR Exiles Leon Trotsky to Mexico
Josef Stalin Begins Purge in the USSR to Liquidate Political Enemies
Germany Reoccupies the Rhineland
The Berlin-Rome Axis Is Established
Japanese Forces Invade Mainland China
Spanish Civil War Starts as Gen. Francisco Franco Leads an Army Uprising
Italy Annexes Ethiopia

NATION

With Roosevelt's Victory over Alf Landon, Both Houses of Congress Are Three Fourths Democratic
The New Gallup Poll Accurately Predicts the Election Results
Social Security Takes Effect. The First Social Security Checks Are Mailed
National Debt is $34 Million; Population Hits 127 million

ENVIRONMENT, SAFETY AND HEALTH

Severe Drought Hits Crops Causing Hardships for Farmers
Farmers Paid to Plant Alfalfa & Clover Instead of Soil-Depleting Crops
President Roosevelt Signs an Omnibus Flood Control Act
Hoover Dam Generators Begin Transmitting Electricity to Los Angeles

LIFESTYLE

Civilian Labor Force Unemployment Rate Is 16.9 %
38% of Families (11.7 million) Have Income Less Than $1,000 Per Year
Poverty Line is Set at $1,330

SCIENCE AND TECHNOLOGY

The BBC Creates the First Electronic Television System
Vitamin B1 Synthesized (Niacin)
Sulfa Drugs From Germany Now Available in the United States
Douglas Aircraft Company Introduces the 21 Passenger DC-3 Aircraft

BUSINESS AND INDUSTRY

S.S. Queen Mary Begins Atlantic Service for Cunard-White Star Line
Willys-Overland Reorganizes and Starts Low-Priced Car Production
The Howard Johnson Restaurant/Hotel Chain Starts in Massachusetts
The Super Chief Train Reduces Chicago to Los Angeles Rail Time to 39 Hours

CONSUMER PRODUCTS AND SERVICES

Bottle Screw Caps Appear
The First Ford V8 Debuts
Life Magazine Publishes Its First Issue
Polaroid Lens Sunglasses Marketed
Lever Brothers Introduces Spry to Compete with Crisco
Mercedes Benz Offers the First Diesel Engine for Production Automobiles
Tampax Produces the First Cotton Tampon
Eastman Kodak Offers Color Kodachrome Film in 35mm Cartridges
Robert C. Wian Jr. Invents "Big Boy" Double Deck Hamburger

As Social Security Starts

SPORTS

Max Schmelling Knocks Out Joe Louis
Jesse Owens Wins Four Olympic Gold Medals at the Berlin Olympic Games
Bob Feller and Joe Dimaggio Start Their Baseball Careers
The Baseball Hall of Fame Opens in Cooperstown, NY

ARTS AND MEDIA

STAGE

Idiot's Delight	Robert Sherwood, Lunt and Fontanne
Red Hot and Blue	Cole Porter, Ethyl Merman, Bob Hope
You Can't Take It with You	George Kaufman, Moss Hart
On Your Toes	Richard Rogers, Ray Bolger,

MOVIE

Modern Times	Charlie Chaplin, Paulette Goddard
Mr. Deeds Goes to Town	Frank Capra, Gary Cooper, Jean Arthur
Swing Time	Fred Astaire, Ginger Rogers
Eh, What's Up Doc?	(animated) Introduces Bugs Bunny

RADIO

The Edgar Bergen and Charley McCarthy Show
Kraft Music Hall   Bing Crosby
Lux Radio Theater
The Kate Smith Show
The Shadow   Orson Wells (others), Agnes Moorehead (others)

BOOK

Winning Bridge Made Easy	Charles Goren
How/Win Friends & Influence People	Dale Carnegie
Gone With the Wind	Margaret Mitchell

MUSIC

Peter and the Wolf   Sergei Prokofiev
Carmina Burana   Carl Orff
I've Got You Under My Skin
Is It True What They Say About Dixie?   *There's a Small Hotel*
Let's Face the Music and Dance   *Swing Time*
Pennies from Heaven   *You Are My Lucky Star*
The Way You Look Tonight   *Good Night, Irene*
    I'm an Old Cowhand...

PEOPLE

King George V of England Dies, Succeeded by Son King Edward VIII
King Edward Abdicates Throne for Divorced American Wallis Simpson
George VI (Brother Alfred) Crowned King of England
Franklin Roosevelt Sweeps the Election Winning Every State Except Maine and Vermont.
    The Electoral Count Is Roosevelt 523 to Alf Landon's 8

CRIME AND PUNISHMENT

Bruno Hauptmann Is Executed for the Kidnap/Killing of the Lindbergh Baby

INCIDENTALS AND TRIVIA

A New Dance Called the Jitterbug Sweeps the Nation
New Slang Includes *Hepcat, In the Groove,* and *Alligator*

1937 *Unions Make Serious Inroads*

WORLD

Nazis Exclude Jews from Trade and Industry. They Must Wear the Yellow Star of David
The USSR Tries Hundreds of Its Citizens as Spies in a Continuing Political Purge
The Japanese Sink a US Gunboat on the Yangtze River in China But Later Apologize

NATION

Four Year Economic Boom Sputters; Many Federal Programs Are Criticized and Challenged
The President Attempts to Increase the Size of the Supreme Court with Younger, More
        Liberal Justices. Congress Balks and His Effort Fails
When One Justice Retires, the President Names Liberal Hugo Black to the Position
President Signs the Neutrality Act, Prohibiting Arms Exports to Warring Nations (see 1939)

ENVIRONMENT, SAFETY AND HEALTH

The Bonneville Dam on Washington's Columbia River Is Dedicated
Standard Oil Drills the First Offshore Oil Wells near Louisiana

DISASTER

German Dirigible Hindenburg Explodes as It Arrives at Lakehurst, NJ

LIFESTYLE

The American Medical Association Strongly Endorses Contraception for Birth Control
Marijuana Traffic Laws Now Prohibit the Sale and Use of the Product
Over Two Million US Households Now Have Refrigerators and Some Have Freezers, But
        Most Homes Still Use an Icebox and Have Ice Delivered on a Regular Basis

SCIENCE AND TECHNOLOGY

Nazis Establish Penemunde a Secret Rocket Base on the Baltic Coast
San Francisco's Golden Gate Bridge Opens
Chester F. Carlson Invents Xerography, First Method for Photocopying
The First Blood Bank Is Established in Chicago
Insulin Is Successfully Used with Diabetics
Studies Suggest that Cigarette Smoking Is a Cause of Cancer
A Yellow Fever Vaccine Is Now Available
Cyclamate, a Sugar Substitute, Is Discovered

BUSINESS AND INDUSTRY

John L. Lewis' United Mine Workers Are Recognized by United States Steel
General Motors Agrees to Recognize the United Auto Workers Union After a Sit-Down Strike
Packard Sells a Record 110,000 Automobiles
The Number of Automakers Shrinks; Stutz Files for Bankruptcy and Pierce-Arrow Is Auctioned

CONSUMER PRODUCTS AND SERVICES

The Marriott Brothers Pioneer In-Flight Meal Service on DC-3 Planes
An "Automatic" Washing Machine Now Washes, Rinses and Extracts Water from Clothes
Hormel Foods Introduces Canned *SPAM*
Women's Day Monthly Magazine Is Sold in A&P Markets for Three Cents an Issue
Look Magazine Begins Publication to Compete with *Life*

Our Beloved Amelia Disappears 1937

SPORTS

Joe Louis Knocks Out James Braddock for the Heavyweight Title

ARTS AND MEDIA

STAGE	*I'd Rather Be Right*	George M. Cohan
	Babes In Arms	Rogers and Hart
	Of Mice and Men	John Steinbeck
	Golden Boy	Clifford Odets
MOVIE	*The Life of Emile Zola*	Jos. Schildkraut, Paul Muni
	Captains Courageous	Spencer Tracy, Mickey Rooney
	The Great Ziegfield	Luise Rainer, William Powell, Myrna Loy
	In Old Chicago	Alice Brady, Tyrone Power, Alice Faye
	Lost Horizon	Ronald Coleman, Jane Wyatt
	A Star Is Born	Fredric March, Janet Gaynor
	Night Must Fall	Robert Montgomery, Rosiland Russell
	Snow White and the Seven Dwarfs	(animated) Disney Studios
RADIO	*The Fitch Bandwagon*	Phil Harris, Alice (Faye) Harris
	Maxwell House Coffee Time	Frank Morgan, Fanny Brice
	Terry and the Pirates	
	Stella Dallas (soap)	
	Our Gal Sunday (soap)	
BOOK		
	The Hobbitt	J.R.R. Tolkien
	To Have and Have Not	Ernest Hemingway

MUSIC

Once In a While	*Sweet Leilani*
Ebb Tide	*The Lady Is A Tramp*
That Old Feeling	*My Funny Valentine*
Harbor Lights	*Whistle While You Work*

PEOPLE

Amelia Earhart Disappears off New Guinea While on an Around the World Flight

QUOTES

"I see one third of a nation ill housed, ill clad, ill nourished."
Franklin D. Roosevelt
Second Inaugural Speech

We'll never recognize the United Auto Workers' Union or any other union."
Henry Ford (1937)

INCIDENTALS AND TRIVIA

Ford Employs Over 600 Private Guards (Goons) with Guns and Blackjacks to Maintain a Peaceful, Non-Union Workforce

1938 *Peace with No German Invasion*

WORLD

To Avoid War, the Munich Pact Gives the Sudetenland Area of Czechoslovakia to Germany
Germany Annexes Austria to Protect the "Rights" of Germans There
Nazis Plunder Jewish Shops and Homes in Austria
Italy Enacts Anti Jewish Legislation

NATION

The Vinson Naval Act Provides for a Two Ocean Navy
The March of Dimes to Fight Polio Is Organized
The Fair Labor Standards Act Passes, Creating a National Minimum Hourly Wage
New York State Requires Blood Tests for Marriage License Applicants
The Civil Aeronautics Act Puts All Civilian Air Transportation under Federal Regulation

DISASTER

New York and New England Are Ravaged by the "Long Island Express," a Hurricane that
        Claims Over 600 Lives
Floods and Landslides in Southern California Claim 144 Lives

LIFESTYLE

Civilian Labor Force Unemployment Rate Is 19.0 %. US Worker's Minimum Wage Is $.25
The Number of Americans Receiving Federal Relief Dropped from 3.2 to 2.1 in One Year
The Conga and the Samba Are Very Popular Dances

SCIENCE AND TECHNOLOGY

Konrad Zuse Builds a Computing Machine Using Binary Technology
First Total Artificial Hip Replacement
Teflon Is Discovered

BUSINESS AND INDUSTRY

Hitler Orders the Manufacture of the Volkswagen (people's car)
Five US Companies Make TV Sets. No Standards and Broadcasting Is Experimental
DuPont Names Its New Synthetic Yarn Nylon
The Congress of Industrial Organizations (CIO) is Formed; John L. Lewis, President
William Green, Head of the AF of L Suggests That the CIO Join Their Organization

CONSUMER PRODUCTS AND SERVICES

Dairy Queen Soft Ice Cream Is Launched
Airwick Room Freshener and Deodorant Appears
The Garrand Turntable Tips a Record Over To Play the Other Side
Tupperware Becomes Available for Food Storage
Duffy-Mott Markets Mott's Apple Juice

RICES

Milk	$.09 per quart
Bread	.25 per pound
Steak	.35 per pound
Chewing Gum (5 sticks)	.05

But Aliens "Invade" New Jersey   1938

SPORTS

Bob Feller Strikes Out 18 Batters in a Single Game
Don Budge Wins the Men's Singles at Wimbledon
Fiberglas Begins to Replace Wood in Boats and Skis

ARTS AND MEDIA

STAGE	*Our Town*	Thornton Wilder
	Knickerbocker Holiday	Kurt Weill, Walter Huston
	Hellzapoppin'	Ole Olsen, Chic Johnson
	Oscar Wilde	Robert Morley
	Abe Lincoln in Illinois	Robert Sherwood, Raymond Massey
MOVIE	*Pygmalion*	Leslie Howard, Wendy Hiller
	Jezebel	Betty Davis, Fay Bainter
	Kentucky	Walter Brennan, Loretta Young
	Crime School	Humphrey Bogart, Leo Gorcey, Huntz Hall
RADIO	*Information Please (quiz show)*	
	Kay Kyser's College of Musical Knowledge	
	Life Can Be Beautiful (soap)	
	Young Widder Brown (soap)	
	The Green Hornet	
BOOK	*The Unvanquished*	William Faulkner

MUSIC

Billy The Kid — Aaron Copeland
Amelia Goes to the Ball — Gian-Carlo Menotti

My Reverie
A-Tisket, A-Tasket
Jeepers Creepers
Love Walked In
Thanks for the Memory

You Must Have Been a Beautiful Baby
Heart and Soul
Whistle While You Work
Falling In Love With Love
September Song

PEOPLE

War of the Worlds, a Mercury Theater Radio Play with Orson Wells, Accidentally Panics
the Nation into Believing That Martians Have Invaded New Jersey
Howard Hughes Sets an Around the World Record Flying Time of 3 Days, 19+ Hours
Frank Lloyd Wright Completes Taliesin West near Phoenix, His Home and Teaching Center

QUOTES

"I believe it is peace for our time...peace with honor."
Neville Chamberlain (1938)

REFLECTION

The Daughters of the American Revolution Refuse to Rent Constitution Hall to Black
Contralto, Marian Anderson, for a Concert. Eleanor Roosevelt, a DAR Member, Resigns and
Arranges a Performance for Anderson Attended by 75,000 at the Lincoln Memorial.

1939 *War Again Returns to Europe*

WORLD

Italy Invades Albania
Franco Takes Madrid. The Spanish Civil War Ends
Czechoslovakia Ceases to Exist. Germany Takes Bohemia and Moravia as Protectorates.
        Slovakia Is Annexed by Hungary
Hitler Invades Poland on September 1
England and France Declare War on Germany September 3
Soviet Forces Invade Finland in November
Germany and the USSR Sign a Non Aggression Treaty

NATION

Roosevelt Orders 571 Airplanes Built for Defense, But Pledges American Neutrality
The New York World's Fair, "The World of Tomorrow," Opens
The President Lays the Cornerstone for the Jefferson Memorial
The Neutrality Act of 1939 Allows US to Sell Arms to Selected Belligerents (see 1937)

LIFESTYLE

US Worker's Minimum Wage Is $.30

SCIENCE AND TECHNOLOGY

Scientists Split the Atom under Laboratory Conditions
Electronic Television Is Demonstrated at the New York World's Fair
DDT Is Discovered to be a Potent, Long-lasting Insecticide (see 1972)
Igor Sikorsky Designs and Flies the First Mass Production Helicopter
John Atansoff & Clifford Berry Complete the First Digital Computer
Bell Laboratories Demonstrates a Stereo Recorder Using Steel Tape
The Rh Factor (a Component of Red Blood Cells) Is Discovered in Human Blood
Edwin Armstrong Demonstrates Frequency Modulation (FM) Radio

BUSINESS AND INDUSTRY

Pan American Airlines Begins Yankee Clipper Air Service between New York and Europe
California Perfume Company, Founded in 1883, Changes Its Name to Avon Products, Inc.
New York's Municipal Airport (later La Guardia) Is Dedicated
General Electric Introduces Fluorescent Lighting, More Efficient Than Incandescent

CONSUMER PRODUCTS AND SERVICES

Col. Harland Sanders Creates a Secret Blend of 11 Herbs and Spices for Seasoning Chicken
Nylon Stockings Challenge Silk as Women's Hose, Going on Sale for the First Time
Lays Potato Chips Are Sold
Ford Introduces the Mercury Auto Line
Cream of Wheat Offers a 5-Minute Cooking Time to Compete with New Quick Quaker Oats

PRICES

Gasoline	$.19 per gallon
Average New Car	$ 680
Average New 3BR House	$ 3,850 @ 5% Interest

The "Iron Man" Quits Baseball   1939

SPORTS

Sir Malcolm Campbell Hits 141 mph in Speedboat, Bluebell
Byron Nelson Wins the US Open Golf Championship
Football Helmets Are Made Mandatory for Collegiate Football
Robert "Bobby" Riggs (21) Takes the Men's Tennis Singles at Wimbledon
Ted Williams (20) Begins His 19 Year Career with the Boston Red Sox

ARTS AND MEDIA

STAGE	The Time of Your Life	William Saroyan
	The Little Foxes	Lillian Hellman
	The Man Who Came To Dinner	Monty Wooley
	Mamba's Daughters	Ethyl Waters
	George White's Scandals	Ben Blue, Ann Miller, Three Stooges
	The Streets of Paris	Carmen Miranda
MOVIE	Gone With The Wind	Vivian Leigh, Hattie McDaniel, Clark Gable
	Good-bye, Mr. Chips	Robert Donat, Greer Garson
	Stagecoach	Thomas Mitchell, John Wayne
	The Wizard of Oz	Judy Garland, Ray Bolger, Bert Lahr, Jack Haley, Frank Morgan, Billie Burke
	Wuthering Heights	Merle Oberon, Laurence Olivier, David Niven
RADIO	The Aldrich Family	
	I Love a Mystery	
	The Milton Berle Show	
	Mr. District Attorney	Jay Jostyn
BOOK	Abraham Lincoln, the War Years	Carl Sandberg
	The Grapes of Wrath	John Steinbeck
	Captain Horacio Hornblower	C.S. Forester

MUSIC

Concierto de Aranjuez   Joachin Rodrigo
Deep Purple   And the Angels Sing
Over the Rainbow   Stairway to the Stars
South of the Border   Heaven Can Wait

PEOPLE

Dwight Eisenhower, a Lt. Colonel under Douglas MacArthur, Will Rise to General in 18 Months
Kate Smith Sings Irving Berlin's God Bless America on Network Radio
Cardinal Eugenio Pacelli Is Elected Pope, Taking the Name, Pius XII
Anna Mary Robertson, Grandma Moses (79), Gains Instant Fame as Her Paintings Are Exhibited

QUOTES

"I might have been given a bad break, but I've got an awful lot to live for."
Lou Gerhig at his Yankee Stadium Retirement Celebration

INCIDENTALS AND TRIVIA

Franklin Roosevelt Is the First President on TV at the Opening of New York's World's Fair
Roadside Restaurant Tray Boys, Tray Girls and Running Boys Now Known as Carhops
1939 Commercial: "Pepsi Cola Hits the Spot. Twelve Full Ounces, That's a Lot"

1940 *Britain Battles for Its Life*

WORLD

Nazi Forces Overrun Belgium, Holland and Luxembourg
England and France Rush Troops to Assist Belgium
Italy Declares War on the Allies and Invades Greece
Nazis Sweep Around the Maginot Line Toward Paris. France Surrenders. Paris Is Occupied
Luftwaffe Bombers Pound London (Aug.-Oct.) in the "Battle of Britain," but Finally Relent
      After Suffering Heavy Losses by the R.A.F.
Polish Jews Must Wear the Star of David Cloth I.D. Badge

NATION

Franklin Roosevelt Defeats Wendell Willkie for an Historic Third Term
First Ever Peacetime Draft Is Instituted
Roosevelt Officially Restates the US Position from Neutrality to Non-Belligerency
      (Will Support the Allies without Going to War)
The 40-Hour Work Week Goes into Effect (Fair Labor Standards Act 1938)
The National Debt is $43 Billion
US Gross National Product Is $99 Billion, Still Below That of 1929 (see 1929,1932)
The Arroyo Seco Parkway, Los Angeles to Pasadena, Is California's First Freeway

DISASTER

The Tacoma Narrows Bridge in Puget Sound Collapses in High Winds

LIFESTYLE

Civilian Labor Force Unemployment Rate Is 14.6 %
6.1 Million US Farms (23% of Population)
US Population Is Now 132 Million. 6.9% Over Age 65
One in Nine Americans Is a High School Graduate
One in Twenty Americans Is a College Graduate
There Are 1.5 Million College Students (see 1947, 1956, 1990)

SCIENCE AND TECHNOLOGY

US Develops a Chemical Synthetic Rubber Substitute
Peter Goldmark Demonstrates First Successful Color Television System
New Radar Towers Along the British Coast Provide Early Air Attack Warning and Give the
      RAF a Critical 2 to 1 Kill Ratio
Penicillin Is Developed as an Antibiotic
First Successful Helicopter Flight in the US

CONSUMER PRODUCTS AND SERVICES

Mac and Dick McDonald Open a Hamburger Stand in San Bernardino, California
Nylon Stockings Are Now Broadly Available
M&M Coated Chocolate Candies. "Candy that melts in your mouth, not in your hand." (see 1954)

PRICES

Gasoline	$.19 per gallon
Average new car	$ 701
Average new house	$ 6,558
Average loan interest	4.5%

US Is the Arsenal of Democracy   1940

SPORTS

Chicago Bears Beat the Washington Redskins 73-0. (Most Lopsided Football Game Score)

ARTS AND MEDIA

STAGE	*The Corn Is Green*	Ethyl Barrymore
	My Sister Eileen	Shirley Booth
	Pal Joey	Gene Kelly
MOVIE	*The Grapes of Wrath*	John Ford, Jane Darwell Henry Fonda
	Pinocchio and *Fantasia*	Disney Studios (Animated)
	The Great Dictator	Charlie Chaplin, Paulette Goddard, Jack Oakie
	Northwest Passage	Spencer Tracy, Robert Young, Ruth Hussey
RADIO	*Arthur Godfrey Time*	
	Beat the Band	Host: The Incomparable Hildegard
	Captain Midnight	
	The Quiz Kids	
	My Favorite Husband	Lucille Ball
	Abie's Irish Rose	"Bud" Collyer, Mercedes McCambridge
BOOK	*For Whom the Bell Tolls*	Ernest Hemingway
	Native Son	Richard Wright
	You Can't Go Home Again	Thomas Wolfe

MUSIC

Blueberry Hill   *When You Wish Upon a Star*
Fools Rush In   *Darn That Dream*
...Swallows Come Back to Capistrano   *The Woodpecker Song*
Imagination   *I'll Never Smile Again*

PEOPLE

"This...Is London," Edward R. Murrow Broadcasts Daily from the Streets of the Ravaged City
Exiled Communist, Leo Trotsky Is Shot and Killed by an Assassin in Mexico City
Glenn Miller and His Orchestra Record *Pennsylvania 6-5000* for RCA
Artie Shaw and His Orchestra Record Hoagy Carmichael's *Stardust*

QUOTES

"I have nothing to offer but blood, toil, tears and sweat."
Winston Churchill

COMMENTARY

"The long Depression finally seems to be ending and jobs are more plentiful. Sadly, we know a lot of the improvement is due to war preparedness. A lot of our young men are entering service and factories are humming with the manufacture of machines and materials for Great Britain and Russia

"The president says he hopes to keep us out of war if at all possible, but that Lend Lease is a logical and moral way for us to provide real support for those nations we believe to be in the right."

Kate Hawthorne

1941   *America Begins Lend Lease*

WORLD

Germany Invades Russia Despite Their Non-Aggression Treaty
Invading Nazi Forces Massacre 90,000 Ukrainian Civilians, Mostly Jews, Near Kiev
The German Battleship Bismark Is Sunk with a Loss of 2,300 Lives
A Sneak Attack on Pearl Harbor by Japanese Aircraft Destroys Most of the US Pacific Fleet
      and Kills 2,403 Americans (12/7)
US Congress Declares War on Japan (12/8)
Germany and Italy Declare War on the US (12/11) Congress Declares War on Germany and
      Italy the Same Day
The Japanese Attack Luzon in the Philippines. Wake Island Falls after a Gallant Defense
Ethiopia Regains Independence as British Forces Drive Out the Italian Occupation Army
Hong Kong Falls to the Japanese on Christmas Day
Jewish Groups in Palestine Resort to Violence in Attempts to Gain Independence from Britain

NATION

The Lend-Lease Bill Provides War Supplies to Countries Fighting the Axis
President Proclaims the *Four Freedoms*, as Cornerstones of a New World: Freedom of Speech and
      Expression, Freedom of Worship, Freedom from Fear and Freedom from Want
The Atlantic Charter Calls for Agreed Upon War Aims Between the US and Britain
The Treasury Department Issues Series E War Bonds at 2.9% Interest
The America First Committee Unites Leading Isolationists Like Robert McCormick (Chicago
      Tribune Publisher), Robert E. Wood (Sears Chairman) and Charles A. Lindbergh
German Consulates and Nazi Propaganda Organizations in the US Are Shut Down
Scrap Iron and Gasoline Shipments to Japan Are Embargoed
German, Italian and Japanese Assets in the US Are Frozen
The National Revenue Act Sharply Raises Taxes for the Defense Effort
German or Italian Vessels Seen in US Waters Will Be Attacked

ENVIRONMENT, SAFETY AND HEALTH

The Federal Wage and Hour Law Prohibits Children Under 18 from Dangerous Occupations
Sculptor Lincoln Berglum Completes Mt. Rushmore National Memorial for His Father,
      Gutzon, Who Retired in 1938
Grand Coulee Dam on the Columbia River in Washington Begins Producing Power

SCIENCE AND TECHNOLOGY

John Rex Whinfield Invents Dacron
The Element Plutonium Is Isolated at Berkeley, California

BUSINESS AND INDUSTRY

Industry Tools Up for Full Scale War Production
Ford Motor Company Signs Its First Contract with a Labor Union
Henry Kaiser Establishes Seven Shipbuilding Yards on the Northern California Coast

CONSUMER PRODUCTS AND SERVICES

Edsel Ford Personally Introduces the Sleek Lincoln Continental
The Pressurized Spray Can Is Introduced, Primarily for Insecticides
General Mills Markets Cheerios Cereal
Parade Magazine Begins Publication

Pearl Harbor Is Attacked

ARTS AND MEDIA

STAGE	Watch on the Rhine	Lillian Hellman
	Lady in the Dark	Gertrude Lawrence, Danny Kaye
	Claudia	Dorothy McGuire
	Blythe Spirit	Noel Coward
MOVIE	How Green Was My Valley	Donald Crisp, Walter Pidgeon, Maureen O'Hara
	Sergeant York	Gary Cooper, Joan Leslie
	Citizen Kane	Orson Welles, Agnes Moorhead
	Dumbo	Disney Studios (animated)
	Tobacco Road	Marjorie Rambeau, Gene Tierney
	The Maltese Falcon	Humphrey Bogart, Mary Astor, Peter Lorre
RADIO	Burns and Allen	George Burns, Gracie Allen, Mel Blanc
	The Great Gildersleeve	Harold Peary
	Inner Sanctum	Boris Karloff
	The Red Skelton Show	
	Duffy's Tavern	Ed Gardner, Shirley Booth
BOOK	My Friend Flicka	Mary O'Hara
	Berlin Diary	William Shirer
	The White Cliffs of Dover	Alice Miller

MUSIC

Anapola

I Don't Want to Set the World on Fire

The Hut Sut Song

There'll Be Some Changes Made

Till Reveille

Intermezzo

There'll Be Bluebirds Over the White Cliffs of Dover

PEOPLE

Nazi Rudolph Hess Parachutes into Scotland in What He Claims Is a Peace Mission. He is Jailed

British P.M. Winston Churchill Launches His "V For Victory" Campaign

Low Budget Movie Cowboy, Gene Autrey, Is in Top Ten Box Office

Glenn Miller's *Chattanooga Choo Choo* Record Sells a Million. First Gold Record Ever

QUOTES

"This was their finest hour."

Winston Churchill

"...a day that shall live in infamy."

Franklin Roosevelt

"Remember Pearl Harbor!"

All Americans

COMMENTARY

"It's off to war soon, but still time to spend Saturday night with your sweetie, listening to the romantic big band sounds on the radio. We love all of the popular bands such as Glenn Miller, Benny Goodman, Harry James, Tommy & Jimmy Dorsey, Cab Calloway, Carmen Cavallero, Bob Crosby, Xavier Cugat, Eddie Duchin, Duke Ellington, Guy Lombardo and Ted Lewis."

"Miss Picky"

Irene English

1942 *War News Is Not Encouraging*

WORLD

Nazi Leaders Determine the "Final Solution" for the Extermination of Europe's Jews
US and Soviet Union Sign a Lend Lease Agreement to Aid the Soviet War Effort
Bataan Peninsula on Luzon and, Later, Corregidor Island Fall to the Japanese
General Douglas MacArthur Leaves Luzon and Sets Up Headquarters in Australia
Thousands of US Soldiers Die in the "Bataan Death March" or Later in Camps
The Weakened US Fleet Scores Victories in the Coral Sea and the Battle of Midway
Lt. Col. James Dolittle's Air Squadron Raids Tokyo from the USS Hornet
US Marines Invade Guadalcanal Island in Our First Major Pacific Offensive
Tank Commander Erwin Rommel Takes Tobruk in Libya and 50,000 Allied Prisoners
US Forces Land in North Africa to Assist British Units

NATION

Office of Economic Stabilization Creates Controls on Farm Prices, Rents, Wages and Salaries
The Women's Auxiliary Army Corps (WAAC). Head Is Houston Post Editor, Oveta Culp Hobby
Congress Establishes the Women Accepted for Voluntary Emergency service (WAVES) to
        Support the Navy. Their Head Is Mildred McAfee, President of Wellesley College
A Lone Japanese Submarine Shells the Oil Fields Near Santa Barbara, California.
The National Birth Control League Becomes Planned Parenthood
The Supreme Court Rules That Nevada Divorces Are Legal in All States

DISASTER

Boston's Coconut Grove Nightclub Fire Kills 487, Mostly from Asphyxia and Trampling

LIFESTYLE

Millions of Men Go to War. Women Take Jobs in War Industries and Military Support Units
The Civilian Labor Force Unemployment Rate Is 4.7 %
In Many States Gasoline Is Rationed to 3 Gallons Per Week for Non-Essential Vehicles
Coffee, Sugar, Meats and Many Other Foodstuffs and Commodities Are Rationed
Milk Delivery Goes to Alternate Days and Horse-Drawn Wagons Begin to Appear Again
45% of US Households Now Have Mechanical Refrigerators
The Term, *Government Issue*, Is Shortened to *GI* to Refer to Almost Everything Military

SCIENCE AND TECHNOLOGY

Enrico Fermi Builds the First Nuclear Reactor
A Self-Sustaining Nuclear Chain Reaction Is Demonstrated at the University of Chicago
First US Jet, the XP-59, Is Tested But Performance Lags Behind Conventional Aircraft
US Develops a "Bazooka" Anti-Tank Weapon

BUSINESS AND INDUSTRY

Most Industry Converts to War Related Production

CONSUMER PRODUCTS AND SERVICES

Sales of New Cars and Trucks Are Banned
With Rationing and Shortages, Consumer Spending Drops to 38 Billion from 69 Billion in 1939
A Banana Shortage Forces the Twinkie To Substitute a Vanilla Cream Filling
The *Sad Sack* Cartoon Appears
There Are 50 Drive-In Theaters in the US (see 1958)

The Home Front Does Without

1942

SPORTS

Joe Louis Defends His Title for the 20th Time, Knocking Out Buddy Baer

ARTS AND MEDIA

STAGE	*Rodeo (ballet)*	Aaron Copeland
	This Is The Army	Irving Berlin
	The Skin Of Our Teeth	Thornton Wilder, Tallulah Bankhead, Fredric March, Montgomery Clift
MOVIE	*Mrs. Miniver*	William Wyler, Greer Garson, Teresa Wright
	Yankee Doodle Dandy	James Cagney, Joan Leslie
	Holiday Inn	Bing Crosby, Fred Astaire
	Now Voyager	Betty Davis, Paul Henreid
	I Married a Witch	Veronica Lake, Fredric March
	This Gun for Hire	Alan Ladd, Veronica Lake
	Bambi	Disney (animated)
RADIO	*Abbott and Costello*	Bud Abbott, Lou Costello
	Stage Door Canteen	(Countless Celebrities)
	People Are Funny	Art Linkletter
BOOK	*The Robe*	Lloyd Douglas
	See Here Private Hargrove	Marion Hargrove

MUSIC

Warsaw Concerto — Richard Addinsell
The Saber Dance — Aram Khachaturian
White Christmas
Don't Sit Under the Apple Tree
Serenade in Blue
Deep in the Heart of Texas

Tangerine
Blues in the Night
When the Lights Go on Again
Praise the Lord and Pass the...

QUOTES

"I shall return."
Gen. Douglas MacArthur, Upon Leaving the Philippines

"Kilroy was here."
Thousands of GIs, Wherever They Went

COMMENTARY

"Along with up-beat popular music, radio comedy helped erase, if only momentarily, our concerns and fears of war and separation. Key to the success of most radio comedies was the announcer who was often integrated into the plots as a main character. Some familiar ones are Don Wilson (Jack Benny), Ken Carpenter (Edgar Bergen), Harry Von Zell (Eddie Cantor), Pierre Andre (Orphan Annie), Harlow Wilcox (Fibber McGee), and Bill Goodwin (Bob Hope).

"Other well known announcers were Fred Foy (Lone Ranger), Andre Baruch (Hit Parade), Milton Cross (Metropolitan Opera) and Franklyn McCormack (Jack Armstrong)."

Hank Hawthorne

1943 *Tide of War Is Slowly Turning*

WORLD

Russians Capture 91,000 German Troops and 24 Generals at Stalingrad as the Nazi Drive Stalls
US and Canadian Troops Retake Kiska Island in the Aleutians from the Japanese
Allies Take 100,000 Prisoners in the North Africa Campaign
Jews in the Warsaw Ghetto Offer Temporary Armed Resistance, But Are Soon Crushed
US and British Troops Invade and Take Sicily by August
Allies Invade Mainland Italy in September. Italy Surrenders Unconditionally, but German
    Forces There Continue the Battle with the Allies
King Victor Emmanuel III Dismisses Benito Mussolini as Italian Premier and Has Him
    Placed Under Arrest
Mussolini Is Rescued from Confinement by German Paratroopers
Chiang Kai-shek Becomes President of China
At the Casablanca Conference, the Allies Agree to Demand Unconditional Surrender
Dwight Eisenhower Is Named Supreme Commander of US Forces in the European Theater
Allies Continue Heavy Bombing of Industrial Areas of Germany and Occupied France

NATION

"Pay-As-You-Go" Income Tax Withholding Begins
Shoes, Meat, Cheese and Canned Goods Are Rationed
The Red Cross Volunteer Organization Has Grown to 4 Million
The Red Cross Is Now Collecting Blood Donations at 2 Million Units/Year
Work Is Completed on the Pentagon Building
The Jefferson Memorial Is Dedicated in Washington DC

ENVIRONMENT, SAFETY AND HEALTH

The Longest Oil Pipeline, "Big Inch," Stretches 1254 Miles from Texas to Pennsylvania

DISASTER

A Polio Epidemic Sweeps the Country. 1,150 Die and Thousands More Are Crippled

LIFESTYLE

From the Start of the War, 8 Million Women Have Entered the Workforce
A One & Two Digit Postal Zone Numbering System for Cities Is Expected to Speed Mail Service
Essential War Workers Are "Frozen" and Cannot Leave Their Jobs at Will

SCIENCE AND TECHNOLOGY

British "Colossus" Electronic Computer Breaks German "Enigma" Codes
Streptomycin Is Developed as an Antibiotic
Volume Production of Much Needed Penicillin Is Made Possible with More Powerful Mold Cultures

BUSINESS AND INDUSTRY

Willys, Ford and Other Carmakers Combined, Produce 75 Jeeps Per Day for the Military

CONSUMER PRODUCTS AND SERVICES

New Movie Cartoon Series, *Private Snafu* (Narrated by Mel Blanc) Warns the Public About
    "Loose Lips" and "Spreading Rumors."
War Bond Sales Drives Greatly Aided by Help from Big Movie Stars

Rosie the Riveter Is Symbolic　　1943

SPORTS

Ace Adams of the New York Giants Pitches in a Record 70 Games This Year
Professional Sports Are Without Their Best Players Because of the War

ARTS AND MEDIA

STAGE

Oklahoma	Rogers & Hammerstein, Alfred Drake, Celeste Holm
One Touch Of Venus	Mary Martin
Something For The Boys	Ethyl Merman
Winged Victory	Moss Hart
The Voice Of The Turtle	Margaret Sullavan

MOVIE

Casablanca	Michael Curtiz, Humphrey Bogart, Ingred Bergman, Paul Henreid, Claude Rains, Conrad Veight, Peter Lorre, Sidny Greenstreet
Watch On The Rhine	Paul Lukas, Bette Davis, Beulah Bondi
Song of Bernadette	Jennifer Jones, Charles Bickford
The More The Merrier	Charles Coburn, Jean Arthur, Joel McCrea
For Whom The Bell Tolls	Katina Paxinou, Gary Cooper, Ingred Bergman
Heaven Can Wait	Don Ameche, Gene Tierney, Spring Byington
Girl Crazy	Judy Garland, Mickey Rooney, June Allyson

RADIO

The Adventures of Nero Wolfe	Sidney Greenstreet
The Cisco Kid	
Blind Date	Arlene Francis

BOOK

A Tree Grows in Brooklyn	Betty Smith
Thirty Seconds Over Tokyo	Captain Ted Lawson
The Human Comedy	William Saroyan
Here Is Your War	Ernie Pyle

MUSIC

You'll Never Know	*Don't Get Around Much Anymore*
Elmer's Tune	*All or Nothing at All*
Paper Doll	*People Will Say We're in Love*
It's Magic	*That Old Black Magic*

PEOPLE

Norman Rockwell's *Rosie The Riveter* Appears on the Cover of the Saturday Evening Post
Lt. John F. Kennedy Is Credited With Saving Crew Members When His Torpedo Boat,
　　PT-109, Is Sheared by a Japanese Destroyer
Eleanor Roosevelt Continues to Visit US Troops Around the World
Fearing U-Boats, President Roosevelt Is Flown to the Casablanca Conference in a Chartered
　　Pan Am Flying Boat Using Civilian Pilots. This Is the First "Official" Presidential Flight

REFLECTION

From 1933-1942, the Civilian Conservation Corps (CCC) Provided Jobs for over Two Million
　　Young Men
Walk Down the Street and in About Every other Window There Is a Blue Banner with One or
　　More Stars to Signify the Number of Family Members Serving in the Armed Forces.
　　Gold Stars Indicate Those Members Who Will Not Be Returning Home

WORLD

US Heavy Bombers Stage the First American Raid on Berlin
V-1 Ballistic Missiles Start Hitting Britain. Of 7,500 Launched, 50% Are Shot Down in Flight
        Later, 1,100 More Deadly V-2 Rockets Cannot Be Stopped Before Detonation
US Amphibian Forces Invade Japanese-Held New Guinea
Rome Is Liberated (6/5)
Operation Overlord (D-Day) an Allied Armada Creates the Western Front with the Invasion of
        Europe at Normandy (6/6)
A Planted Bomb Explodes During a Nazi Conference but Hitler Escapes Serious Injury
Paris Is Liberated (8/29)
Gen. George Patton's Third Army Sweeps Through France and US Troops Enter Germany
        Near Trier (9/12)
Iceland Gains Independence from Denmark
Nazi Troops in October Finally Crush a Two-Month Warsaw Uprising.
Gen. Douglas MacArthur Returns to the Philippines After 2½ Years
Adm. William "Bull" Halsey Commands a Decisive Victory at the Battle of Leyte Gulf
Chester Nimitz Is Honored by Being Named a Five Star Admiral for His Leadership
George Marshall Becomes General of the Army (5 Star)
The Battle of the Bulge in December Is the Nazi's Last Major Attack of the War

NATION

The National Budget is a Whopping $70 Billion, Mostly for the War Effort
President Signs the Servicemen's Readjustment Act That Will Become Known as the GI Bill
FDR Drops VP Henry Wallace from the Ticket and Replaces Him with Little-Known Missouri
        Senator, Harry S Truman
Franklin Roosevelt Defeats Thomas E. Dewey for an Unprecedented 4th Presidential Term
US Withdraws Its Recognition of Argentina for Lack of Cooperation with the Allies

LIFESTYLE

Civilian Labor Force Unemployment Rate Is a Mere 1.2 %
Rationing on Most Grades of Meat Ends in May
Bobby Socks Appear—Fashion Statement or Youthful Rebellion?
The GI Bill Offers 4% Interest and No Down Payment on Homes for Veterans and Offers an
        Opportunity to Get a College Education
Bare Midriffs, Slim Skirts and Large Hats Are Much in Vogue with American Women

SCIENCE AND TECHNOLOGY

Wilem Kolff Develops the Kidney Dialysis Machine
DNA Is Proven to be a Blueprint of Heredity
The First Eye Bank Is Established in New York
Streptomycin Is Isolated; Proves to Be Effective in Destroying the Tuberculosis Bacterium

BUSINESS AND INDUSTRY

Total US Aircraft Production Peaks at One Plane Every Six Minutes!
Douglas Aircraft Outfits a C-54 with Desk, Workspace After Decision to Set Aside One Military
        Plane for the President. No Official Markings But Pilots Dub It, "The Sacred Cow."
The US Military XP-80 Jet Aircraft Exceeds 600 mph
Quinine Is Synthesized
Eastman Kodak Creates Kodacolor, a Color Film That Will Lead to Low-Cost Color Photographs

As We Retake Pacific Islands 1944

ARTS AND MEDIA

STAGE

Harvey	Frank Fay, Josephine Hull
Bloomer Girl	Celeste Holm
On the Town	Leonard Bernstein
Appalachian Spring,	Martha Graham, Aaron Copeland

MOVIE

Going My Way	Bing Crosby, Barry Fitzgerald
Gaslight	Ingred Bergman, Charles Boyer
None But The Lonely Heart	Ethyl Barrymore, Cary Grant, Jane Wyatt
Laura	Jean Tierney, Dana Andrews
To Have and Have Not	Humphrey Bogart, Lauren Bacall
Thirty Seconds Over Tokyo	Spencer Tracy, Van Johnson, Robert Walker
Keys of the Kingdom	Gregory Peck, Peggy Ann Garner
Since You Went Away	Claudette Colbert, Jennifer Jones, Joseph Cotton
Meet Me in St. Louis	Judy Garland, Margaret O'Brien

RADIO

The Adventures of Ozzie & Harriet	Ozzie, Harriet (Hilliard), David, Ricky Nelson
The Billie Burke Show	
The Danny Kaye Show	
The Saint	
The FBI in Peace and War	

BOOK

Forever Amber	Kathleen Winsor
Brave Men	Ernie Pyle

MUSIC

I'll Walk Alone
Don't Fence Me In
Long Ago and Far Away
I'll Be Seeing You
Mairzy Doats

The Trolley Song
Swinging on a Star
Besame Mucho
Back in the Saddle Again
You Are My Sunshine

PEOPLE

Frank Sinatra Leaves the Tommy Dorsey Band to be a *Your Hit Parade* Regular
Comic Joe E. Brown Travels a Record 150,000 Miles Entertaining Troops
Tommy Dorsey and Orchestra Record *Opus No. 1* for RCA Victor
Cartoonist, Bill Mauldin, Creates the Long-Suffering GI's, Joe and Willie, to Entertain the Troops

QUOTES

"NUTS!"
> Gen. Anthony McAuliffe, responding to a Nazi demand that he surrender his troops

"I'm Chiquita Banana and I've come to say, bananas have to ripen in a certain way. When they are flecked with brown and..."
> Radio Jingle

INCIDENTALS AND TRIVIA

With So Many US Service Personnel in England, There's Bound To Be Some Rivalry. The Tommies Say the Yanks Are 1.) *Over Paid*, 2.) *Over Sexed* and 3.) *Over Here*. The Yanks Reply That the Tommies Are 1.) *Under Paid*, 2.) *Under Sexed* and 3.) *Under Eisenhower*

1945 *Roosevelt Dies; the Nation Mourns*

WORLD

The Burma Road to China Is Reopened
The Yalta Conference Deals With the Reorganization of Post-War Europe
US and Soviet Forces Link at the Elbe River. The Collapse of Nazi Germany Is Near
Delegates of 50 Nations Meet in San Francisco to Form the United Nations
Benito Mussolini and His Mistress Are Executed by Italian Partisans on April 28
US Soldiers Liberate the Dachau Concentration Camp on April 29
Soviet Forces Enter the Devastated City of Berlin
Adolph Hitler Designates Admiral Karl Doenitz as His Successor on April 29
Hitler and Wife, Eva Braun, Commit Suicide in the Berlin Bunker on April 30
Germany Surrenders Unconditionally on May 8   (V-E Day)
Allies Divide Germany into Four Occupation Zones: Soviet, British, French and American
Japanese Lose 450,000 Troops as US Retakes the Philippines
British Voters Oust Churchill's Conservatives in Favor of the Labour Party
The Final Big Three Meeting at Potsdam Is with Truman, Stalin, and Clement Atlee
An Atomic Bomb Is Dropped on Hiroshima (8/6) and on Nagasaki (8/9)
Japan Surrenders (V-J Day) on August 15, on the Battleship Missouri in Tokyo Bay

NATION

The Atomic Bomb Is Tested in Secret at Alamogordo, NM
Franklin Delano Roosevelt Dies on April 12 in Warm Springs, GA. The Entire Nation Mourns
Harry S Truman Is Sworn in as the 33rd US President
Lone Japanese Balloon Bomb Explodes in Oregon, Killing Six
The National Debt Is $259 Billion
President Truman Signs the United Nations Charter

DISASTER

A B-25 Bomber Crashes into the Fog Shrouded Empire State Building Killing Thirteen

LIFESTYLE

800,000 Women Fired as War Ends and Men Return to Reclaim Jobs
Radio Is Part of Everyday Life with 56 Million Sets Nationwide
Nylon Stockings Return After Wartime Shortages, Triggering "Nylon Riots." In Many Stores

SCIENCE AND TECHNOLOGY

The ENIAC Computer Is Developed (30 Tons & 18,000 Vacuum Tubes)
An Operation Now Can Save "Blue Babies" with Oxygen Deficiencies

CONSUMER PRODUCTS AND SERVICES

Burton Baskin and Irving Robbins Open an Ice Cream Parlor
Gasoline Rationing Ends
Tupperware Is Born
Frozen Orange Juice Becomes Available

PRICES

Gasoline	$ .21 per gallon
Steak	.41 per pound
Milk	.14 per quart

We Welcome V-E, V-J Days 1945

ARTS AND MEDIA

| STAGE | *The Glass Menagerie* | Tennessee Williams |
| | *Carousel* | Rogers and Hammerstein |

MOVIE	*The Lost Weekend*	William Wyler, Ray Milland, Jane Wyman
	Mildred Pierce	Joan Crawford, Zachary Scott, Eve Arden
	A Tree Grows In Brooklyn	James Dunn , Dorothy McGuire, Joan Blondell
	National Velvet	Anne Revere, Elizabeth Taylor
	State Fair	Jeanne Crain, Dana Andrews, Dick Haymes
	The Picture of Dorian Gray	Donna Reed, Angela Lansbury, Peter Lawford

RADIO	*The Andrews Sisters*	Patti, Maxine, LaVerne Andrews, Gabby Hayes, Judy Canova
	The Whistler	Marvin Miller
	Maisie	Ann Sothern, Lurlene Tuttle
	The Bob Hawk Show (Quiz)	

| BOOK | *Cass Timberlain* | Sinclair Lewis |
| | *Black Boy* | Richard Wright |

MUSIC

Till the End of Time
Sentimental Journey
Accentuate the Positive
I'll Buy That Dream
Laura

On the Atchison Topeka and Santa Fe
There, I've Said It Again
If I Loved You
It Might As Well Be Spring
You'll Never Walk Alone

PEOPLE

Millions Cheer a NYC Parade Honors War Hero Dwight D. Eisenhower on June 19
Emperor Hirohito Broadcasts the Surrender. First Time His Subjects Have Heard His Voice
Low Budget Movie Cowboy, Roy Rogers, Is in Top Ten Box Office
"Boy" and "Girl" Singers Dominate the Radio and Record Music Scene: Frank Sinatra, Perry Como, Dick Haymes, Peggy Lee, Jo Stafford, Doris Day, Helen O'Connell, Kay Starr
Juan Peron Stages a Coup and Becomes Ruler of Argentina
Eleanor Roosevelt Is Named as the First US Delegate to the United Nations

REFLECTION

The Cost of World War II in US Service Personnel: Died, 405,400; Injured 670,800

INCIDENTALS AND TRIVIA

Truman Is the Only 20th Century President with No College Education
Correct Answers on the Bob Hawk Quiz Show to Win Money, Become a "Lemac" (Camel Backwards) and Be Serenaded with, "You're a Lemac Now."

COMMENTARY

"The returning vets knew about the GI Bill, and the millions who took advantage of it to buy a low-cost home in the suburbs and to finance a college education, would change the US lifestyle forever. Then, with education, home and prosperity, the baby boom was about to begin."

Bill Goodpage

1946 *The Men Are Back at Work*

WORLD

US Forces Occupy Japan and Share Occupation of Germany with Britain, France and the USSR
The Philippines Become Independent of US Sovereignty
The Nuremberg Tribunal Sentences 12 Leading Nazis to Death

NATION

President Truman Takes Control of the Nation's Railroads to Avoid a Threatened Strike
The Atomic Energy Commission (AEC) Is Established
The Strategic Air Command (SAC) Is Created But Lacks Intercontinental Flight Capability
US Brings Scientist Werhner von Braun to White Sands, NM for Army Rocket Research

ENVIRONMENT, SAFETY AND HEALTH

Smokey Bear Begins to Appear as the US Forestry Service Mascot

DISASTER

Tidal Waves in the Hawaiian Islands Kill 170

LIFESTYLE

There are 6,000 Television Receivers in the US (see 1951). But Mostly Show Test Patterns
The Daring New Two-Piece "Bikini" Swimsuit for Women Has Everyone Talking
Housing Shortages Abound and Inflation Grows as Goods Go off Rationing

SCIENCE AND TECHNOLOGY

Dry Ice Crystals Are Used to Seed Clouds and Produce Rain
ENIAC Computer (J. Presper Eckert Jr. & John W. Mauchley) Is Built, Primarily to
        Calculate Ballistic Trajectories for the Military
John von Neumann Claims that Computer Instructions Can Be Stored Inside the Computer
The US Explodes a 20 Kiloton Atomic Bomb near Bikini Atoll in the Pacific

BUSINESS AND INDUSTRY

US Produces Only 600 Military Propeller Driven Aircraft (see 1944)
The Air Force Buys a Douglas DC-6 (C-118) for the President. Named "Independence,"
Haloid Company Buys the Rights to Chester Carlson's Xerography Process (see 1938, 1960)

CONSUMER PRODUCTS AND SERVICES

Willys Offers Consumers a Modified Jeep, the Two Wheel Drive Jeepster
7-Eleven Stores Are Born in Dallas-Fort Worth
FM Radios, Developed Years Earlier, Finally Go into Mass Production
Record Sales Soar, Particularly Those Featuring Popular Vocalists
Survey Indicates That 100,000 Watched the Joe Louis-Billy Conn Heavyweight Title Bout on TV
        Sponsored by Gillette. TV Critics Are Impressed but TVs Cost $375 or More
The Italian Vespa Moped Is a Novelty Here in the States

SPORTS

Baseball Stars Returning from Military Service Make the 1946 Season Exciting
Ben Hogan Is Golf's Top Money Winner at $42,000

Housing Is in Short Supply

ARTS AND MEDIA

STAGE	*Anne Get Your Gun*	Ethyl Merman
	The Iceman Cometh	Eugene O'Neill
	St. Louis Woman	Pearl Bailey
	Born Yesterday	Paul Douglas, Judy Holliday
MOVIE	*The Best Years... Our Lives*	William Wyler , Fredric March,
	To Each His Own	Olivia de Havilland, John Lund
	The Razor's Edge	Anne Baxter, Tyrone Power
	The Harvey Girls	Judy Garland, John Hodiak
	Anna snd The King Of Siam	Irene Dunn, Rex Harrison
	The Jolson Story	Larry Parks, Evelyn Keyes
	Duel In The Sun	Jennifer Jones, Gregory Peck
RADIO	*Twenty Questions*	
	Sam Spade	Howard Duff
BOOK	*This Side of Innocence*	Taylor Caldwell
	Mr. Roberts	Thomas Heggen

MUSIC

The Girl That I Marry
Doin' What Comes Natur'lly
The Old Lamp-Lighter
Zip-a Dee-Doo-Dah
They Say It's Wonderful
Shoofly Pie and Apple Pan Dowdy
Five Minutes More

It's a Good Day
There's No Business Like Show Business
South America, Take It Away
Come Rain or Come Shine
That's How Much I Love You

PEOPLE

Eva "Evita" Peron Begins to Establish Herself as the "Patron Saint of the Poor" in Argentina
Mother Frances Xavier Cabrini Is Canonized as the First American Saint
"Bugsy" Siegal and Associates Open the Flamingo Hotel in the Desert Town of Las Vegas
Hermann Goering Poisons Himself Hours Before His Scheduled Execution

QUOTES

"Television won't be able to hold onto any market it captures after the first six months. People will soon get tired of staring at a plywood box every night."
Darryl F. Zanuck, 20th Century Fox (1946)

"...an iron curtain has descended across the Continent."
Winston Churchill (former Prime Minister)

"If you ever plan to motor west, travel my way,
that's the highway that's the best, get your kicks on Route 66
Bobby Troup

INCIDENTALS AND TRIVIA

The ENIAC Computer Weighs 50 Tons, Uses 18,000 Vacuum Tubes, Stores 20 Words in Memory
Several Top Bands Dissolve and the Golden Days of Big Bands Ends

1947 *Communists Are Gaining Abroad*

WORLD

The Truman Doctrine Helps Greece and Turkey Resist Communism
India Attains Independence after 200 Years of British Rule
King Michael of Romania Is Forced to Abdicate by the Communists
France Closes the Dreaded French Guyana and Devil's Island Prisons

NATION

Congress Enacts the Taft-Hartley Labor Law, Overriding a Presidential Veto. It Will Take Some
    Powers Away from the Unions
The Department of Defense, National Security Council, Central Intelligence Agency and the
    Joint Chiefs of Staff Are Created
The US Air Force Finally Becomes a Separate Military Service Branch
House Un-American Activities Committee Begins Investigation of Suspected Communist
    Infiltration in Films, Theater and Television. Hundreds Will Be Blacklisted
George C. Marshall, Secy.of State, Proposes the Marshall Plan for European Reconstruction

DISASTER

Tornadoes in Texas, Oklahoma and Kansas Kill 169

LIFESTYLE

Builder, William Leavitt, Creates Levittown, the First Low Cost, Mass Produced Suburb.
    Identical Cape Cod Style Houses Are Priced at $6,990
93% of All Homes Have Radios
1.6 Million Vets (49% of Students) Enter College Under the GI Bill (see 1940, 1956, 1990)
Wartime Rationing Ends as Sugar Is Now Available without Coupons

SCIENCE AND TECHNOLOGY

Col. Chuck Yeager Exceeds the Sound Barrier in the Bell X-1 Plane and Creates a Sonic
    Boom (see 1997)
Bell Laboratory Scientists Invent the Transistor
Dennis Gabor Develops Holography
Chloromycetin, the First Broad Spectrum Antibiotic Is Tested on Typhus
Willard F. Libby Develops a Process for Radiocarbon Dating, a Major Tool in Exploring
    Human Prehistory
The B-47 Bomber Is Added to the Strategic Air Command. It Can Be Refueled In-Flight,
    Creating the Necessary SAC Intercontinental Capability
Ampex Corporation Develops a Tape Recorder
Pan American Becomes a Globe-Circling Airline. An Around the World Fare Is $1,700

CONSUMER PRODUCTS AND SERVICES

New Polaroid Land Camera Can Produce B/W Photo in One Minute
Reynolds Wrap Aluminum Foil Is Great for Saving Leftovers

SPORTS

Jackie Robinson, First Black Major League Player, Debuts with the Brooklyn Dodgers.
Larry Doby Signs with Cleveland; the First Black Player in the American League
New York A.L. Bests Brooklyn N.L. in World Series, First to Be Broadcast on Television

Are They Gaining at Home Too? 1947

ARTS AND MEDIA

STAGE	*Brigadoon*	Lerner and Loewe
	A Streetcar Named Desire	Tennessee Williams, Marlon Brando, Jessica Tandy
	All My Sons	Elia Kazan. Ed Begley, Arthur Kennedy
MOVIE	*Gentleman's Agreement*	Celeste Holm, Gregory Peck, Dorothy McGuire, John Garfield
	Miracle on 34th Street	Edmund Gwenn, Maureen O'Hara, John Payne, Natalie Wood
	The Egg and I	Claudette Colbert, Fred MacMurray
	Life With Father	William Powell, Irene Dunne, Elizabeth Taylor
RADIO	*Candid Microphone*	Allen Funt
	You Bet Your Life	Groucho Marx, George Fenneman
	My Friend Irma	Marie Wilson
	Sky King	Earl Nightengale
TV	*Howdy Doody*	"Buffalo" Bob Smith
	Kukla, Fran and Ollie	Fran Allison, Burr Tillstrom
	Meet The Press	Lawrence Spivak, Martha Roundtree
BOOK	*The Pearl*	John Steinbeck

MUSIC

Open the Door Richard
How Are Things In Glocka Morra?
Old Devil Moon
If This Isn't Love
Feudin' and Fightin'
Mam'selle
Almost Like Being In Love

Beyond the Sea
All I Want for Christmas Is My Two Front Teeth
Heather on the Hill
Papa, Won't You Dance with Me?
It's a Sin
Smoke, Smoke, Smoke (That Cigarette)

PEOPLE

Howard Hughes Briefly Flies the Spruce Goose in Long Beach Harbor. (Its Only Flight)
Thor Heyerdahl Sails in Primitive Balsa Raft from Peru to Polynesia
In Spain, Renowned Bullfighter Manolete Is Mortally Wounded by a Bull

INCIDENTALS AND TRIVIA

"Alien Flying Saucer Spacecraft" Debris Found Near Roswell, NM, The Army Insists That It Is Only Remnants of a Weather Balloon. The Flying Saucer Scare Begins

COMMENTARY

"Things were now getting back to normal. Prices for a lot of goods were higher than when they were last available before the war, but with money to spend, most families went on a buying spree.

"Furniture and appliances were priorities. And, finally, new Dodges, Fords and Buicks were available. Many families looked for inexpensive housing in new tracts carved out of farmers' fields outside the city limits. Suburbs were being created and commuting soon became a way of life.

"The good life had finally arrived after long years of Depression and war—and not a moment too soon."

Kate Hawthorne

1948 Truman's Win Surprises Everyone

WORLD

Communists Take Over Czechoslovakia with the Resignation of Eduard Benes
Soviets Seal Off West Berlin from the West
The British, French and US Begin a Massive Air Lift to the Beleaguered City
The Marshall Plan Begins Infusing Money and Materials to Rebuild Western Europe, Greece,
　　　　Turkey and Economic and Military Aid to China
British Rule in Palestine Ends. The Independent State of Israel Is Proclaimed in Tel Aviv
The New State of Israel Is Immediately Attacked by Jordan, Egypt, Syria, Iraq, and Lebanon
The People's Democratic Republic of Korea (North Korea) Is Established
UN General Assembly Adopts Universal Declaration on Human Rights
Britain Grants Independence to Burma

NATION

Harry S Truman Wins a Surprise Presidential Election over Republican Thomas E. Dewey, Despite
　　　　the Third Party Breakaway Democratic "Dixiecrats."
US Supreme Court Says Prohibitions on Real Estate Sales to Minorities Are Unenforceable
Truman Signs an Executive Order Ending Segregation in the Military

LIFESTYLE

June: 175,000 TV Sets in American Homes, December: 750,000 TV Sets

SCIENCE AND TECHNOLOGY

The Big Bang Theory on the Origin of the Universe Is Proposed
The Smear or "PAP" Test for Cervical Cancer Is Adopted
Georges de Mestral Invents Velcro
Cortisone Is Synthesized to Treat Arthritis
The Mammoth 200 Inch Palomar Telescope and Observatory Is Dedicated
New York International Airport (later John F. Kennedy) Is Completed

BUSINESS AND INDUSTRY

IBM, Bell Telephone and Sperry Rand Begin Production of Computers
First Use of Cost-Of-Living Raises in a Labor Contract
Preston Tucker Produces 51 Radical Tucker Torpedo Cars. The Auto Has a Helicopter-
　　　　Type Rear Engine and a Third, "Cyclops" Headlight That Turns with the Front Wheels

CONSUMER PRODUCTS AND SERVICES

Earl "Madman" Muntz Introduces Muntz TV at an Incredibly Low $170
Small Tailfins Appear on the Cadillac
Columbia Introduces the 33 1/3 rpm Long Play Record. The 78 rpm Record Is Obsolete
Silly Putty, Packaged in a Plastic "Eggshell," Is Introduced
General Mills and Pillsbury Introduce Packaged Cake Mixes
Selchow & Richtor Market a New Game Called *Scrabble*

PRICES

McDonald Brothers Hamburger Stand (No Tipping)
　　　　Hamburger　　　　$.15
　　　　French Fries　　　　.10
　　　　Milk Shake　　　　.20

But Tucker's Surprise Fizzles   1948

SPORTS

Leroy "Satchel" Paige (42), the Oldest Rookie in Pro Baseball, Signs with Cleveland.

ARTS AND MEDIA

STAGE	*Mister Roberts*	Henry Fonda, David Wayne
	Kiss Me Kate	Cole Porter, Alfred Drake
MOVIE	*Johnny Belinda*	Jane Wyman, Lew Ayres
	Easter Parade	Judy Garland, Fred Astaire
	The Snake Pit	Olivia de Havilland, Mark Stevens
	The Babe Ruth Story	William Brendix, Claire Trevor
RADIO	*Life With Luigi*	J. Carrol Naish, Hans Conried
	My Favorite Husband	Lucille Ball, Richard Denning
	Our Miss Brooks	Eve Arden, Jeff Chandler
TV	*The Texaco Star Theater*	Milton Berle
	Toast of the Town	Ed Sullivan
	Republican and Democratic National Conventions	
BOOK	*The Big Fisherman*	Lloyd C. Douglas
	The Naked and the Dead	Norman Mailer
	How to Stop Worrying...Start Living	Dale Carnegie

MUSIC

Buttons and Bows
On a Slow Boat to China
Baby, It's Cold Outside
It's a Most Unusual Day
Lavender Blue (Dilly Dilly)
Once In Love With Amy
Tennessee Waltz

It's Magic
The Syncopated Clock
Sabre Dance
So In Love
Wunderbar
Another Openin' Another Show

PEOPLE

Margaret Chase Smith of Maine Is Elected to the US Senate and Becomes the First Woman
    to Serve in Both Houses of Congress
Alger Hiss, Former State Department Employee, Is Convicted of Perjury in Spy Case
Bernard Baruch Coins the Term, *Cold War*, to Describe Current East-West Relations

CRIME AND PUNISHMENT

Nazi Propagandist, Mildred Gillars (Axis Sally), Is Convicted and Serves
    12 years in Prison

COMMENTARY

"Though he was well known in the auto industry, Harley Earl of G.M. is hardly a household name. However, he impacted American tastes and buying habits for many years—for better or for worse.
"Earl put the tail fins on the Cadillac, a trend the entire industry followed. He was the brainchild behind two-tone paint, pillarless hardtops, and wrap around windshields."

Hank Hawthorne

1949 *We Win the Battle for Berlin*

WORLD

The Berlin Blockade Is Lifted by the USSR After 10+ Months
The Soviet Union Announces that It Has the Atomic Bomb
East and West Germany Form Separate Governments
Communist Leader Mao Zedong Proclaims the People's Republic of China, as
　　　　　Chiang Kai-shek's Nationalist Army Retreats to the Island of Formosa
Josef Cardinal Mindzenty Is Found Guilty if Treason in Hungary
Israel Is Accepted into the United Nations
The North Atlantic Treaty Is Signed for Mutual Western Defense
British Troops Successfully Defend Hong Kong from a Mainland Threat
The Last World War II US Forces Are Withdrawn from Korea

NATION

President Truman Asks Congress for a Health Insurance Bill
The United Nations Gets a Permanent Home in New York City

ENVIRONMENT, SAFETY AND HEALTH

Holland Tunnel Disaster in New York
The Puget Sound Narrows Bridge Is Rebuilt (see 1940)

LIFESTYLE

There Are Now 4 Million TV Sets in US, But Still Receive Test Patterns Most of the Day
"Bring a Buck" Pyramid Clubs Spawn a False Easy Money Craze
The US Minimum Wage is $.75

SCIENCE AND TECHNOLOGY

US Viking Rocket Replaces the Rapidly Dwindling Supply of German V-2 Rockets
Lucky Lady, a B-50 Superfortress, Completes the First Non-Stop Around-the-World Flight
An Air Force XB-47 Jet Crosses the US in 3 hrs., 46 min.
Schizophrenia Is Now Treatable with Lithium
Albert Einstein Outlines a New Theory on Gravitation and Electromagnetism

CONSUMER PRODUCTS AND SERVICES

Direct Dial Long Distance Telephone Service Begins
The Emmy Awards Show Debuts
RCA Introduces the 45 rpm Record With a Large Center Hole. It Competes With Columbia's
　　　　　33 1/3 Speed. The Record Industry Is in Turmoil
Elmer's Glue (Borden's Scowling Bull Label) Goes on Sale
The German Volkswagen Is Introduced to America. Curious Isn't It?
Mr Magoo Cartoon Character Appears
Motor Trend Magazine Will Cover the Post War Fascination with Automobiles

PRICES

Television Set (Sears Catalog)	$149.95
Butter	.73 per pound
Steak	.60 per pound
Eggs	.60 per dozen
Bread	.15 per pound

SPORTS

Heavyweight Boxer, Joe Louis, Retires after 12 Years as Champion
Ezzard Charles Defeats Jersey Joe Walcott for Heavyweight Boxing Title
Connie Mack Marks 50 Years as a Manager
The Ladies Professional Golf Association Is Founded with Patty Berg as President

ARTS AND MEDIA

STAGE	*Death of a Salesman*	Arthur Miller, Lee J. Cobb, Mildred Dunnock
	Gentlemen Prefer Blondes	Carol Channing
	South Pacific	Rogers & Hammerstein, Mary Martin, Ezio Pinza

MOVIE	*All The King's Men*	Broderick Crawford, Mercedes McCambridge
	A Letter To Three Wives	Jeanne Crain, Linda Darnell, Ann Sothern
	The Heiress	Olivia de Havilland, Montgomery Clift
	Twelve O'clock High	Gregory Peck, Dean Jagger
	She Wore A Yellow Ribbon	John Wayne, Joanne Dru
	Pinky	Jeanne Crain, William Lundigan, Ethyl Waters
	Home Of The Brave	Mark Robeson, James Edwards, Frank Lovejoy

RADIO	*Dragnet*	Jack Webb
	Father Knows Best	Robert Young
	The Halls of Ivy	Ronald and Benita Hume Coleman
	Hopalong Cassidy	William Boyd
	Man Against Crime	Ralph Bellamy

TV	*Mama*	Peggy Wood
	Garroway at Large	Dave Garroway
	The Camel News Caravan	John Cameron Swayze
	Your Show of Shows	Sid Caesar, Imogene Coca, Carl Reiner, Howard Morris
	Kay Kyser's Kollege of Musical Knowledge	Kay Kyser, Ish Kabibble

| BOOK | *Death of a Salesman* | Arthur Miller |
| | *1984* | George Orwell |

MUSIC

Some Enchanted Evening
Rudolph the Red Nosed Reindeer
That Lucky Old Sun
Riders In the Sky
Mockin'bird Hill
Mule Train

This Nearly Was Mine
I'm Gonna Wash That Man Right Out of My Hair
Younger Than Springtime
Wedding Bells
Candy Kisses

PEOPLE

Rita Hayworth Marries the Ali Khan
Milton Berle Appears on the Cover of Both *Time* and *Newsweek*
American-Born Iva Toguri D'Aquino (Tokyo Rose) Gets 10 Years in Prison

QUOTES

"Computers in the future may, perhaps, only weigh 1.5 tons."
Popular Mechanics Magazine 1949

1950 *It's Back to War Again...*

WORLD

Communist North Korean Troops Invade South Korea
President Truman Orders US Troops to Korea after the UN Security Council Requests
       Assistance from Member Nations
After Numerous Setbacks, Allied Forces Land at Inchon and Drive Toward Seoul.
Red Chinese Troops Cross Into North Korea to Counter the US Drive

NATION

US Population Now 150.7 Million. The National Debt Is $256 Billion
An Attempted Assassination of President Truman by Puerto Rican Extremists Is Foiled at
       Washington's Blair House
The FBI Creates the *Ten Most Wanted* List and Relies on the Media for Its National Publicity
Blacklisting of Performers and Others with Alleged Communist Affiliations or Sympathies
       Reaches a Peak. Many Careers Are Ruined or Put on Hold for Years
Inflation Remains a Nagging Problem and a Key Issue for Unions

ENVIRONMENT, SAFETY AND HEALTH

The Grand Coulee Dam on Washington's Columbia River Is Completed

LIFESTYLE

49.3 Million Automobiles Are Registered
The Federal Minimum Hourly Wage Is $.75 and Average Factory Weekly Gross Is $60
The Hell's Angels Motorcycle Gang Forms
A Dance Called the Mambo Is Introduced from Cuba
The Card Game, Canasta, Is a US and World-Wide Craze

SCIENCE AND TECHNOLOGY

The EDVAC Computer Uses Magnetic Storage Disks
The Public Loves Antihistamines for the Common Cold Despite Medical Warnings

BUSINESS AND INDUSTRY

Kaiser Frazer Corporation Introduces the *Henry J* Compact Automobile
Nash Introduces a Smaller Sedan Called the Rambler
John Crean Starts Fleetwood Enterprises to Build Travel Trailers and Mobile Homes

CONSUMER PRODUCTS AND SERVICES

Marlboro Runs Its First Craggy Cowboy Advertisements
Diners Club Card Offers Instant Credit for Business Travelers
The Hopalong Cassidy Lunchbox Sells 600,000 Copies
The Xerox Copier Is Introduced. Compared to Peel-Apart Wet Copies, It Is Wonderful!
Minute Rice Is Very Convenient
Kellogg Introduces Sugar Pops Cereal

PRICES

Ford 2 Door (entry level))	$ 1,417
Henry J (entry level)	1,363

Or Is It a Police Action?

SPORTS

Associated Press Names Man o' War the Horse of the Half Century
Ben Hogan Wins the US Open Golf Championship

ARTS AND MEDIA

STAGE	*The Member of the Wedding*	Ethyl Waters, Julie Harris
	Come Back Little Sheba	Shirley Booth, Sidney Blackmer
	The Cocktail Party	Alec Guinness, Cathleen Nesbitt
	Peter Pan	Jean Arthur, Boris Karloff
	Guys and Dolls	Robert Alda, Sam Levene, Vivian Blaine
MOVIE	*All About Eve*	Jos. L. Mankiewicz, Betty Davis, George Sanders
	Sunset Boulevard	William Holden, Gloria Swanson
	Harvey	James Stewart, Josephine Hull, Jesse White
	The Third Man	Joseph Cotton, Orson Welles
RADIO	*The Big Show*	Tullulah Bankhead
	Dangerous Assignment	Brian Dunlevy
TV	*Your Hit Parade*	Dorothy Collins, Snookie Lanson, Russell Arms, Giselle Mackenzie
	What's My Line?	Dorothy Kilgallen, Bennett Cerf, John Daly, Arlene Francis
	Arthur Godfrey & Friends	Arthur Godfrey, Julius LaRosa
	You Bet Your Life	Groucho Marx, George Fenneman
	Burns and Allen	George Burns, Gracie Allen
BOOK	*Dianetics*	L. Ron Hubbard
	The Wall	John Hersey

MUSIC

If I Knew You Were Comin' I'd've Baked a Cake
Rag Mop
A Bushel and a Peck
Silver Bells
If I Were a Bell
Frosty the Snowman

Luck Be a Lady Tonight
I'm Going to Live Till I Die
It's a Lovely Day Today
Good Night Irene
Long Gone Lonesome Blues
Chattanooga Shoe Shine Boy

PEOPLE

Ralph Bunche Becomes First Black Leader to Win the Nobel Peace Prize.
Cartoonist Charles Schultz Syndicates *L'il Folks*, Later Named *Peanuts*

QUOTES

"If all economists were laid end to end they would not reach a conclusion."
George Bernard Shaw (1856-1950)

INCIDENTALS AND TRIVIA

Underarm Deodorants Are Becoming as Necessary as Toothpaste for Middle Class Americans
Burglars Steal 2.5 Million From the Brinks Headquarters Building in Boston

1951 *The Korean Conflict Continues*

WORLD

Chinese Troops Drive UN and South Korean Units Back, Temporarily Taking Seoul
Allies Retake Seoul and the Battle Lines Shift Around the 17th. Parallel
MacArthur Wants to Bomb China Across the Yalu River but the UN Disagrees
The United Nations Finally Condemns China for Aggression in Korea
President Truman Relieves Gen. Douglas MacArthur of All His Commands
Armistice Talks to End the Korean Conflict Begin in Kaesong

NATION

Anxiety Is High as Anti-Communist Hysteria Begins to Grip the Nation
Estes Kefauver Opens Senate Televised Hearings on Organized Crime
The 22nd. Amendment to the Constitution Limits a President to Two Elected Terms
US Detonates an Atomic Bomb over the Nevada Desert in a Test with Live Troops

LIFESTYLE

There Are Now Over 11,000,000 B/W TV Sets in the US (see 1946)
Airstream Inventor, Wally Byam, Leads the First Trailer Caravan
The First Portion of the New Jersey Turnpike Opens
Marlon Brando Gives the Tee-Shirt Rebel Status in His *Streetcar* Role and Transforms the
    White Undershirt into the Most Popular Garment of the Century

SCIENCE AND TECHNOLOGY

UNIVAC Computer Is Installed at the Bureau of the Census. It Uses Magnetic Tape for Input
CBS Transmits a One-Hour Commercial Color Telecast from New York
First All Jet Dogfights as Soviet MIG 15 and US F-86 Sabre Jets Meet in Korea
The First Atomic Powered Generator Begins Producing Electricity in Idaho
Pittsburgh's Alcoa Building Is Completed with 30 Stories Clad in Aluminum

BUSINESS AND INDUSTRY

Wang Laboratories Is Founded
AT&T Is First Corporation to Claim More Than a Million Shareholders
Major Movie Studios Are Resisting TV by Refusing to Sell Old Films to Networks
Filmed Shows Are Replacing Live TV. Production Rapidly Shifts From New York to Hollywood

CONSUMER PRODUCTS AND SERVICES

Topps Bubble Gum Is Marketed With Baseball Cards
Zenith Radio Launches a Pay-TV System. Viewers Pay $1.00 Per Film
Hickory Farms Opens a Store in Toledo and the Cheese Ball Is Born
Dennis the Menace Cartoon by Hank Ketcham, Appears in Newspapers

PRICES

Local Pay Telephone Call	$.10 (Double from Last Year)
Café Coffee	$.10 Per Cup (Double from Last Year)
Gasoline	$.27 Per gallon
Average New Car	$1,480
Average 3 BR House	$9,000
Mortgage Interest Rate	4½%

SPORTS

Mickey Mantle Joins the Yankees as Joe Dimaggio Retires
Jersey Joe Walcott Knocks Out Ezzard Charles for Heavyweight Title

ARTS AND MEDIA

STAGE		
	The King and I	Yul Brunner, Gertrude Lawrence
	The Rose Tattoo	Tennessee Williams, Maureen Stapleton, Eli Wallach

MOVIE		
	An American In Paris	Gene Kelly, Leslie Caron
	A Place In The Sun	Montgomery Clift, Elizabeth Taylor, Raymond Burr
	The African Queen	Humphrey Bogart, Katherine Hepburn
	A Streetcar Named Desire	Marlon Brando, Vivian Leigh, Karl Malden, Kim Hunter
	Strangers On A Train	Robert Walker, Ruth Roman, Farley Granger
	The Great Caruso	Mario Lanza, Ann Blyth, Dorothy Kirsten

TV		
	Dragnet	Jack Webb, Ben Alexander
	I Love Lucy	Lucille Ball, Desi Arnaz, William Frawley, Vivian Vance
	See It Now	Edward R. Murrow
	The Roy Rogers Show	Roy Rogers, Dale Evans, Pat Brady

BOOK		
	The Caine Mutiny	Herman Wouk
	The Grass Harp	Truman Capote
	The Sea Around Us	Rachel Carson
	The Catcher in the Rye	J.D. Salinger

MUSIC

Amahl and the Night Visitors Gian Carlo Menotti
Unforgettable
Kisses Sweeter Than Wine
On Top of Old Smokey
The Little White Cloud That Cried
Come On-a My House

We Kiss In a Shadow
Whistle a Happy Tune
Hello Young Lovers
Cold, Cold Heart
There's Been a Change in Me

PEOPLE

Due to TV, Julius LaRosa Sells 750,000 Copies of His Recording of *Anywhere I Wander*
Judy Garland Breaks All Records at the Palace Theater in New York

QUOTES

"Old soldiers never die, they just fade away."
Gen. Douglas MacArthur (1951)

COMMENTARY

"Another war. This time it's against the communists who seem to be taking over everywhere. Some of our own citizens are being called subversives or sympathizers. Is there a communist plot to take over the country? It's difficult for the average American to understand."

INCIDENTALS AND TRIVIA

"Miss Picky"

Irene English

Flying Saucers and Mysterious Objects Are Being Sighted Everywhere. Even the Air Force Has Some Photographs That Can't Be Explained. Newspapers and Magazines Love It

Yes, We Sure Do Like Ike

WORLD

George VI Dies. Queen Elizabeth Will Rule the Shrinking British Empire
UN Reports That the Korean Truce Talks Are Deadlocked
South Africa's Supreme Court Rules that Apartheid Is Discriminatory but the Parliament
    Says It Is the Highest Court in the Land and the Policy Continues
Native Uprisings Begin in Kenya against White Settlers

NATION

US Policy Is to Arm Europe and Make it Too Costly for the USSR to Start a War
President Temporarily Seizes the Steel Mills, Anticipating a Major, Prolonged Strike
A GI Bill of Rights for Korean Vets Is Passed and Implemented
Truman Announces He Will Not Be a Candidate. The Democratic Race Is Wide Open
Eisenhower Defeats Sen. Robert A. Taft (Mr. Republican) for the GOP Presidential Nomination
VP Candidate Richard Nixon Is Accused of Taking Illegal "Slush Fund" Money and Successfully
    Defends Himself in His Famous "Checkers" Speech on Television
Dwight D. Eisenhower Defeats Democrat Adelai E. Stevenson for President
Puerto Rico Becomes a Self-Governing Commonwealth of the United States

DISASTER

Polio Epidemic in US Strikes 57,600, Killing 3,300 and Crippling Most Others

LIFESTYLE

Cheerleading Is Very Popular in High School Athletics
17 Million US Homes Now Have a TV

SCIENCE AND TECHNOLOGY

The UNIVAC Computer Predicts a Landslide Victory for Eisenhower
Rapid Eye Movement (REM) Is Discovered To Be a Specific Stage in Sleep
The B-52, an Intercontinental Bomber, Joins the SAC Bomber Command
US Detonates the First Thermonuclear Bomb (Hydrogen) in a Test at Enewetok Island
Thalidomide, a Drug Sold as a Sedative for Pregnant Women, Is Banned for Causing Horrific
    Birth Defects in Babies. It Is Not Officially Sold in the US, but Many Women Acquire It

BUSINESS AND INDUSTRY

Holiday Inn, First National Hotel Chain, Starts in Memphis
George Meany Is Appointed Head of the AFof L, Replacing William Green, Who Died
Walter Reuther, President of the United Auto Workers, Now Heads the CIO

CONSUMER PRODUCTS AND SERVICES

Sony Offers an Amazing Pocket-Sized Transistor Radio
PEZ Candy Comes to America in a Mickey Mouse Head Dispenser
Mad Magazine Begins Publication
Mr. Potato Head Toy Is Created. Plastic Parts Are Stuck into a Real Potato
Hollywood Offers, *This Is Cinerama*, a Wide Curved Screen With Stereophonic Sound
Household Rubber Gloves Are Sold to Protect Hands from Hot Water and Solvents
Kellogg Introduces Sugar Frosted Flakes Cereal
Proctor and Gamble Markets *Gleem* Toothpaste
No-Cal Ginger Ale Uses Cyclamate Instead of Sugar. Will Revolutionize the Industry

And Dick Is O.K. Too 1952

SPORTS

Rocky Marciano Defeats Jersey Joe Wolcott for Heavyweight Boxing Title
Dick Button Again (7th Time) Wins the Men's US Figure Skating Championship
Eddie Arcaro Wins His Fifth Kentucky Derby

ARTS AND MEDIA

STAGE	*Venus Observed*	Rex Harrison, Lilli Palmer
MOVIE	*Greatest Show On Earth*	Betty Hutton, Cornel Wilde, Dorothy Lamour
	High Noon	Gary Cooper, Grace Kelly
	Come Back Little Sheba	Shirley Booth, Burt Lancaster
	Viva Zapata	Anthony Quinn, Jean Peters, Marlon Brando
	The Bad and the Beautiful	Gloria Grahame, Lana Turner, Kirk Douglas
TV	*Ozzie and Harriet*	Ozzie, Harriet, David and Ricky Nelson
	American Bandstand	Dick Clark
	Victory At Sea (documentary)	
	Mr. Peepers	Wally Cox
	Today	Dave Garroway
	Jack Benny	
	The Jackie Gleason Show	Art Carney, Audrey Meadows and Joyce Randolph
BOOK	*Charlotte's Web*	E.B. White
	The Silver Chalice	Thomas B. Costain
	A Man Called Peter	Catherine Marshall
	Power of Positive Thinking	Norman Vincent Peale

MUSIC

That Doggie In the Window
I Saw Mommy Kissing Santa Claus
Lullaby of Birdland
Wheel of Fortune
Till I Waltz Again With You
Do Not Forsake Me
Botch-a Me
I Believe
Jambalaya
When I Fall In Love
Kiss of Fire
Slow Poke

PEOPLE

Albert Schweitzer Receives the Nobel Peace Prize
The Dave Brubeck Quartet Pioneers "Progressive" Jazz
Marilyn Monroe Makes the Cover of Life Magazine
Malcolm X (27), Now Out of Prison, Joins Elijah Mohammed, Black Muslim Leader
Rex Humbard Begins His Television Ministry
Emmy Awards Name Bishop Fulton J. Sheen the "Most Outstanding Television Personality"
George Jorgensen Receives a Sex Change Operation in Denmark, Becoming Christine Jorgensen

QUOTES

"I will go to Korea." (Promising to end the conflict)
Candidate Dwight D. Eisenhower

INCIDENTALS AND TRIVIA

Across the Nation, College Men Make "Panty Raids" on Sororities and Girls' Dormitories

1953 *A New Leader in the US*

WORLD

The Korean War Armistice Is Signed Ending 3 Years of Warfare
Elizabeth II Is Crowned Queen of England at Westminster Abbey
300,000 East Berliners Escape to the West
Joseph Stalin Dies in Moscow. He is Succeeded by Georgei Malenkov
Dag Hammarskjold of Sweden Is Named Secretary General of the United Nations

NATION

Nation Has the First Republican Administration in 24 Years
Congress Establishes the Department of Health, Education and Welfare (HEW)
Presidential Plane in a Near Miss Via Number Confusion. Will Now Be Known as *Air Force One*

LIFESTYLE

25% of Motion Picture Theaters Close, Largely Due to Television. Drive-In Theaters Thrive
Bermuda Shorts Get Men Out of Long Pants During the Summer Months

SCIENCE AND TECHNOLOGY

Dr. Jonas Salk Tests an Experimental Polio Vaccine
The DNA Structure Is Believed to Be the Basis of Heredity
John Gibbon Jr. Uses a Heart-lung Machine He Invented for Successful Open Heart Surgery
US Army Demonstrates "Amazon Annie," an Atomic Cannon
U.S. Announces That It Has Developed a Hydrogen Bomb
The Soviet Union Explodes a Hydrogen Bomb

BUSINESS AND INDUSTRY

IBM Introduces the 701 Computer Using Proven Punch Card Technology
Rail Cargo Efficiency Improves with the Introduction of Semi-Trailer Piggyback Technology
Nash Merges with Cash-Short Hudson Motor Company

CONSUMER PRODUCTS AND SERVICES

Chevrolet Introduces the Corvette
Hugh Hefner (27) Publishes *Playboy* Magazine. *TV Guide* Magazine Begins Publication
Cheez Whiz Is Born
Burger King Opens Its First Restaurant
Many Wide Cinemascope Pictures Are Introduced to Bolster Sagging Movie Attendance
You Can Also Don 3-D Glasses to View Films Like *Bwana Devil*
The Collapsible Steering Wheel Is a New Safety Improvement
Filter Tipped L&M Cigarettes Are Advertised as " Just What the Doctor Ordered."

PRICES

Steak	$.92 per pound
Milk	.22 per quart
Bread	.16 per pound

SPORTS

The Boston Braves Become the Milwaukee Braves as Baseball Begins to Realign Teams

New Leaders in the USSR 1953

ARTS AND MEDIA

STAGE   *Can Can*   Cole Porter, Gwen Verden
                  Wonderful Town   Leonard Bernstein, Rosalind Russell

MOVIE   *From Here To Eternity*   Frank Sinatra. Donna Reed
                  Stalag 17   William Holden, Don Taylor, Peter Graves
                  Shane   Alan Ladd, Jean Arthur, Van Heflin
                  Call Me Madam   Ethyl Merman, Donald O'Conner, Vera-Ellen
                  Moulin Rouge   Jose Ferrer, Zsa Zsa Gabor

TV   *Make Room For Daddy*   Danny Thomas
                  Omnibus   Alistair Cooke
                  Person To Person   Edward R. Murrow
                  You Are There   Walter Cronkite

BOOK   *The Robe*   Lloyd C. Douglas

MUSIC

Vaya Con Dios	*Don't Let the Stars Get In Your Eyes*
Cry Me a River	*Stranger In Paradise*
Secret Love	*This Is My Beloved*
My One and Only Heart	*I Love Paris*
Oh! My Pa-pa	*Your Cheating Heart*

PEOPLE

General George C. Marshall Receives the Nobel Peace Prize
Sir Edmund Hillary and Tenzing Norkay Reach Mt. Everest Summit
Earl Warren Is Named Chief Justice of the US Supreme Court
Fred M. Rogers (later Mr. Rogers) Starts a Children's TV Program
L. Ron Hubbard Establishes the Church of Scientology
Ethyl and Julius Rosenberg Are Executed as Spies for the Soviet Union
Sen. Joseph McCarthy Says the Prior Administration Was "Crawling" With Communists

QUOTES

"I'm crying all the way to the bank."
                 Liberace (To His Musical Critics)

REFLECTION

The Cost of the Korean Conflict in US Service Personnel: Died, 25,700; Injured, 103,300; Missing In Action, 8,000

COMMENTARY

     "This year and the next several, we witnessed some of television's finest acting and directing performances through such shows as Philco Playhouse, Goodyear Playhouse, Kraft Theater, Studio One, Robert Montgomery Presents and the U.S. Steel Hour.
     "This was drama at its finest but some sponsors were not happy with these 'realistic' shows, believing that simpler, happy-ending programs would sell more products."

Bill Goodpage

1954   *An End to the Dreaded Polio?*

WORLD

Fighting Ends in Indochina Between the French and the Communist Vietminh after 7 Years.
Vietnam Is Split into North and South at the 17th Parallel

NATION

US Supreme Court Rules That Racially Segregated Public Schools Are Inherently Unequal.
    Chief Justice Earl Warren Says Schools Must Integrate with "All Deliberate Speed."
Televised Senate Army-McCarthy Hearings Begin Downfall of Sen. Joseph McCarthy
The Senate Censures Sen. Joseph McCarthy for His Conduct in Senate Subcommittees
Ellis Island Immigration Station Is Officially Closed. 13 Million Entered US Through Ellis
President Eisenhower Proposes a Highway Modernization Program
The US and Canada Announce Plans for a 3,000 Mile Early Warning Radar System

LIFESTYLE

Everybody Loves the New "California Dip" (Dry Onion Soup Mix & Sour Cream)
Transparent "Murgatroid" Plastic Raincoats Are All the Rage
The ChaChaCha Is Introduced to American Dance Floors

SCIENCE AND TECHNOLOGY

The First Successful Kidney Transplant Operation Is Performed
Production of the Supersonic B-58 Bomber Begins
Salk Polio Vaccine Inoculations Begin on Pittsburgh School Children
Nautilus, the First Atomic Submarine, Is Launched at Groton, CT

BUSINESS AND INDUSTRY

Ray Kroc Obtains Franchise Rights to the 12 McDonald Brothers Restaurants
Howard Johnson Goes into the Motor Lodge Business
First Network Color Broadcast Is the Tournament of Roses Parade on NBC
A Lockheed Super Constellation (VC-121E) Is Modified as Air Force One
American Motors Corporation Is Formed from the Nash and Hudson Merger
Studebaker-Packard Corporation Is Created Through Merger

CONSUMER PRODUCTS AND SERVICES

More Than a Million Davy Crockett Hats Are Sold Because of the Popular TV Show
Sports Illustrated Magazine Begins Publication
Mars Now Offers Peanut M&M Covered Chocolate Candies (see 1940)
General Mills Introduces *TRIX*, a Cereal with Lots of Sugar

PRICES

15" RCA Color Television Set	$1,000.00
19" Black and White Television Set	190.00 or less

SPORTS

Roger Bannister Breaks the "Unbreakable" Four Minute Mile
The St. Louis Browns Become the Baltimore Orioles

Can You Shake, Rattle and Roll? 1954

ARTS AND MEDIA

STAGE
	The Pajama Game	Carol Haney, Shirley MacLaine
	The Bad Seed	Nancy Kelly, Patty McCormack
	Peter Pan	Mary Martin

MOVIE
	On The Waterfront	Elia Kazan, Marlon Brando, Eva Marie Saint
	The Barefoot Contessa	Ava Gardner, Edmund O'Brien
	Three Coins in the Fountain	Clifton Webb, Jean Peters, Dorothy McGuire, Louis Jourdan
	Rear Window	James Stewart, Grace Kelly, Thelma Ritter, Raymond Burr
	A Star Is Born	Judy Garland, James Mason
	White Christmas	Bing Crosby, Rosemary Clooney, Danny Kaye, Vera-Ellen
	Carmen Jones	Dorothy Dandridge, Harry Belafonte

TV
	The Tonight Show	Steve Allen, Skitch Henderson
	Lassie	June Lockhart, Tommy Rettig
	Caesar's Hour	Sid Caesar, Nanette Fabray, Carl Reiner, Howard Morris
	People Are Funny	Art Linkletter
	Father Knows Best	Robert Young, Jane Wyatt, Elinor Donihue
	The Spike Jones Show	Spike Jones, Helen Grayco, Billy Barty, Bill Dana

BOOK
	Lord of the Flies	William Golding

MUSIC

Hernando's Hideaway	The High and the Mighty
That's Amore	Mister Sandman
I Left My Heart in San Francisco	Young at Heart
Earth Angel	Hey There
Shake Rattle and Roll	Baubles, Bangles and Beads

PEOPLE

Hollywood Starlet, Marilyn Monroe, Marries Baseball's Joe Dimaggio
Elvis Presley Records *That's All Right*, His First Song
Oral Roberts Begins His Television Ministry
Miss California, Lee Ann Meriwether, Is the Winner in the First TV Miss America Pageant
Marian Anderson Is the First Black Singer Hired by the Metropolitan Opera
Nelson Mandella Is Convicted of Treason in South Africa and Jailed

INCIDENTALS AND TRIVIA

154 Americans Have Incomes of One Million Dollars or More, Compared to 513 in 1929
The Stock Market Finally Has a Higher Valuation than It Had in 1929

COMMENTARY

"After the fall of many eastern European nations to Soviet rule and the loss of Mainland China, many Americans fear that Communism will spread into the US through infiltration. Are there Communists among us? Are they already running the government?

"There are many reactionaries eager to exploit the issue of domestic Communism. Most noted is Sen. Joseph McCarthy of Wisconsin who claims to 'have lists of names.' Since 1950, McCarthy has increased the fury of his attacks. Late in the year the Senate censures him, ending an ugly period in this country's history."

Kate Hawthorne

1955 *The Magic Kingdom Opens*

WORLD

Nikolai A. Bulganin Replaces Georgei Malenkov as Premier of the USSR
The Soviet Union and 8 Communist Bloc Countries Form the Warsaw Pact (see 1993)
Hundreds Die as Anti-French Riots Sweep Morocco and Algeria
Winston Churchill Quits as British Prime Minister. Anthony Eden to Form a New Government
Dictator, Juan Peron, Is Overthrown in Argentina

NATION

The US Air Force Academy Is Established in Colorado
Private Atomic Energy Plants Are Authorized by the Atomic Energy Commission
Racial Desegregation on Interstate Trains and Busses Is Ordered by the ICC

ENVIRONMENT, SAFETY AND HEALTH

The Salk Polio Vaccine Is a Resounding Success. Albert Sabin Develops an Oral Vaccine

LIFESTYLE

Consumers Purchase 4 Million New Refrigerators, Ridding Themselves, of Units That Had
     Little Space for Frozen Foods and TV Dinners
High Density Molded Boards Create New Waves of "Hot Dogger" Surfers
Half of US Homes Have a Television Receiver, Now Known Simply as a TV
Rock and Roll Is Sweeping the Country
One in Every Eight Autos Sold Is a Station Wagon

SCIENCE AND TECHNOLOGY

Exposure to Asbestos Has a Link to Lung Cancer

BUSINESS AND INDUSTRY

The AF of L and the CIO Merge. The Combined Organization Has 15 Million Members
Volkswagen Produces Its Millionth Automobile

CONSUMER PRODUCTS AND SERVICES

Disneyland, "The Magic Kingdom," Opens in Anaheim with A, B, C, D & E Ride Tickets
Ford Introduces the Thunderbird
Chrysler Offers a More Aggressive and Powerful 300 Model
Revamped Chevrolet Includes Power and Options Limited to Luxury Cars in the Past
Toothpastes with Fluoride Additives Appear
T-Fal Non-Stick Cookware Is Marketed

PRICES

McDonald's Drive-In
Hamburger $.15
French Fries   .10
Milk Shake   .20

SPORTS

US Takes First Place in Team Sports at the Pan-American Games in Mexico

ARTS AND MEDIA

STAGE	*Damn Yankees*	Gwen Verden, Ray Walston
	Diary of Anne Frank	Susan Strasberg, Joseph Schildkraut
	A Hatful Of Rain	Shelley Winters, Ben Gazzara, Anthony Franciosa
	The Matchmaker	Thornton Wilder, Ruth Gordon
MOVIE	*Marty*	Delbert Mann, Ernest Borgnine, Betsy Blair
	Mister Roberts	Jack Lemmon, Henry Fonda, James Cagney
	Rebel Without A Cause	James Dean, Natalie Wood, Sal Mineo
	To Hell and Back	Audie Murphy, Jack Kelly, David Janssen
	Blackboard Jungle	Sidney Poitier, Glenn Ford
	Guys and Dolls	Marlon Brando, Frank Sinatra, Stubby Kaye, Jean Simmons,
TV	*The Mickey Mouse Club*	
	Captain Kangaroo	Bob Keeshan
	Davy Crockett	Fess Parker
	Highway Patrol	Broderick Crawford
	Gunsmoke	James Arness, Dennis Weaver, Amanda Blake, Milburn Stone
	The Honeymooners	Jackie Gleason, Art Carney, Audrey Meadows, Joyce Randolph
	Alfred Hitchcock Presents	
	The Ernie Kovacs Show	
BOOK	*The Man in the Gray Flannel Suit*	Sloan Wilson

MUSIC

Cherry Pink and Apple Blossom White	*The Yellow Rose of Texas*
Tutti Frutti	*Whatever Lola Wants*
Moments to Remember	*The Great Pretender*
Que Sera' Sera'	*All of You*
Arrivederci, Roma	*Heartbreak Hotel*

PEOPLE

Rosa Parks of Montgomery, Alabama, Refuses to Give Up Her Seat in the White Section of a Bus
Esther "Eppie" Friedman Begins the *Ann Landers* Advice Column (see Abagail Van Buren 1956)
Robert Schuller Begins His Television Ministry from the Roof of A Drive-In Theater Snack Shack
Tom Parker Acquires the Management Contract of Elvis Presley
Salvador Dali Paints *The Sacrament of the Last Supper*

QUOTES

"The ability to get to the verge without getting into the war is the necessary art."
John Foster Dulles, Secretary of State

COMMENTARY

Bill Goodpage

"For years summer struck fear in the hearts of parents. Far too many friends and family members had been crippled by polio; wore braces, crutches, needed wheelchairs or even an iron lung to breathe.

"By 1955, millions had already received the miraculous Salk vaccine, and the disease would soon be eradicated. Salk received numerous honors but refused any personal profit from his work."

WORLD

Chinese Who Resist Communization Continue to Be Liquidated
A Hungarian Anti-Stalinist Revolt Is Crushed by Soviet Troops
US Takes No Action to Support the Short-Lived Revolt
Egyptian President Gamal Nasser Nationalizes the Suez Canal
Israel Invades Egypt's Sinai Peninsula
Morocco Becomes an Independent Nation

NATION

Democrats Nominate Stevenson for President, Estes Kefauver for Vice President
"Ike" Eisenhower Defeats Adelai E. Stevenson in a Landslide Election
The National Highway Interstate Project Begins
Congress Approves a Bill to Pay Farmers for Not Planting Crops Under the "Soil Bank" Program
Martin Luther King Organizes a Boycott of Montgomery, Alabama, Public Transportation

LIFESTYLE

The Federal Minimum Hourly Wage Is $1.00
There Are 37 Million TV Sets in America and Movie Goers Are Now Half That of 1946
The GI Bill Ends But 2.2 Million Veterans Have Gone to College (see 1940, 1947, 1990)

SCIENCE AND TECHNOLOGY

IBM Invents a Computer Hard Drive. Size: 2 Refrigerators Output: 5 mb
US Explodes an Airborne Hydrogen Bomb over Bikini Atoll
The Polaris Missile Can Be Launched from Under Water and Carries an Atomic Warhead
An Aeroflot Tupolev-104 Takes off from Moscow. First Scheduled Jet Airliner Flight

BUSINESS AND INDUSTRY

Ampex Corp. Develops a Commercial Video Tape Recorder. Most TV Shows Will Quickly
        Adopt Taping and the "Live" Studio Broadcast Will Become the Exception
Zenith Engineer, Robert Adler, Invents the TV Remote Control

CONSUMER PRODUCTS AND SERVICES

Play Doe for Children Is Introduced
AM Corporation Produces Ramblers under Both the Nash and Hudson Nameplates
R.J. Reynolds Markets *Salem*, a Mentholated Cigarette
Proctor and Gamble Offers *Comet* Cleanser to Compete with *Ajax*
Anheuser-Busch Adds *Busch Bavarian* Beer to Its Traditional Budweiser and Michelob Brands

PRICES

Volkswagon $ 1,280.00

SPORTS

Edson "Pele" do Nascimento (15) Begins His Incredible 18 Year Soccer Career
Yankee's Don Larsen Pitches a Perfect Game Five. The Only One in Wold Series History
Floyd Patterson Takes the Heavyweight Boxing Championship by Beating Archie Moore.

While the World Takes No Action   1956

ARTS AND MEDIA

STAGE
- *Middle of the Night* — Paddy Chayefsky, Gena Rowlands, E.G. Robinson
- *My Fair Lady* — Rex Harrison, Julie Andrews
- *Long Day's Journey Into Night* — Fredric March, Florence Eldridge, Jason Robards Jr.
- *Auntie Mame* — Rosiland Russell

MOVIE
- *Around The World In 80 Days* — David Niven, Shirley MacLaine, Cantiflas
- *Giant* — James Dean, Elizabeth Taylor, Rock Hudson
- *The King And I* — Yul Brynner, Deborah Kerr
- *Lust For Life* — Anthony Quinn, Kirk Douglas
- *Picnic* — William Holden, Kim Novak
- *Written On The Wind* — Dorothy Malone, Rock Hudson
- *Man With The Golden Arm* — Otto Preminger, Frank Sinatra, Eleanor Parker
- *Godzilla - King of the Monsters* — Raymond Burr
- *Forbidden Planet* — Walter Pidgeon, Leslie Nielson, Anne Francis
- *The Ten Commandments* — Charleton Heston, Debra Paget, Anne Baxter, Yvonne De Carlo,

TV
- *The Huntley-Brinkley Report*
- *Requiem for a Heavyweight* — Jack Palance, Keenan Wynn
- *The Millionaire* — Marvin Miller
- *The Nat "King" Cole Show*

BOOK
- *Peyton Place* — Grace Metalious
- *The Last Hurrah* — Edwin O'Conner

MUSIC

Blue Suede Shoes
Love Me Tender
Heartbreak Hotel
Don't Be Cruel
Standing On a Corner
Bells Are Ringing

Memories Are Made of This
Mr. Wonderful
Moonglow
Mack the Knife
I Could Have Danced All Night
On the Street Where You Live

PEOPLE

Elvis Presley Appears on the Ed Sullivan Show. Close-In TV Shots Do Not Show His Gyrating Hips
Pauline "Popo" Friedman (Eppie's twin) Begins the *Dear Abby* Column. (see Ann Landers 1955)
Jerry Falwell Broadcasts the *Old Time Gospel Hour* Television Ministry
Chet Huntley and David Brinkley Now Anchor the NBC Nightly News
Grace Kelly (26) Marries Prince Ranier III of Monaco
Maria Callas Makes Her Debut with the Metropolitan Opera

QUOTES

"You can be sure if it's Westinghouse"
Betty Furness, Westinghouse TV Spokesperson

"See the USA in your Chevrolet."
Dinah Shore, Chevrolet TV Spokesperson

"History is on our side. We will bury you!"
Nikita Khrushchev, Soviet TV Spokesperson

1957 *Black Students Denied Access*

WORLD

The Eisenhower Doctrine Expands US Power to Protect Middle East Nations
US Orders the Sixth Fleet to the Middle East to Counter a Communist Threat to Jordan
Kremlin Shakeups Oust V.M. Molotov, Georgei Malenkov, Lazar Kaganovich & Georgi Zhukov
The US and Canada Create the North American Air Defense Command (NORAD)

NATION

Governor Orval Faubus Uses the National Guard to Stop Nine Black Students from
        Enrolling in Little Rock, AK, Central High School
The President Sends Federal Troops to Little Rock to Avoid Anarchy

ENVIRONMENT, SAFETY AND HEALTH

Soviet Urals Nuclear Waste Explodes, Contaminating 1,000s of Square Miles
Hurricane Audrey Rips Through Louisiana and Texas. Over 500 Killed

LIFESTYLE

97% of US Adults Are Married and Do Things as Couples
In General, Women Stay Home and Have Children
Trying to "Keep Up with the Jones's" Is Pretty Normal
US Factory Workers Average $2.08 per hour or $83 Per Week.
20% of Americans Still Are Considered to Be Below the Poverty Line

SCIENCE AND TECHNOLOGY

The USSR Launches Sputnik 1 on 10/4; The First Earth Orbiting Satellite
Sputnik 2 Carrying Laika, First Dog in Space, Burns Up in the Atmosphere
The US Tests an Intercontinental Ballistic Missile (ICBM)
Gordon Gould Develops an Idea for the Laser. (See 1986)
Interferon, a Protein That Interferes with Viral Reproduction, Is Discovered
Major John Glenn Jets Across US from Long Beach to Brooklyn in Record 3 hrs. 23 min.
US Conducts Initial Underground Nuclear Tests in the Nevada Desert
The First Heart Pacemaker Is Employed
Spandex Is Invented and Is Available for Clothing Use
The Mackinac Straits Bridge in Michigan Is the World's Longest Suspension Bridge

CONSUMER PRODUCTS AND SERVICES

Ford Introduces Its Much Publicized Edsel Automobile
American Motors Corporation Makes Rambler a New and Separate Nameplate
Dr. Suess Books Make a Major Impact on Children's Literature
Toyota Introduces the "Toyopet" Automobile in the US. 280 Are Sold in the First Year
Wham-O Corp. Markets the Hula Hoop and Pluto Platters (later called Frisbees)
Fast Food Burger King Offers a New Sandwich Called the "Whopper."
Pink Plastic Flamingos Begin to Roost in Front Yards
Stereophonic Music Equipment Is Marketed in Large Walnut and Oak Cabinets
The "Sack" Dress Is Introduced. Most Women Hate It. Men Do Too!

PRICES

Chicken	$ .47 per pound
Milk	.23 per quart

Federal Troops Clear a Path 1957

SPORTS

Althea Gibson Is the First Black Woman Tennis Player to Win at Wimbledon
The Giants Leave the Polo Grounds for San Francisco at Season's End
The Brooklyn Dodgers Play Their Last Game at Ebbets Field Before Moving to Los Angeles
Middleweight Champ Sugar Ray Robinson (36) Has Won and Lost His Title Several Times

ARTS AND MEDIA

STAGE

West Side Story	Leonard Bernstein, Stephen Sondheim
The Music Man	Meredith Wilson, Robert Preston
Look Homeward Angel	Anthony Perkins
Dark at the Top of the Stairs	William Inge, Pat Hingle, Teresa Wright, Eileen Heckert

MOVIE

The Bridge On The River Kwai	David Lean, Alec Guinness , William Holden Jack Hawkins, Sessue Hayakawa
The Three Faces of Eve	Joanne Woodward , David Wayne
Sayonara	Red Buttons, Miyoshi Umeki
An Affair To Remember	Cary Grant, Deborah Kerr, Richard Denning
Jailhouse Rock	Elvis Presley, Dean Jones
And God Created Woman	Roger Vadim, Brigitte Bardot, Curt Jurgens

TV

The Tonight Show	Jack Paar (new host)
Leave It To Beaver	Jerry Mathers, Tony Dow, Barbara Billingsley, H. Beaumont
American Bandstand	Dick Clark
Maverick	James Garner, Jack Kelley, Roger Moore
Have Gun Will Travel	Richard Boone
Perry Mason	Raymond Burr, Barbara Hale, William Talman
Wagon Train	Ward Bond, Robert Horton, Frank McGrath

BOOK

The Cat in the Hat	Theodor Geisel (Dr. Suess)
Atlas Shrugged	Ayn Rand
Profiles in Courage	John F. Kennedy (wins Pulitzer Prize)

MUSIC

April Love	*Jailhouse Rock*
Love Letters In the Sand	*Tammy*
Seventy Six Trombones	*Maria*
Old Cape Cod	*Tonight*
It's Not For Me to Say	*Somewhere*
Chances Are	*Wake Up Little Susie*
Jingle-Bell Rock	

PEOPLE

Elvis Presley Takes a Military Physical and Is Drafted
James R. Hoffa Is Under Criminal Indictment. His Teamster's Union Is Expelled by the AFL-CIO

QUOTES

"California is a fine place to live—if you happen to be an orange."
Fred Allen (1894-1957)

"Does she or doesn't she?"

Clairol Hair Coloring Advertisement

1958 Explorer 1 Puts the US in Space

WORLD

Nikita Khrushchev Becomes Premier of the USSR, Ousting Nickolai Bulganin
Charles De Gaulle Is Named Premier of France After an Algerian Crisis
Mainland China Shells the Nationalist Islands of Quemoy and Matsu
The United Arab Republic Is Formed by the Union of Egypt, Sudan and Syria
VP Nixon Is Attacked by Anti-American Protestors on Trip to Venezuela and Peru

NATION

The Alaska Statehood Bill Becomes Law
The Hawaii Statehood Bill Becomes Law
Robert Welch Jr. and 11 Others Form the John Birch Society
First Class Postage Goes from Three Cents to Four Cents

ENVIRONMENT, SAFETY AND HEALTH

Whalers Kill 6,908 Blue Whales and Will Soon Decimate the Species

LIFESTYLE

Beehive Hairdos Become Very Popular, Due Largely to Better Hairsprays
Americans Love Drive In Theaters. There Are Now over 4,000 in the US (see 1942)
The Average Annual Income for Physicians Is $16,000
The US Median Family Income Is $5,020

SCIENCE AND TECHNOLOGY

US Launches Explorer 1; First US Satellite to Orbit the Earth
The National Aeronautics and Space Administration (NASA) Is Born
James Van Allen Discovers Radiation Belts in Space Surrounding Earth
The First Integrated Circuits Are Developed by Intel Corp. & Texas Instruments
The Implantable Artificial Pacemaker Is Developed
Nuclear Submarine, USS Nautilus, Crosses the North Pole, Underwater
Nuclear Submarine, USS Seawolf Sets a 60-Day Underwater Endurance Record

BUSINESS AND INDUSTRY

National Airlines Begins Jet Airliner Passenger Service Between New York and Miami

CONSUMER PRODUCTS AND SERVICES

Chevrolet Offers the Upscale Impala Model with Dual Headlights and Triple Taillights
Ford's Recently Introduced Edsel Meets Low Public Acceptance
The AM Rambler Ambassador Replaces the Full Size Hudson and Nash Brands
Sweet and Low Artificial (saccharin) Sweetener Is Marketed
Pizza Hut Restaurants Are Launched in Kansas
American Express Cards Appear
Stereo Records and Players Are Introduced
Procter & Gamble Markets Mr. Clean Detergent

PRICES

Gasoline	$.33 per gallon
Average New Car	$3,275

Hula Hoops Have US "Spaced" 1958

SPORTS

Arnold Palmer (28) Wins Golf's Masters Tournament and a Hefty $42,000 Prize
New York Giants (NL) Relocate the Team to San Francisco
Brooklyn Dodgers (NL) Relocate the Team to Los Angeles
Intercollegiate Football Inaugurates a Two Point Alternate Conversion Rule

ARTS AND MEDIA

STAGE

Suddenly Last Summer	Tennessee Williams
Sunrise at Campobello	Ralph Bellamy
Two for the Seesaw	Henry Fonda, Anne Bancroft
Vanessa (opera)	Samuel Barber

MOVIE

Gigi	Vicente Minelli, Leslie Caron, Maurice Chevalier
Separate Tables	David Niven, Wendy Hiller, Deborah Kerr
I Want To Live	Susan Hayward, Theodore Bikel
The Big Country	Burl Ives, Gregory Peck, Jean Simmons
The Old Man And The Sea	Spencer Tracy, Harry Bellaver
The Long Hot Summer	Joanne Woodward, Paul Newman
Auntie Mame	Rosalind Russell, Forest Tucker
Cat on a Hot Tin Roof	Elizabeth Taylor, Paul Newman
South Pacific	Mitzi Gaynor, Rossano Brazzi

TV

Peter Gunn	Craig Stevens, Lola Albright, Herschel Bernardi
The Donna Reed Show	Donna Reed, Carl Betz, Shelly Fabares
77 Sunset Strip	Efram Zimbalist, Jr., Roger Smith, Edd Byrne
Sea Hunt	Lloyd Bridges

BOOK

The Affluent Society	John Kenneth Galbraith
Lolita	Vladimir Nabokov

MUSIC

Volare
The Chipmunk Song
I Remember It Well
Thank Heaven For Little Girls
The Purple People Eater
Gigi

Periwinkle Blue
The Ways of a Woman in Love
Send Me the Pillow You Dream On
Jingle Bell Rock

PEOPLE

Cardinal Roncalli (John XXIII) Becomes Pope After Pope Pius XII Dies (Pontiff for 19 Years)
Van Cliburn (23) Wins the Tchaikovsky International Piano Festival
Bertrand Russell (86) Leads a Nuclear Disarmament Rally in England

QUOTES

"Work expands so as to fill the time available for its completion."
Parkinson's Law (Cyril Northcote Parkinson)

INCIDENTALS AND TRIVIA

Americans Buy Over a Million Hula Hoops (Wham-O) But the Fad Soon Dies

1959 Alaska and Hawaii Become States

WORLD

Fidel Castro Leads Cuban Revolutionaries to Victory Over Fulgencio Bautista
In Moscow, Vice President Nixon and Premier Khruschev Hold Their "Kitchen Debate"
The UN General Assembly Votes to Condemn Racial Discrimination Anywhere in the World

NATION

Alaska Is Admitted to the Union as the 49th State
Hawaii Is Admitted to the Union as the 50th State
The St. Lawrence Seaway Opens the Great Lakes to World Shipping
The House Oversight Committee Holds Hearings on Rigged TV Quiz Shows
The FTC and FCC Go After Record Companies for Bribing Disk Jockeys
Congress Authorizes Food Stamps to Distribute Surplus Food to Impoverished Americans
High Schools Reopen in Little Rock, AK, with Limited and Tense Integration

ENVIRONMENT

The Cranberry Cancer Scare Ruins Many Washington and Oregon Growers

LIFESTYLE

Bomb Shelters Are Now Being Dug in Many American Back Yards
Columnist Herb Caen Suggests the Term "Beatnik" for Non-Conforming Rebels of All Types
There Are 32 TV Western Series on the Three National Television Networks
Americans Now Love Little Foreign Cars: US Volkswagen Sales Top 200,000. Other Imports
        Such as British Ford, G.M. Opel, Renault Dauphine and Chrysler's Simca Sell Very Well
10% of Americans Live on the "Poverty Line" and 20% Live Below It
College Men Compete in a New, Creative Activity, Called Phone Booth Stuffing

SCIENCE AND TECHNOLOGY

Soviet Lunik III Photographs the Dark Side of the Moon
Air Force Conducts Weightlessness Experiments Thru Dive and Climb
The Integrated Electronic Circuit Is Born
NASA Announces the Selection of the First Seven Astronauts
Louis Leakey Discovers a Man-Ape Skull and Tools in Tanganyika That Are 1.8 Million Years Old

BUSINESS AND INDUSTRY

New York's 40 Story Bronze-Clad Seagram Building, Is Completed by Architects
        Mies van de Rohe and Phillip Johnson
The RCA 501 Is the World's First Fully Transistorized Computer
Supermarkets Now Account for 70% of Sales Even Though They Are Only 11% of Food Stores
Japanese Automakers Produce a Total of 79,000 Cars up from Less Than 200 in 1947

CONSUMER PRODUCTS AND SERVICES

Mattel Corporation Begins Marketing the Barbie Doll
Ford Introduces the Compact Falcon Model to Combat Growing Import Sales
Chevrolet Offers Its Compact Rear Engine Corvair Automobile
General Foods Offers a Powdered Breakfast Beverage Called Tang
Panti-Legs, the First Panty Hose Are Marketed
General Mills Advertises Frost-O's Sugared Breakfast Cereal
Sony Corporation Introduces a Fully Transistorized Television Set

America Meets the Astronauts 1959

ARTS AND MEDIA

STAGE

Raisin in the Sun	Lorraine Hansberry, Sidney Poitier, Ruby Dee
The Miracle Worker	Anne Bancroft, Patty Duke
The Sound of Music	Mary Martin
Once Upon a Mattress	Carol Burnett

MOVIE

Ben Hur	William Wyler, Charlton Heston, Hugh Griffith
Room At The Top	Simone Signoret, Laurence Harvey
Anatomy of a Murder	James Stewart, Lee Remick, Ben Gazzara
Some Like It Hot	Billy Wilder, Tony Curtis, Jack Lemmon, Marilyn Monroe
North By Northwest	Cary Grant, Eva Marie Saint, James Mason
The Diary of Ann Frank	Shelly Winters, Lou Jacobi, Diane Baker
Porgy and Bess	Dorothy Dandridge, Sidney Poitier, Pearl Bailey, Sammy Davis Jr.

TV

Bonanza	Lorne Greene, Pernell Roberts, Michael Landon, Dan Blocker (First Series Broadcast in Color)
The Twilight Zone	Rod Serling
The Untouchables	Robert Stack, Narrated by Walter Winchell

BOOK

Advise and Consent	Alan Drury
Columbus	Phillip Roth
Breakfast at Tiffanys	Truman Capote

MUSIC

Everything's Coming Up Roses
A Teenager In Love
High Hopes
He's Got the Whole World In His Hands
Personality

Put Your Head On My Shoulder
Climb Ev'ry Mountain
My Favorite Things
Do-Re-Mi
Dream Lover

PEOPLE

Daniel K. Inouye of Hawaii Becomes the First Japanese-American US Representative
Benjamin O. Davis USAF, Becomes the First Black to Achieve the Rank of Major General
US Security Prohibits Nikita Khruschev from Visiting Disneyland While in Los Angeles
Gus Hall Is Named General Secretary of the Now Dwindling American Communist Party
Walter Williams, the Last Surviving Civil War Veteran Dies at 117
John Foster Dulles Resigns as Secretary of State Due to Illness
Charles van Doren Admits He Was Coached in Quiz Show Scandal.
Hiram A. Fong of Hawaii Is the First Chinese-American Senator

COMMENTARY

"Miss Picky"
Irene English

"We see them on TV in uniform and in their civilian best. They are clean cut, articulate American sons who will undergo the brutal training necessary to fly into space in the planned Mercury Program. So far we have only been able to orbit small satellites but Scott Carpenter, Gordon "Gordo" Cooper, John Glenn, Virgil "Gus" Grissom, Wally Shirra, Alan Shepard and Donald "Deke" Slayton look like they have the right stuff to make it happen."

1960 *US Spy Plane Shot Down*

WORLD

US U-2 Spy Plane Shot Down Over Russia. Pilot Gary Powers Is Captured, Tried and Convicted, and Sentenced to Ten Years in Soviet Prison
US Cancels All Similar Soviet Overflights as the USSR Demands an Apology
Cuba Takes an Anti-American Posture through Propaganda and Property Seizure
US Declares an Embargo on All Exports to Cuba

NATION

Public Has Concerns About US Prestige in the World Due to Problems in Laos, Congo and Cuba
Democrats Pick John F. Kennedy on the First Ballot. Lyndon Johnson Agrees to Second Place
Republicans Nominate Richard Nixon by Acclamation. Henry Cabot Lodge Is His Running Mate
John F. Kennedy Narrowly Defeats Richard M. Nixon for President. Popular Vote Almost Even
Congress Investigates Payola in the Music Industry
Integration of Southern Schools Remains Slow Despite Federal Efforts
Blacks Begin "Sit In" Demonstrations at Greensboro, NC, Lunch Counters

ENVIRONMENT, SAFETY AND HEALTH

Massive Hurricane Donna Rips the East Coast
American Heart Association Says Men Who Are Heavy Smokers Have a 50%-150% Higher Chance of Heart Attack
Fish in the Mississippi River Die by the Millions as Pollution Reduces Water Oxygen Levels
Coal Still Supplies 45% of US Energy Requirements
Aluminum Cans Are Introduced for Food and Beverage Use. They are Non-Biodegradable

LIFESTYLE

25% Now Live in the Suburbs and Have Activities Centered Around the Home
Jet Travel Is Chic. The Term "Jet Setters" Appears
A Dance Called the Twist is Popular
US Annual Beef Consumption Reaches a Record 99 Pounds Per Person

SCIENCE AND TECHNOLOGY

Sputnik 5 Carries Dogs Belka and Streika for 18 Orbits and Safely Returns Them to Earth
Heart Pacemakers for Humans Come into Use
Discoverer 13 Capsule Becomes the First Vehicle Recovered from Space
The USS Enterprise, the First Nuclear Aircraft Carrier, Is Launched
The FDA Refuses to Approve the Experimental Tranquilizer, Thalidomide, for US Use

BUSINESS AND INDUSTRY

Election Night TV Coverage Reaches 92% of Homes.
A Digital Equipment Company (DEC) Computer Uses a Keyboard and Monitor Instead of Punched Cards

CONSUMER PRODUCTS AND SERVICES

Nissan Corporation Introduces the Datsun Automobile into the US Market
Domino's Pizza Opens in Detroit
A Playboy Club Opens In Chicago. It Is Considered Very Risqué (see 1972, 1988)
Just Introduced, the Xerox 914 Copier, Will Revolutionize the World of Business
Enovid 10, the First Commercially Available Oral Contraceptive. "The Pill" Sells for $.55 Each
Bulova Offers the Accutron Watch with a Vibrating Fork Mechanism

J.F.K. Wins a Narrow Election 1960

SPORTS

Boxing Is Under Fire for Concerns About the Extent of Underworld Influence in the Sport
Dolph Schayes of Syracuse Is the First NBA Player to Reach the 15,000 Point Scoring Level

ARTS AND MEDIA

STAGE
Camelot	Richard Burton, Julie Andrews, Robert Goulet
Unsinkable Molly Brown	Tammy Grimes
Bye Bye Birdie	Dick Van Dyke, Kay Medford, Chita Rivera
All the Way Home	Arthur Hill
Toys in the Attic	Maureen Stapleton, Ann Revere, Jason Robards Jr.
A Taste of Honey	Angela Lansbury, Joan Plowright
An Evening with...	Mike Nichols and Elaine May

MOVIE
The Apartment	Fred MacMurray, Jack Lemmon, Shirley MacLaine, Ray Walston
Elmer Gantry	Burt Lancaster, Shirley Jones
Butterfield 8	Elizabeth Taylor, Eddie Fisher
Spartacus	Peter Ustinov, Kirk Douglas, Jean Simmons
Exodus	Paul Newman, Eva Marie Saint, Lee J. Cobb
Never On Sunday	Melina Mercouri, Jules Dassin
Song Without End	Dirk Bogarde, Capucine,
Psycho	Alfred Hitchcock, Anthony Perkins, Janet Leigh, Vera Miles
Bells Are Ringing	Judy Holliday, Dean Martin
The Time Machine	Rod Taylor, Alan Young, Yvette Mimieux
The Bellboy	Jerry Lewis

TV
Andy Griffith Show	Andy Griffith, Don Knotts, Jim Nabors, Ron Howard
My Three Sons	Fred MacMurray, William Frawley, William Demarest
Route 66	Martin Milner, George Maharis, Glenn Corbett
The Flintstones (animated)	

BOOK
To Kill a Mockingbird	Harper Lee
Green Eggs and Ham	Theodor Geisel (Dr. Suess)

MUSIC

The Manger (oratorio)   Pablo Casals
Camelot   Lollipops and Roses
Hey, Look Me Over   Mr. Lucky
Are You Lonesome Tonight   How to Handle a Woman
                                                            If Ever I Would Leave You

PEOPLE

Dick Clark Features Chubby Checker and the Twist on His American Bandstand
Berry Gordy Starts Motown Records and Creates the "Motown Sound"

QUOTES

"It is an unfortunate fact that we can secure peace only by preparing for war."
John F. Kennedy (1960)

INCIDENTALS AND TRIVIA

John F. Kennedy, at 43, Is the Youngest Elected US President (see 1901)

1961 *The Bay of Pigs Fiasco*

WORLD

Fidel Castro Declares That He Will Lead Cuba to Communism
US Severs Diplomatic Relations with Cuba
The CIA Backed Bay of Pigs Invasion of Cuba by Cuban Rebels Fails
East Germany Erects a Perimeter Wall in Berlin to Stop the Exodus to the West
Chancellor Konrad Adenauer Visits the New President to Discuss West German Issues
The Alliance for Progress Bill Provides Assistance to Latin American Nations
The UN General Assembly Condemns South Africa's Apartheid Policy
Hostilities Continue in the Congo and Elsewhere in Africa
A Second, Severe Year of Crop Shortages Hits China
Zhou En-lai Leaves the Soviet Party Congress, Signaling a Break in Sino-Soviet Relations

NATION

President Kennedy Proposes a Peace Corps
The Twenty Third Amendment Provides Congressional Representation for the District
of Columbia

ENVIRONMENT

Acid Rain Has Been Found to Kill Some Lake Species

LIFESTYLE

The Federal Minimum Hourly Wage Is $1.15

DISASTER

A Fire in the Brentwood-Bel Air District of Los Angeles Destroys 447 Homes

SCIENCE AND TECHNOLOGY

Soviet Cosmonaut Yuri Gagarin in Vostok 1 Spaceship Completes One Earth Orbit and
Becomes the First Man in Space
NASA Sends a Chimpanzee into Sub Orbital Flight as a Prelude to Later Manned Flights
Alan Shepard Jr. (Mercury 3) and Virgil Grissom (Mercury 4) Fly Sub Orbital US Missions
Louis and Mary Leakey Discover *Homo Habilis*, a Human Ancestor
Bell Laboratories Announces Development of the Laser
Dr. Albert B. Sabin Develops a Second Polio Vaccine. It and the Salk Vaccine Virtually
Eradicate the Dreaded Disease

BUSINESS AND INDUSTRY

Chrysler Discontinues Producing the Slow-Selling DeSoto Auto Line (see 1928)

CONSUMER PRODUCTS AND SERVICES

Barbie's Boyfriend, the Ken Doll, Is Created by Mattel Toys
Pampers, Disposable Baby Diapers, Are Introduced
Stereophonic Broadcasting Begins for FM Stations
Squib Promotes the Value of an Electric Toothbrush
Coca Cola Offers *Sprite* to Compete with 7UP
General Mills Advertises the Nutritional Value of *Total,* Their Vitamin Enriched Cereal

East Germany Builds a Wall 1961

SPORTS

NY Yankee Roger Maris Hits a Record 61 Home Runs in a 162 Game Season (see 1927,1998)
The Minnesota Twins and the Los Angeles Angels Play Their First Season

ARTS AND MEDIA

STAGE	The Caretaker	Alan Bates, Robert Shaw, Donald Pleasance
	A Man for All Seasons	Paul Scofield
	Night of the Iguana	Betty Davis, Patrick O'Neal
	How To Succeed in Business...	Robert Morse, Rudy Vallee
MOVIE	West Side Story	George Chakiris, Rita Moreno, Natalie Wood
	Judgement At Nuremberg	Maximilian Schell, Marlene Dietrich, Richard Widmark
	Two Women	Sophia Loren, Raf Vallone
	Breakfast At Tiffany's	Audrey Hepburn, George Peppard
	The Hustler	Paul Newman, Jackie Gleason
TV	Sing Along With Mitch	Mitch Miller
	Hazel	Shirley Booth, Don DeFore, Whitney Blake
	The Defenders	E.G. Marshall, Robert Reed
	Dr. Kildare	Richard Chamberlain, Raymond Massey
	Ben Casey	Vince Edwards, Sam Jaffe, Bettye Ackerman
BOOK	The Agony and the Ecstasy	Irving Stone

MUSIC

Can't Help Falling in Love
Hit the Road Jack
Moon River
I Believe in You

Where the Boys Are
Yellow Bird
I Fall to Pieces
Foolin' Around

PEOPLE

While in Paris, Soviet Ballet Dancer, Rudolph Nureyev Defects to the West
Newton Minow, New FCC Chairman Blasts Television as a "Vast Wasteland."
Speed Reading Expert, Evelyn Wood, Apparently Once Had the President as a Pupil

QUOTES

"My fellow Americans, ask not what your country can do for you—ask what you can do for your country."

John F. Kennedy (Inaugural Address)

"He who hesitates is sometimes saved."

James Thurber (1894-1961)

COMMENTARY

"Americans hated the thought of a Communist regime just 90 miles from Florida. So, when a 1,500 man invasion force of US backed Cuban exiles invaded Bahia de Cochinos on April 17, we thought Castro would be overthrown. Most were killed or captured in what became known as the Bay of Pigs disaster. The new president took full responsibility and the US had yet another black eye."

Hank Hawthorne

1962 *The World Holds Its Breath*

WORLD

Nuclear Test Ban Talks Adjourn. They Are Deadlocked Over How to Monitor
US Resumes Nuclear Testing in the Atmosphere Near Christmas Island
Algeria Gains Independence from 132 Years of French Rule
Jamaica Becomes an Independent Dominion within the British Commonwealth
Trinidad and Tobago Also Gain Independence from Britain
U Thant of Burma Becomes the United Nations Secretary General
Fighting Rages Over Disputed Border Areas of China and India
US Navy Blockades All Shipping to Cuba in Retaliation for Deployment of Soviet Missiles
US Demands Missiles Be Removed as the Specter of Nuclear War Looms
Nikita Khrushchev Dismantles and Removes the Soviet Missile Bases in Cuba

NATION

President Federalizes Mississippi's National Guard; Orders State to Yield
James Meredith Is the First Black to Attend the University of Mississippi
President Bans Housing Discrimination
Dulles International Airport Opens Near Washington, DC

LIFESTYLE

90% of US Homes Now Have at Least One TV Set; 13% Have Two or More

SCIENCE AND TECHNOLOGY

John Glenn (Mercury 6) and Scott Carpenter (Mercury 7), Each Makes Three Earth Orbits
US Ranger IV Space Probe Reaches the Moon
US Space Probe Mariner 2 Reaches the Atmosphere of Venus
Telstar 1, the First Communications Satellite Goes into Orbit
JFK News Conference Is Televised Live to Europe Via Telestar
Secret, High Altitude, F-101 Reconnaissance Jet Provides Detailed Photo Proof of Offensive
      Missile Site Construction in Cuba

BUSINESS AND INDUSTRY

The First K-Mart Opens in Detroit
Sam Walton Opens the First Wal-Mart Store in Arkansas (see 1990)
Glen Bell Opens a Taco Bell Store in Downey, California
H. Ross Perot Founds Electronic Data Systems
William P. Lear Introduces the Lear Jet for Business

CONSUMER PRODUCTS AND SERVICES

Ford's Thunderbird Is Enlarged to Seat Four
8 Track Cassette Players and Tapes
Diet Rite Cola
Soft Contact Lenses
All-Aluminum Cans with Tab Openers for Beer and Soft Drinks (See 1935)

PRICES

Taco Bell Taco	$.19 each
B/W 19 inch TV	139
Chrysler Newport	2,964

And the Soviets Blink First

SPORTS

The New York Mets Are Added to the National League, Managed by Casey Stengel
Jack Nicklaus Wins His First Major Golf Tournament
Wilt Chamberlain Scores 100 Points in a Basketball Game
New, Springy Fiberglass Pole Results in the First Vaults Over 16 Feet

ARTS AND MEDIA

STAGE	*I Can Get It for You Wholesale*	Elliot Gould, Barbra Streisand
	Stop the World, I Want To Get Off	Anthony Newley
MOVIE	*Lawrence Of Arabia*	David Lean, Peter O'Toole, Omar Sharif
	To Kill A Mockingbird	Gregory Peck, Mary Badham
	The Miracle Worker	Anne Bancroft, Patty Duke
	The Longest Day	John Wayne, Rod Steiger, Robert Ryan
	Days Of Wine And Roses	Jack Lemmon, Lee Remick
	Lolita	James Mason, Sue Lyons
	How the West Was Won	Debbie Reynolds, All-Star Cast
	Music Man	Robert Preston, Shirley Jones
TV	*Tour of the White House*	Jacqueline Kennedy, Charles Collingwood
	The Tonight Show	Johnnie Carson (new host)
	CBS Evening News	Walter Chronkite (new anchor)
BOOK	*Silent Spring*	Rachel Carson
	Calories Don't Count	Herman Taller
	Making of a President	Theodore H. White

MUSIC

Days of Wine and Roses
I Can't Stop Loving You
The Girl from Ipanema
Ramblin' Rose

Blowin' In the Wind
Breaking Up Is Hard to Do
What Kind of Fool Am I?

PEOPLE

Walter Cronkite Succeeds Douglas Edwards as *CBS Evening News* Anchor
Marilyn Monroe Found Dead in Her Hollywood Apartment
Captured U2 Pilot Gary Powers Is Exchanged for Soviet Spy, Rudolph Abel

QUOTES

"I am prepared to wait until Hell freezes over." (for a Soviet missile explanation)
Adelai Stevenson (US Ambassador to the UN)

"A man would prefer to come home to an unmade bed and a happy woman than to a neatly made bed and an angry woman."
Marlene Dietrich, *Unmade Bed* (1962)

"You won't have Nixon to kick around anymore."
Richard Nixon after His Loss to Gov. Pat Brown

1963 *John Kennedy is Assassinated*

WORLD

US and Soviet Union Set up a Hot Line Link to Reduce the Possibility of Accidental Nuclear War
US, Soviet Union and Britain Agree to Prohibit Testing Nuclear Weapons in the Atmosphere,
in Space, or Underwater

NATION

200,000 Civil Rights Marchers Led by Dr. Martin Luther King, Converge on Washington D.C.
The University of Alabama Is Integrated as Gov. George Wallace Is Forced to Step Aside
Required Reading of the Bible in School Is Declared Unconstitutional
The US Post Office Inaugurates Its Five-Digit Zip Code Program with the Mr. Zip Character
Alcatraz Federal Penitentiary Closes (see 1934)
Medicare, a Medical-Hospital Finance Plan Is Submitted to Congress
President Signs a Bill for Equal Pay for Equal Work, Regardless of Sex
The President Asks Congress for a Far-Reaching Civil Rights Bill
John F. Kennedy Is Assassinated in Dallas on November 22; Gov. John Connally Wounded
Lyndon B. Johnson Is Sworn in as the 36th US President Aboard Air Force 1, Carrying
Kennedy's Body Back to Washington
Shooting Suspect, Lee Harvey Oswald Is Arrested, Then Shot and Killed by Jack Ruby while
Being Transported by the Dallas Police

ENVIRONMENT

Congress Passes the First Clean Air Act
Sensing Interest in the Environment, CBS Offers, *The Silent Spring of Rachel Carson*
Only 417 Breeding Pairs of American Bald Eagles Remain in the Lower 48 States Due to
Hunting, Lack of Prey and Use of Pesticides Such as DDT (see 1999)

LIFESTYLE

The Federal Minimum Hourly Wage Is $1.25
Jean Nidetch Founds Weight Watchers in New York
US Factory Workers Average Just Over $100 a Week for the First Time in History
Two Thirds of All Autos in the World Are in the US, Which Has 6% of the World's Population

SCIENCE AND TECHNOLOGY

Russian Valentina Tereskova Becomes the First Woman in Space
Dr. Thomas Starzl Performs a Human Liver Transplant Operation
Gordon Cooper Completes the Last Mercury Mission; Sends First Pictures Back from Space

CONSUMER PRODUCTS AND SERVICES

General Motors Introduces the Small, Rear Engine CORVAIR
Vallium Becomes Available for Use as a Tranquilizer
Push Button Telephones Replace Dials.   236-1313 Replaces CEntral 1313
Audio Cassette Recorder/Players are Marketed
The Ronald McDonald Clown Character Is Born

SPORTS

Stan "The Man" Musial Retires After 22 Years with the St. Louis Cardinals

Suspect Oswald is Also Killed   1963

ARTS AND MEDIA

STAGE		
	Oliver!	Clive Revill
	Strange Interlude	Geraldine Page
	Luther	Albert Finney

MOVIE		
	Tom Jones	Tony Richardson, Albert Finney, Susannah York
	Lilies of the Field	Sidney Poitier, Lilia Scala, Lisa Mann
	Hud	Patricia Neal, Melvyn Douglas, Paul Newman
	Cleopatra	Elizabeth Taylor, Richard Burton (All Star Cast)
	The Ugly American	Marlon Brando, Pat Hingle, Arthur Hill
	Dr. NO	Sean Connery, Ursula Andress

TV		
	McHale's Navy	Ernest Borgnine, Tim Conway
	Beverly Hillbillies	Buddy Ebsen, Max Baer Jr., Irene Ryan, Donna Douglas
	The Fugitive	David Janssen, Barry Morse
	East Side, West Side	George C. Scott, Cicily Tyson
	General Hospital (soap)	Tony Geary, Genie Francis

BOOK		
	The Feminine Mystique	Betty Friedan

MUSIC

Call Me Irresponsible
Charade
Puff the Magic Dragon
Hello Muddah Hello Faddah
Blue Velvet

Go Away Little Girl
Dominique
Our Day Will Come
As Long As He Needs Me
Ring of Fire

PEOPLE

Bob Dylan Releases His Second Album, *Freewheelin',* Solidifying His Protest Position
Harvard Professor, Timothy Leary, Extols the Virtues of LSD
A Young Vocal Group Called *The Beatles* Are a Smash in London
Stevie Wonder (12) Records, *I Call It Pretty Music*

QUOTES

"All free men, wherever they may live, are citizens of Berlin and therefore, as a free man, I take pride in the words, *Ich bin ein Berliner.*"
John F. Kennedy (Berlin Visit in June)

"I have a dream that my four little children will one day live in a nation where they will not be judged by the color of their skin but by the content of their character."
Dr. Martin Luther King

"Segregation today, segregation tomorrow and segregation forever!"
George Wallace

COMMENTARY

"If you were 10 or older on November 22, 1963, you can remember exactly who you were with, what you were doing, and the massive grief you felt. Handsome, charismatic, visionary, Jack Kennedy was the youngest elected president, the first Catholic president and the first president born in the 20th Century. Good-bye, Mr. President. Good-bye Camelot."

Kate Hawthorne

1964 Sweeping Civil Rights Bill Passes

WORLD

Khrushchev Is Removed from Office and Succeeded by Alexi Kosygin and Leonid Brezhnev
China Explodes an Atomic Bomb
Japanese Students Demonstrate Against Planned Visits by US Nuclear Submarines
Three Vietnamese PT Boats Attack the USS Destroyer Maddux. Called *the Gulf of Tonkin Incident;* the Event Starts a Major US Escalation of Military Effort in the Area

NATION

The Twenty-Fourth Amendment Makes Poll Taxes Unconstitutional
Lyndon B. Johnson Handily Defeats Barry M. Goldwater for President
Washington D.C. Residents Cast First Votes in a Presidential Election
Civil Rights Act Is Finally Approved After 83 Day Senate Filibuster
President Johnson Signs a Billion Dollar Anti-Poverty Measure
Actor George Murphy Beats Pierre Salinger for the US Senate from California
Robert Kennedy Wins Senate Seat in His "New" Home State, New York
Edward Kennedy Takes a Senate Seat from Massachusetts
The Free Speech Protest Movement Is Born at the University of California, Berkeley

ENVIRONMENT, SAFETY AND HEALTH

Congress Establishes the National Wilderness Preservation System
Major Earthquake Centered in Anchorage, Alaska, Kills 117 and Causes Enormous Damage

LIFESTYLE

US Surgeon General Concludes That Smoking Causes Lung Cancer. Warnings Will Go on Packs
Beatlemania Has Taken Hold in the US. Beatles Merchandise Sales Here Tops 50 Million Dollars
Popular Rock and Roll Dances Are the **Dog**, the **Monkey**, the **Chicken**, the **Watusi** and the **Frug**
Aqua Color Keyed Kitchen Appliances Are in Demand as White Is Passe. (see 1972, 1978)

SCIENCE AND TECHNOLOGY

Surgeon, James Hardy, Performs a Human Lung Transplant
Ranger VII Spacecraft Returns Detailed Moon Surface Photographs
The B-70 Bomber Is Rolled Out
AT&T Displays a Prototype Videophone at the New York World's Fair

CONSUMER PRODUCTS AND SERVICES

Ford Introduces the Soon-To-Be-Classic Mustang Coupe
GI Joe Toy Action Figures are Marketed
Children Love the New Toaster Treat, Kellogg's *Pop Tarts*
General Mills Gives Us *Lucky Charms*
American Tobacco Introduces *Carlton*, a Filtered Cigarette. "Filters" Not Very Popular
Kaiser Jeep Corporation Offers the Wagoneer
Studebaker-Packard Offers Seat Belts as Standard Equipment, But Closes Shop by Yearend
Audio Tape Cassette Players
Pillsbury Introduces Ready-To-Spread Frosting

PRICES

A "Base" Mustang $2,368.00
Gasoline $.30 per gallon

A Landslide Victory for LBJ   1964

SPORTS

Cassius Clay Defeats Sonny Liston for the Heavyweight Boxing Title and Changes His Name
   to Muhammad Ali
Jim Bunning of the Phillies Pitches the First "Perfect" Game Since 1922

ARTS AND MEDIA

STAGE	*Funny Girl*	Barbra Streisand
	Fiddler on the Roof	Zero Mostel
	Hello Dolly	Carol Channing
	The Subject Was Roses	Jack Albertson, Martin Sheen, Irene Dailey
MOVIE	*My Fair Lady*	Rex Harrison, Audrey Hepburn, Stanley Holloway
	Mary Poppins	Julie Andrews, Dick Van Dyke
	Zorba the Greek	Anthony Quinn, Lila Kedrova
	Topkapi	Peter Ustinov, Melina Mercouri
	A Hard Day's Night	John Lennon, Ringo Starr, Paul McCartney, George Harrison
TV	*Man From U.N.C.L.E.*	Robert Vaughn, David McCallum
	Bewitched	Elizabeth Montgomery, Agnes Moorehead, Dick York
	Peyton Place (soap)	Ryan O'Neal, Mia Farrow, Lee Grant
	Gilligan's Island	Bob Denver, Alan Hale Jr., Jim Backus, Tina Louise
	The Munsters	Fred Gwynne, Yvonne DeCarlo, Al Lewis
BOOK	*Herzog*	Saul Bellow
	Little Big Man	Thomas Berger
	The Spy Who Came in From the Cold	John le Carre

MUSIC

People	*Matchmaker, Matchmaker*
A Spoonful of Sugar	*Everybody Loves Somebody*
And I Love Her	*Don't Rain on My Parade*
A Hard Day's Night	*Pink Panther Theme*
Downtown	*I Want To Hold Your Hand*
If I Were a Rich Man	*Times They Are A-Changin'*
Sunrise, Sunset	*I Don't Love You Anymore*
King of the Road	*Understand Your Man*

PEOPLE

The Beatles Come to America and Appear on the Ed Sullivan Show
Rudy Genreich Designs a Topless Bathing Suit
Civil Rights Leader Martin Luther King Jr. Wins the Nobel Peace Prize

CRIME AND PUNISHMENT

James Hoffa, Teamsters Union Head Is Found Guilty of Jury Tampering; Sentenced to 8 Years
Jack Ruby Is Convicted and Sentenced to Death for the Killing of Lee Harvey Oswald

INCIDENTALS AND TRIVIA

Biggest TV Laugh Ever: Thrown Tomahawk into a Target "Crotch" on *The Tonight Show*
Refrigerator Magnets Begin to Multiply

1965 *The "Great Society" Begins*

WORLD

US Increases Troops in Vietnam to 75,000 and the Number Is Expected to Climb
Rhodesia Proclaims Its Independence from Britain

NATION

President Outlines Programs for a "Great Society" in His Inaugural Speech
The Federal Voting Rights Act Becomes Law
Medicare and Medicaid Guarantee Medical Insurance Coverage for the Aged and the Poor
The Job Corps Program Is Implemented
The Department of Housing and Urban Development (HUD) Is Created
The National Endowment for the Arts and Humanities Is Approved
Anti-War Protests Are Becoming Common

ENVIRONMENT, SAFETY AND HEALTH

Abandoned Ellis Island Is Declared Part of the Statue of Liberty Monument
The Highway Beautification Act Bans Many Highway Billboards
Water Quality Act and Solid Waste Disposal Act Become Law
Massive Power Failure Blacks Out New York City for 13 Hours

DISASTER

A Series of Tornadoes Sweep through the Midwest Killing 271. Worst in 40 Years
Several Days of Rioting and Looting Occurs in Los Angeles' Watts Area

LIFESTYLE

Average Hourly Production Wage Is $3.15 (see 1975)
Federal Law Requires Surgeon General's Warning on Cigarette Packs
Mini-Skirts, Two Inches Above the Knee Are Common, But Four Inches Is Modeled in Paris.
Young Men Grow Shoulder-Length Hair; Women Love Vidal Sassoon Inspired Bangs and Shingles
Hippies, Are Colorful, Happy, Holy, Dancing Idealists, Believing in World Peace and Free Love

SCIENCE AND TECHNOLOGY

Cosmonaut Alexander Leanov Becomes First Human to Walk in Space
Astronaut Ed White Is the First American To Walk in Space
Mariner IV Probe Finds No Life on Mars
F-111 Aircraft Can Attain Speeds of Three Times That of Sound
A Kidney Dialysis Machine Is Tested
The Gateway Arch in St. Louis, Designed by Eero Saarinen, Is Completed

CONSUMER PRODUCTS AND SERVICES

Bank of America Offers BankAmericard (will later become VISA)
Digital Equipment Corporation Markets a "Mini" Computer
Telephone Answering Machines Become Available
Sony Corporation Sells the Betamax, a Home Video Recording Machine
Eight-Track Cartridge Player for Cars (Invented by William Lear)

PRICES

Ford Galaxie 500 Hardtop Coupe $3,321

War Protests Become Commonplace 1965

SPORTS

University of Alabama Quarterback, Joe Namath, Signs with the New York Jets for $400,000
Peggy Fleming Wins the US Figure Skating Championship
Gary Player Wins the US Open Golf Championship
The Massive Astrodome, an Enclosed Stadium, Opens in Houston

ARTS AND MEDIA

STAGE	*The Odd Couple*	Neil Simon, Art Carney, Walter Matthau
	Cactus Flower	Lauren Bacall
	Generation	Henry Fonda
	Flora, The Red Menace	Liza Minelli
	Man of La Mancha	Richard Kiley

MOVIE	*Sound of Music*	Robert Wise, Julie Andrews, Christopher Plummer, Peggy Wood, Eleanor Parker
	Cat Ballou	Lee Marvin, Jane Fonda
	A Thousand Clowns	Martin Balsam, Jason Robards Jr
	Doctor Zhivago	Omar Sharif, Julie Christie
	Ship of Fools	Vivien Leigh, George Segal, Simone Signoret
	The Pawnbroker	Rod Steiger, Geraldine Fitzgerald

TV	*I Spy*	Bill Cosby, Robert Culp
	Get Smart	Don Adams, Barbara Felden
	The Big Valley	Barbara Stanwyck, Richard Long, Lee Majors, Linda Evans
	Green Acres	Eddie Albert, Eva Gabor
	Run for Your Life	Ben Gazzara
	Hogan's Heroes	Bob Crane, Werner Klemperer, John Banner
	Lost In Space	Guy Williams, June Lockhart, Billy Mumy,

| BOOK | *Unsafe At Any Speed* | Ralph Nader |
| | *The Source* | James A. Michener |

MUSIC

The Shadow of Your Smile
What the World Needs Now Is Love
Yesterday
Like a Rolling Stone
It's Not Unusual
I've Got You Babe

Dulcinea
I Hear a Symphony
Satisfaction
The Impossible Dream
King of the Road

PEOPLE

Pope Paul VI (Giovanni Montini), Addresses the UN General Assembly
M.L. King Jr. Leads 25,000 on a March for Civil Rights from Selma to Montgomery
Black Activist Malcolm X (Malcolm Little) Is Assassinated in Harlem

INCIDENTALS AND TRIVIA

Painter, Andy Warhol, Gives Us *Campbell's Tomato Soup Can*
The Hippie Subculture Introduces New Meanings to **Bag, Blow Your Mind, Freak, Out of Sight, Scene** and **Thing**
US Convertible Automobile Sales Peak at 507,000 (see 1974)
Amos 'n Andy Is Withdrawn From Syndication Because of Protests Over Its Black Stereotypes

1966 *The Vietnam Buildup Continues*

WORLD

Harvests Are Up in the USSR but India Suffers Severe Famine
US Troop Strength in Vietnam Is Now Well above 200,000 and Increasing
Protests in Major Cities Around the World Criticize US Policy in Vietnam
Indira Ghandi Is Elected Prime Minister in India

NATION

Supreme Court Rules That Police Must Read the "Miranda" Rights to Suspects in Custody
President Johnson Signs the Freedom of Information Act
The Department of Transportation (DOT) Is Created
Congress Passes the Fair Packaging and Labeling Act
The National Organization for Women (NOW) Is Founded by Betty Friedan

ENVIRONMENT, SAFETY AND HEALTH

The First Rare and Endangered Species List Contains 78 Species

LIFESTYLE

The Vatican Now Allows US Catholics to Eat Meat on Fridays Except for Lent
US Adults Consume an Average of 210 Packs of Cigarettes a Year

SCIENCE AND TECHNOLOGY

Fiber Optics Are Demonstrated as a Way of Transmitting Data
A Vaccine Now Exists for Rubella (German Measles)
Insulin Is Synthesized
US Surveyor I Lands on the Moon to Take Surface Photographs
Gemini 10 and 11 Flights Demonstrate Successful Space Dockings with a Target Vehicle
Gemini 12, with James A. Lovell and Edwin "Buzz" Aldrin Jr. Is the Last Gemini Flight
Surgeon, Michael DeBakey, Uses an Artificial Heart Pump

BUSINESS AND INDUSTRY

Color Television Broadcasting Has Reached 100% During the Prime Time Evening Hours
Freddy Laker Founds Laker Airlines

CONSUMER PRODUCTS AND SERVICES

Ampex and Norelco Introduce Stereo Cassette Decks
The Interbank Card Is Offered to Counter BankAmericard, Becomes Master Charge in 1969
General Motors Debuts Luxury Front Drive Models: Olds Toronado and Cadillac Eldorado
Chevrolet Introduces the Camaro "Pony" Car
Pampers Disposable Diapers Are Marketed. They Will Revolutionize the Diaper Market

PRICES

Average 3 Br. Home	$17,600	6% interest
Average New Car	3,480	
Gasoline	$.33 per gallon	

TV Goes Where No Man Has Ever... 1966

SPORTS

The Milwaukee Braves Move and Become the Atlanta Braves
Giant's Willie Mays Signs a Record Two Year Salary Agreement at $130,000 Per Year
Peggy Fleming Wins the Women's World Figure Skating Championship
Evel Knievel Invents the Sport of Motorcycle Jumping
Nolan Ryan Begins a 27-Year Career in which He Will Strike Out a Record 5,714 Batters
The LA Dodgers Have to Pay Sandy Koufax $130,000, But He Wins 27 Games
Billy Casper Is Golf's Top Money Winner at $122,000

ARTS AND MEDIA

STAGE		
	Cabaret	Lisa Minelli, Joel Gray
	Mame	Angela Lansbury, Beatrice Arthur
	Sweet Charity	Gwen Verdon
	Wait Until Dark	Lee Remick
	Mark Twain Tonight!	Hal Holbrook

MOVIE		
	A Man for All Seasons	Fred Zinnemann, Paul Scofield
	Alphie	Michael Caine, Shelley Winters
	Georgie Girl	James Mason, Lynn Redgrave
	Fantastic Voyage	Raquel Welch, Stephen Boyd
	One Million Years B.C.	Raquel Welch, John Richardson

TV		
	Star Trek	William Shatner, Leonard Nimoy, DeForest Kelley, James Doohan, Nichelle Nichols, Walter Koenig, George Takei
	Mission Impossible	Peter Graves, Barbara Bain, Martin Landau, Greg Morris, Peter Lupus
	That Girl	Marlo Thomas, Ted Bessell
	Batman	Adam West Burt Ward, Neil Hamilton
	Family Affair	Brian Keith, Sebastian Cabot, Johnnie Whittaker

BOOK		
	In Cold Blood	Truman Capote
	Valley of the Dolls	Jacqueline Suzanne

MUSIC

Yellow Submarine
On a Clear Day You Can See Forever
Strangers in the Night
Born Free
Cabaret

Georgie Girl
Feelin' Groovy
Mame
Hey Big Spender
If My Friends Could See Me Now

PEOPLE

Edward Brooke of Massachusetts Is the First Black US Senator
Robert C. Weaver Becomes the First Black Cabinet Member as Secretary of HUD
Jimi Hendrix (23) Shows the Potential of the Electric Guitar
Nightclub Comedian and Cult Hero, Lenny Bruce Dies of a Drug Overdose

QUOTES

"Money is like a sixth sense without which you cannot make complete use of the other five."

W. Somerset Maugham (1874-1966)

WORLD

Israel's Six-Day War with Arab States Results in Land Acquisition in the Sinai Desert
The US, Britain and USSR Ratify a Treaty Banning Nuclear Weapons in Outer Space
US Troop Strength in Vietnam Reaches 475,000

NATION

Thurgood Marshall Becomes the First Black US Supreme Court Justice
The 25th Constitutional Amendment Clarifies Presidential Disability and Succession
The Corporation for Public Broadcasting Is Created to Aid Non-Commercial Television
Demonstrations Continue Nationwide Against the War in Vietnam
College Students Arrested in Anti-War Demonstrations Will Lose Their Draft Deferments

ENVIRONMENT, SAFETY AND HEALTH

Scientists Say Increased Carbon Dioxide in the Atmosphere May Lead to Global Warming
Smoking Withdrawal Clinics Appear as Americans Take Heed of Cigarette Warnings

DISASTER

Flash Fire in Experimental Apollo Capsule Test Kills Gus Grissom, Ed White and Ed Chaffee
Race Riots in Newark and Detroit Leave 70 Dead. Riots Occur in Scores of Other Cities

LIFESTYLE

The US Population Passes 200 Million
The Federal Minimum Hourly Wage Is $1.40
Pantyhose Sales Soar as Women Adopt the Miniskirt

SCIENCE AND TECHNOLOGY

Christian Barnard Performs a Human Heart Transplant Operation
Rene Favaloro Performs a Successful Human Heart Bypass Operation
Mammography Is Introduced to Screen for Breast Cancer
Stanford Biochemists Produce Synthetic DNA
The Saturn Three-Stage Rocket Powers an Unmanned Apollo Capsule into Earth Orbit
Mariner 5 Determines That the Surface of Venus Is Not Fit for Human Habitation

BUSINESS AND INDUSTRY

Boeing Introduces Its 727-200 Passenger Airliner
Chicago's John Hancock Building Is Slightly Shorter Than New York's Empire State

CONSUMER PRODUCTS AND SERVICES

Mastercharge Credit Cards Are Marketed (later called Master Card)
Amana Introduces the RadaRange Microwave Oven
Quartz Watches Are the New Rage
Rolling Stone Magazine Begins Publication

PRICES

Amana Microwave Oven	$495.00
Bread	$.25 per pound

Protests and Riots Divide the US 1967

SPORTS

Muhammad Ali Is Stripped of Heavyweight Title for Refusing to Serve in the Army, and
    Receives a Five Year Draft Evasion Sentence
Billie Jean King Wins the Women's Singles at Wimbledon

ARTS AND MEDIA

STAGE	*Black Comedy*	Lynn Redgrave, Michael Crawford
	Hallelujah Baby!	Leslie Uggams, Lillian Hayman
MOVIE	*In the Heat of the Night*	Rod Steiger, Sidney Poitier, Lee Grant
	The Graduate	Mike Nichols, Anne Bancroft, Dustin Hoffman, K. Ross
	Guess Who's Coming...Dinner?	Katherine Hepburn, Spencer Tracy
	Cool Hand Luke	Paul Newman, George Kennedy, Patricia Neal
	Bonnie and Clyde	Estelle Parsons, Warren Beatty, Faye Dunaway, W. Oates
	Dr. Dolittle	Rex Harrison, Samantha Eggar
	The Dirty Dozen	Lee Marvin, Robert Ryan, Charles Bronson
TV	*Laugh-In*	Dick Martin, Dan Rowan, Lily Tomlin, Arte Johnson, Ruth Buzzi, Henry Gibson, Goldie Hawn, Gary Owens, Judy Carne, Jo Anne Worley
	The Flying Nun	Sally Field
	The Smothers Brothers	Tom and Dick Smothers
	The Carol Burnett Show	Carol Burnett, Harvey Korman, Tim Conway
BOOK	*The Arrangement*	Elia Kazan
	Confessions of Nat Turner	William Styron

MUSIC

By the Time I Get to Phoenix	*Gentle on My Mind*
All You Need Is Love	*Alice's Restaurant*
Can't Take My Eyes off You	*Ode to Billy Joe*
Michelle	*Sgt. Pepper's Lonely Hearts Club Band*
Light My Fire	*Alfie*

PEOPLE

George Romney's Presidential Bid Is Damaged When He Tells Reporters He Was
    "Brainwashed" by US Officials During a 1965 Vietnam Visit
Phil Donahue's Daytime Show Starts in Dayton, Ohio
A Paris Exhibit of Sculptures Honors Pablo Picasso on His 85th Birthday
Dr. Benjamin Spock, Poet, Alan Ginsberg and Singer Joan Baez, Are Among the Celebrities
    Arrested in Anti-War Protests
Stokely Carmichael Urges Blacks to Arm for "Total Revolution."
Che Guevara (39) Is Killed in Bolivia, While Fighting to Overthrow That Government

CRIME AND PUNISHMENT

Seven Ku Klux Klan Members Are Convicted of Violating the Civil Rights of Three Slain
    Civil Rights Workers in Meridian, Mississippi

INCIDENTALS AND TRIVIA

The Monkees Are the Most Popular Band on Earth

1968 *America Writhes in Pain*

WORLD

A Massive "Tet" Offensive by North Vietnamese Forces Shows They Are Not Losing
The USSR and Other Warsaw Pact Nations Invade Czechoslovakia to Crush the "Prague
     Spring" Liberalization Movement
A Nuclear Nonproliferation Treaty Is Signed by 61 Nations Including the USSR and the US
The Vietnam Conflict Drags on as Both Sides Cite Truce Violations

NATION

Race Riots Break Out in Chicago, Boston, Detroit and the District of Columbia
George Wallace of Georgia Enters the Political Race as a Third Party Candidate
President Johnson Announces That He Will Not Seek Reelection
With King Dead, the Poor People's March on Washington Is Led by Ralph Abernathy
Republicans Nominate Richard Nixon with Spiro Agnew as His Running Mate
The Democratic Convention in Chicago Is Marred by War Protests and Police Overreaction
Democrats Nominate VP Hubert Humphrey with Edmund Muskie as His Running Mate
Richard M. Nixon Defeats Democrat Hubert H. Humphrey for President
Nixon Pledges to End the War in Vietnam
The First 911 Emergency Telephone System Begins in Haleyvillle, Alabama

LIFESTYLE

The Federal Minimum Hourly Wage Is $1.60
Afro Hairdos Go Mainstream
Hemlines Remain High. The Midi-Skirt (mid calf length) Finds Little Support

SCIENCE AND TECHNOLOGY

Astronauts, Frank Borman, William Anders and James Lovell Circle the Moon and Return to
     Earth in Apollo 8
Soviets Develop the Tupolev TU-144, First Supersonic Airliner

CONSUMER PRODUCTS AND SERVICES

McDonalds Offers a Big Mac for the First Time
Motion Picture Association of America Establishes The Voluntary Ratings of G, PG, R, X
Color TV Sets Outsell B/W Receivers 6 Million to 5.5 Million

PRICES

Bread	$.29 per loaf
Coffee	.69 per pound can
Milk	.48 per half gallon
Cigarettes	.30 per pack (see 1999)
First Class Postage Stamp	.06

SPORTS

Longtime Chicago Bears' Owner and Coach, George Halas, Retires
Peggy Fleming Wins the Olympic Gold Medal in Figure Skating
Jim "Catfish" Hunter of Oakland Pitches the First American League Perfect Game Since 1922
Lee Trevino Wins the US Open Golf Tournament

Nixon Pledges to Bring Peace 1968

ARTS AND MEDIA

STAGE

The Great White Hope	James Earl Jones, Jane Alexander
The Man in the Glass Booth	Donald Pleasance
Hair	
Forty Carats	Julie Harris
Plaza Suite	Neil Simon, George C. Scott, Maureen Stapleton

MOVIE

Oliver	Carol Reed, Ron Moody, Oliver Reed
Charly	Cliff Robertson, Claire Bloom
The Lion in Winter	Katherine Hepburn, Peter O'Toole
Funny Girl	Barbra Streisand, Omar Sharif
The Subject Was Roses	Jack Albertson, Patricia Neal
Rosemary's Baby	Ruth Gordon, Mia Farrow
The Thomas Crown Affair	Steve McQueen, Faye Dunaway
Planet of the Apes	Charlton Heston, Roddy McDowall, Kim Hunter
2001 A Space Odyssey	Stanley Kubrick, Gary Lockwood, Kier Dullea

TV

Julia	Diahann Cannon, Lloyd Nolan
The Ghost & Mrs. Muir	Hope Lange, Edward Mulhare
Hawaii Five-O	Jack Lord, James MacArthur, Kam Fong
60 Minutes	Dan Rather, Harry Reasoner, Mike Wallace, Morley Safer

BOOK

Soul On Ice	Eldridge Cleaver

MUSIC

Mrs. Robinson
Hair
Good Morning Starshine
Aquarius
The Windmills of Your Mind
Harper Valley PTA

This Guy's in Love with You
I Say a Little Prayer
Jumpin' Jack Flash
Those Were the Days
I'll Never Fall in Love Again

PEOPLE

Martin Luther King Jr. Is Assassinated in Memphis
Presidential Candidate Robert "Bobby" Kennedy Is Assassinated in Los Angeles
Cesar Chavez of the Farm Worker's Union, Leads a National Boycott on Table Grapes
Jacqueline Kennedy Marries Shipping Magnate Aristotle Onassis
Ronald McDonald (Willard Scott) Makes His First TV Appearances

QUOTES

"In the future, everyone will be famous for fifteen minutes."
Andy Worhol

COMMENTARY

"Our personal and collective grief as a nation continues. John and Bobby Kennedy are dead. Rev. King is dead. The war in Vietnam continues and we increasingly wonder why our boys are there. There are riots in the cities. There is fire, destruction, hatred and blame. Worst of all there appear to be no solutions. These are, indeed, very dark days for our nation."

Bill Goodpage

1969   *A Small Step for a Man*

WORLD

Vietnam Peace Talks Drag on in Paris
US Begins a Reduction of Forces in Vietnam. South Vietnam To Assume a Broader Role
US Reared, Golda Meir, Becomes Premier of Israel

NATION

Nixon Freezes Wages, Rents and Prices for 90 Days to Fight Inflation
Peace Demonstrators Stage Numerous Activities Including a Candlelight Vigil by the White House
Warren Burger Succeeds the Retiring Earl Warren as Chief Justice of the US Supreme Court

ENVIRONMENT, SAFETY AND HEALTH

Residential Use of DDT Is Banned as Part of a Total Phase Out
The Artificial Sweeteners, Cyclamates Are Banned from Most Consumer Products
Baby Food Makers Eliminate Monosodium Glutamate (MSG) from Their Products

LIFESTYLE

The Woodstock Festival in New York Draws 400,000 for Music, Drugs, Love and Fun. Only 3 Die
Relaxed "Jogging" Is Turning into Serious Running
The Saturday Evening Post Ceases Publication After 148 Years

SCIENCE AND TECHNOLOGY

Apollo 11 Astronauts, Neil Armstrong and then Edwin "Buzz" Aldrin, Walk on the Moon on
     July 20. Pete Conrad Handles the Command Ship
Apollo 12 Astronauts, Charles Conrad Jr., and Alan Bean, Walk on the Moon in November.
     Richard Gordon Jr. Handles the Command Ship
Jonathan Beckwith Isolates a Single Gene
Denton Cooley Implants the First Artificial Heart in a Human
The First Internet Message Is Transmitted

BUSINESS AND INDUSTRY

The Boeing 747 Makes Its First Public Flight
The Concorde Supersonic Jet Is Introduced by a British-French Consortium

CONSUMER PRODUCTS AND SERVICES

Sesame Street Is Born; a Product of Public Television
American Motors Introduces the Compact Gremlin Automobile
Ford Offers the Maverick and General Motors Shows Off the Camaro
Hanes Markets L'eggs in Supermarkets and Convenience Stores
Dave Thomas Founds the Wendy's Fast Food Restaurant Chain
The Interbank Charge Card Is Renamed *MasterCharge*
Kelloggs Introduces Frosted Mini Wheats
Cartoonist, Gary Trudeau (20), Pens *Doonesbury* for Syndication

PRICES

Big Mac Sandwich	$.49
Volkswagen Beetle	$1,990.00

A Giant Leap for Mankind

SPORTS

Major League Baseball Celebrates Its 100th Year, Adding Teams and Splitting Into Divisions
The National League Adds San Diego and Montreal; American Adds Kansas City and Seattle

ARTS AND MEDIA

STAGE	*1776*	
	Oh Calcutta!	
	Play It Again Sam	Woody Allen, Diane Keaton
MOVIE		
	True Grit	John Wayne, Kim Darby
	The Prime of Miss Jean Brodie	Maggie Smith, Ronald Neame
	They Shoot Horses Don't They?	Gig Young, Jane Fonda
	Cactus Flower	Goldie Hawn, Walter Matthau
	Butch Cassidy … Sundance Kid	Paul Newman, Robert Redford, Katherine Ross
	Easy Rider	Dennis Hopper, Peter Fonda
TV	*The Brady Bunch*	Florence Henderson, Robert Reed, Ann B. Davis
	Marcus Welby M.D.	Robert Young, James Brolin, Elena Verdugo
	The Bill Cosby Show	Bill Cosby, Lillian Randolph, Beah Richards
BOOK	*The Godfather*	Mario Puzo
	Portnoy's Complaint	Phillip Roth
	Slaughter-house-Five	Kurt Vonnegut, Jr.

MUSIC

Raindrops Keep Falling on My Head
I've Got To Be Me
I'll Never Fall in Love Again
Leaving on a Jet Plane
My Cherie Amour
Sugar, Sugar

Wedding Bell Blues
Honky Tonk Women
Hungry Eyes
Only the Lonely
Darling, You Know I Wouldn't Lie

PEOPLE

Elvis Presley Has Three Gold Albums and Breaks Concert Records Everywhere
Shirley Chisolm of Brooklyn Becomes First Black Woman Elected to Congress

QUOTES

"That's one small step for a man, one giant leap for mankind."
Neil Armstrong (July 20, 1969)

"I was born at the age of twelve on a Metro-Goldwyn-Mayer lot."
Judy Garland (1922-1969)

COMMENTARY

"Man has left the earth and physically stepped onto the surface of another celestial body. It seems unreal, yet we have accomplished it. Even more astonishing is that we did it only 66 years after man first managed powered flight. What joy and pride for America amid all of the chaos we have been enduring."

"Miss Picky"
Irene English

1970 *The US Economy Falters*

WORLD

US Troop Strength in Vietnam Is Now Down to 340,000 from a Peak of Over 500,000
West Germany and Poland Sign a Pact Recognizing Post-WWII Borders
The Polish Government Is Toppled by Food Riots
Anwar Sadat Is Elected President of Egypt After Gamal Nasser Dies of a Heart Attack

NATION

Congress Creates the Public Broadcasting System (PBS)
Four Kent State University Students Are Killed by Guardsmen During an Anti-War Protest
The Lutheran Church Approves Women as Priests
Eighteen-Year-Olds Receive the Right to Vote
The National Rail Passenger Corporation (AMTRAC) Is Created
Harry Blackmun Is Appointed to the Supreme Court to Replace Abe Fortas, Who Resigned
Recession Is a Commonly Heard Word as Inflation Grows and the US Economy Falters
The Postal Reorganization Act Creates an Independent Postal Service System
The RICO Act Will Be Used to Prosecute Mafia Kingpins and White Collar Criminals

ENVIRONMENT, SAFETY AND HEALTH

A Bill Banning Cigarette Advertising on Radio and TV Becomes Law
The Occupational Health and Safety Act (OSHA) Requires Stronger Job Safety Standards
Congress Approves the Environmental Protection Agency (EPA)
First Earth Day Is Celebrated on April 22
No US Deaths from Polio Were Reported This Year
Linus Pauling Claims That High Doses of Vitamin C Can Ward off the Common Cold and Flu

LIFESTYLE

3.0 Million Live on US Farms, Down to 4.8% of the Population (see 1901, 1980)
US Population Is Now 203 Million. 9.8% Over Age 65
There Are Now 59 Million TV Sets in America, 42% Are Color
Miniskirts Up To Ten Inches Above the Knee Are Now Common

SCIENCE AND TECHNOLOGY

Apollo 13 Astronauts James Lovell Jr., Fred Haise Jr. and John Swigert Jr. Splash Down
Safely in their Crippled Spacecraft

BUSINESS AND INDUSTRY

Intel Corporation Develops the Microprocessor

CONSUMER PRODUCTS AND SERVICES

Lexitron Offers the Word Processor, a Dedicated Function Computer
The Floppy Disk Is Introduced for Data Storage
Nissan Markets the Highly Successful Datsun 240Z Sports Car
Nautilus Exercise Machines Introduced

PRICES

Datsun 240Z	$3,526
AMC Rebel	$3,500

Military Expenditures Reduced 1970

SPORTS

The Seattle Pilots Become the Milwaukee Brewers as That City Has Baseball Once Again

ARTS AND MEDIA

STAGE

Applause	Lauren Bacall
Company	Hal Prince, Stephen Sondheim
Two By Two	Danny Kaye
The Rothschilds	Hal Linden
Home	John Gielgud, Sir Ralph Richardson
The Gingerbread Lady	Maureen Stapleton
Child's Play	Fritz Weaver, Pat Hingle
Effect of Gamma Rays On Man-In-The-Moon Marigolds	Sada Thompson

MOVIE

Patton	Frances F. Coppola, George C. Scott, Karl Malden
Ryan's Daughter	John Mills, Robert Mitchum, Sara Miles, Trevor Howard
Airport	Helen Hayes, Burt Lancaster, Jean Seberg (all star cast)
Love Story	Ali MacGraw, Ryan O'Neal
Lovers and Other Strangers	Gig Young, Bea Arthur, Bonnie Bedelia
Five Easy Pieces	Jack Nicholson, Karen Black, Fanny Flagg
Little Big Man	Dustin Hoffman, Martin Balsam, Faye Dunaway, Richard Mulligan

TV

Monday Night Football	Howard Cosell, Frank Gifford
The Mary Tyler Moore Show	Mary Tyler Moore, Ed Asner, Betty White, Ted Knight, Valerie Harper
The Odd Couple	Tony Randall, Jack Klugman
The Flip Wilson Show	Flip Wilson

BOOK

Everything You Ever...About Sex	David Reuben
The Greening of America	Charles Reich
QBVII	Leon Uris
Future Shock	Alvin Toffler
Hard Times	Studs Terkel
Up The Organization	Robert Townsend

MUSIC

Bridge Over Troubled Water
For All We Know
Rubber Duckie
The Candy Man
Let It Be
We've Only Just Begun

What Are You Doing the Rest of Your Life?
Band of Gold
Hello Darlin'
He Loves Me All the Way

PEOPLE

Buckminster Fuller Receives the American Institute of Architects Award for His Geodesic Dome
Pope Paul VI, in Manila, Is Wounded by a Knife Wielding Painter Posing as a Priest
Spiro Agnew Blasts Music and Media for Promoting Drug Culture
Artist, Andrew Wyeth, Has a One Man Exhibition at the White House
Entertainers Jimi Hendrix and Janis Joplin Succumb to Drug Overdoses.

1971 *UN Admits Communist China*

WORLD

UN Seats Peking as the Official Government of China; Taiwan Is Ousted
East Pakistan Proclaims Its Independence and Calls Itself Bangladesh
Indian-Pakistan War Erupts Over Bangladesh Independence
Heaviest Bombing of Vietnam Since 1968

NATION

Supreme Court Upholds the Right to Publish the Pentagon Papers
CIA Admits the Existance of a "Secret" Army in Laos
With Inflation Rising, President Nixon Invokes Wage and Price Controls
William Rehnquist Takes a Seat as a Supreme Court Justice

DISASTER

An Alaska Airlines Jet Crashes Near Juneau, Killing 111
A Four-Day Inmate Rebellion at Attica Prison in Upstate New York Claims 43 Lives
The Sylmar Earthquake in Southern California Kills 65 and Injures 880

LIFESTYLE

Five Thousand March for Gay Rights in New York's Central Park
Granola Captures the Appetite of the Health Food Movement

SCIENCE AND TECHNOLOGY

Spacecraft Mariner 9 Orbits the Planet Mars
Apollo 14 Astronauts David Scott and James Irwin Use a Lunar Rover to Explore the Moon's
        Surface. Alfred Worden Is in the Command Ship
The Microprocessor is Born. Many Integrated Circuits on One Chip
Soviet Souyez 11 Spacecraft Returns to Earth. All 3 Cosmonauts Dead

BUSINESS AND INDUSTRY

Xerox Researchers Develop a Computer with Mouse Pointer. Corporate Isn't Interested
Hardcore Pornographic Movies Try to Establish Themselves as Legitimate Entertainment

CONSUMER PRODUCTS AND SERVICES

To Counter Rising Small Car Imports, Chevrolet Offers the Vega, Pinto from Ford
        and Gremlin from AMC
Disney World Opens in Orlando Florida
Texas Instruments Markets a "Pocket" Calculator at 2½ Pounds.
Look Magazine Ceases Publication
America Falls in Love with the Recently Introduced Datsun 240Z Sports Car
Rival Introduces the Crock-Pot, a Low-Heat, Slow-Cook Appliance
The LED (Light Emitting Diode) Watch Appears. It Is Novel But Expensive

PRICES

Electronic Pocket Calculator	$ 150.00
Pulsar LED Watch	300.00
Loaf of Bread	.39
First Class Postage	.08 (see 1968, 1975)

SPORTS

Billy Jean King Becomes First Female Athlete to Earn $100,000 Per Year
Gordie Howe Retires from the NHL Detroit Redwings at Age 43
The Washington Senators Become the Texas Rangers

ARTS AND MEDIA

STAGE		
	Lenny	Cliff Gorman
	Prisoner of Second Avenue	Mike Nichols, Peter Falk, Lee Grant
	Follies	Stephen Sondheim, Alexis Smith
	Jesus Christ Superstar	Andrew Lloyd Weber, Tim Rice, Ben Vereen
	All Over	Colleen Dewhurst, Jessica Tandy
	Miss Reardon Drinks a Little	Julie Harris, Estelle Parsons

MOVIE

The French Connection — William Friedkin, Gene Hackman
                                              Fernando Rey, Roy Scheider
Klute — Jane Fonda, Donald Sutherland
The Last Picture Show — Cloris Leachman, Ben Johnson, Cybill Shepherd
Shaft — Richard Roundtree, Moses Gunn
The Summer of '42 — Jennifer O'Neill, Gary Grimes
Fiddler on the Roof — Chaim Topol, Norma Crane
Straw Dogs — Dustin Hoffman, Susan George
A Clockwork Orange — Stanley Kubrick

RADIO

Rock Music Is Rapidly Gaining Ground in Station Formats
An Exception: Public Radio Offers the In-Depth News, *All Things Considered*

TV

All in the Family — Carroll O'Conner, Jean Stapleton, Rob Reiner
                                    Sally Struthers
Sonny and Cher Comedy Hour — Sonny and Cher Bono

BOOK

Wheels — Arthur Hailey
Bury My Heart at Wounded Knee — Dee Brown

MUSIC

Go Away Little Girl
Rainy Days and Mondays
Country Roads
Joy to the World
She's a Lady

Take Me Home
You've Got a Friend
Knock Three Times
When You're Hot, You're Hot

PEOPLE

Charles Manson Is Convicted for the Tate-LaBianca Killings in 1969
Indira Ghandi Wins a Gallup Poll as the World's Most Admired Person
Werner Erhardt Creates the Cult-Like **est,** (Erhardt Seminars Training)
Wayne Newton Is the Darling of Las Vegas
Hijacker, D.B. Cooper, Parachutes from a Northwest 727 with $200,000 Ransom. He is Never Found

INCIDENTALS AND TRIVIA

Hot Pants Are Hot and Getting Hotter
The Yellow, Grinning Happy Face Sweeps across America: **"Have a Nice Day."**
Spiro Agnew Watches Are Popular as a Political Lampoon

1972 *It's Nixon In a Landslide*

WORLD

President Nixon Makes a Historic Visit to Communist China in February and the USSR in March
The Last US Combat Troops Leave Vietnam
Britain Imposes Direct Rule Over Northern Ireland
Okinawa Is Returned to Japan after 27 Yeas of US Occupation
Philippine President, Ferdinand Marcos, Declares Martial Law and Assumes Near
     Dictatorial Powers as He Claims to Be Countering a Communist Rebellion

NATION

Burglars Break into the Democratic National Headquarters at the Watergate
Richard Nixon Is Re-nominated with Spiro Agnew Again on the Republican Ticket
Democrats Nominate George McGovern. Sen. Tom Eagleton Is His Running Mate
Eagleton Confirms That He Had Psychiatric Treatments for Nervous Disorders and Exhaustion
Thomas Eagleton Withdraws from the Ticket and Is Replaced by R. Sargent Shriver
Richard Nixon Wins Landslide Second Term over George McGovern
Title IX, Education Amendment of 1972, Passage Prohibits Gender Discrimination (Sports)
     in Schools Receiving Federal Funds
US Supreme Court Rules That the Death Penalty as Currently Administered Constitutes
     "Cruel and Unusual Punishment." (see 1976)

ENVIRONMENT, SAFETY AND HEALTH

The Clean Water Act Forbids Pollutant Discharge into Navigable Waters
Oregon Leads the Nation with a Bottle Recycling Law
Sale of DDT Is Prohibited Due to Its Accumulation in the Food Chain (see 1939)
30% of US Oil Needs Are Now Imported

LIFESTYLE

The Health Food Era: Tofu, Sprouts, Lentils, Whole Grains, with Wine, of Course
The Words, Biodegradable and Non-Biodegradable, Enter Our Vocabulary
Avocado Is the New Color of Choice in Kitchen and Laundry Appliances (see 1964, 1978)
Wall-to-Wall Shag Carpeting in Burnt Orange and Brown Is Very Popular

SCIENCE AND TECHNOLOGY

The CAT Scan Is Introduced to Medicine
Apollo 17, the Last of the Series with Astronauts Eugene Cernan, Ronald Evans and
     Harrison Schmitt, Collects Rock and Soil Samples from the Moon
NASA Begins work on a Reusable Space Shuttle

BUSINESS AND INDUSTRY

The Dow Jones Industrial Average Breaks 1,000

CONSUMER PRODUCTS AND SERVICES

MS. Magazine Debuts
Pulsar Sells a High-Tech Status Symbol LED "Martian Watch" for $2,100 (see 1976)
McDonalds Restaurants Introduce the Egg McMuffin
Polaroid's SX-70 Camera Ejects the Photo; It Develops Outside the Camera As You Watch
The Playboy Organization Has 22 Clubs and One Million Male Members (see 1960, 1988)

Is a Peace Accord Near?

SPORTS

Mark Spitz Wins Seven Olympic Gold Medals in Swimming
Jack Nicklaus Takes Golf's Masters Tournament

ARTS AND MEDIA

STAGE	*The Sunshine Boys*	Sam Levene, Jack Albertson
	Pippin	John Rubenstein, Ben Vereen
MOVIE	*The Godfather*	F.F. Coppola, Marlon Brando, Al Pacino, Robert Duvall, James Caan, Diane Keaton
	Cabaret	Bob Fosse, Lisa Minelli, Joel Grey
	Butterflies Are Free	Eileen Heckart, Goldie Hawn, Edward Albert
	Poseidon Adventure	Ernest Borgnine, Shelley Winters,
	Dirty Harry	Clint Eastwood, Harry Guardino
	Diamonds Are Forever	Sean Connery, Jill St. John
	Deliverance	Jon Voight, Burt Reynolds, Ned Beatty
TV	*M*A*S*H*	Alan Alda, Loretta Swit, Wayne Rogers, Larry Linville, Gary Burghoff, McLean Stevenson, Jamie Farr, Harry Morgan, Mike Farrell, David Stiers, Wm. Christopher
	The Bob Newhart Show	Bob Newhart, Suzanne Pleschette
	Sanford and Son	Redd Foxx, Demond Wilson
	Bridget Loves Bernie	Meredith Baxter, David Birney
	The Waltons	Ralph Waite, Michael Learned, Will Geer, Richard Thomas
	Maude	Bea Arthur, Adrienne Barbeau, Rue McClanahan
BOOK	*Jonathon Livingston Seagull*	Richard Bach
	I'm O.K., You're O.K.	Thomas Harris

MUSIC

Song Sung Blue	*Brian's Song*
Lean on Me	*I Am Woman*
The City of New Orleans	*I'll Still Be Around*
Help Me Make It Through the Night	*Diamonds Are Forever*
Speak Softly Love	*Chantilly Lace*
I'd Like to Teach the World to Sing	*One's on the Way*

PEOPLE

Gov. George Wallace of Alabama Is Shot and Paralyzed While Campaigning for the
  Democratic Presidential Nomination
Johnny Carson's Tonight Show Moves from New York to Los Angeles
Bobby Fischer Beats Boris Spassky of the Soviet Union for the International Chess Crown
Margaret Kuhn (67) Founds the Gray Panthers to Combat Discrimination Against the Elders

REFLECTION

The Cost of the Vietnam War in US Service Personnel: Died or Missing	58,200
Injured	153,300

INCIDENTALS AND TRIVIA

The Purported Howard Hughes Autobiography Is Exposed as a Fake

1973   *Vietnam Peace Pact Signed*

WORLD

Vietnam Peace Pacts Are Signed in January, Ending America's Longest War
Egypt and Syria Attack Israel During the Yom Kippur Holiday
Arab Oil Producing Countries Begin a Six-Month Embargo on Sales to Western Nations
The Oil Embargo and Rising Grain Prices Create a World Monetary Crisis

NATION

Draft Calls End
Archibald Cox Is Sworn in as a Special Watergate Prosecutor
John Dean Implicates Himself, H.R. Haldeman and John Erlichman in the Watergate Cover Up
Aide, Alexander Butterfield, Reveals the Existence of a Secret White House Taping System
President Nixon Agrees to Turn Over White House Tape Recordings
VP Spiro Agnew Resigns for Accepting Bribes and Kickbacks over 10 Years
Gerald R. Ford of Michigan Replaces Agnew as Vice President
"Saturday Night Massacre!" A.G. Elliot Richardson and Deputy, William Ruckelshaus Are
        Fired for Refusing to Fire Archibald Cox. Solicitor General Robert Bork Then Fires Cox
Leon Jaworski Is Named the New Watergate Prosecutor
Roe vs. Wade Decision By Supreme Court (7-2) Allows Women the Right to Abort a Fetus
        During the First Trimester of Pregnancy
Militant American Indians Hold South Dakota Hamlet of Wounded Knee Ten Weeks Before
        Surrendering to Authorities

ENVIRONMENT

80 Nations Agree to Stop Trade in 375 Endangered Animal Species

LIFESTYLE

The Watergate Hearings Telecasts Are Carried by All Three Networks
Banks Begin Installing 24 Hour Automated Teller Machines. The Public Is Lukewarm
Vodka Outsells Whiskey for the First Time in the US

SCIENCE AND TECHNOLOGY

A Single Gene Is Placed into Bacterium; First Genetic Engineering
The Computer Disc Drive Is Developed
US Launches Skylab, Its First Manned Space Station
Mariner 10 Probe Is Off to Mercury and Will Pass Venus on the Way

CONSUMER PRODUCTS AND SERVICES

Xerox Corporation Markets a Hand Held Mouse for Computers
Sales of Desk and Pocket Calculators Soar Over Two Million as Prices Drop Below $100
The Very Upscale and Pricey Cuisinart Food Processor Goes on Sale
The Universal Product Code (UPC) Is Recommended by Producers and Grocers. The Public
        Balks, Wanting Prices on All Grocery Items

PRICES

Median Sales Price of an Existing Home Is $28,800

Oil Embargo Drives Up Prices 1973

SPORTS

Baseballs American League Introduces the Designated Hitter to Bat for the Pitcher
Billie Jean King Defeats Bobby Riggs in Straight Sets in Tennis' "Battle of the Sexes"
Robyn Smith Is the First Woman Jockey to Win a Stakes Race
Secretariat Wins the Kentucky Derby in a Record Time of Just a Hair under Two Minutes
Willie Mays of the NY Mets Retires After 22 Years. He Hit 660 Home Runs

ARTS AND MEDIA

STAGE	*A Little Night Music*	Stephen Sondheim, Glynis Johns, Hermione Gingold
	Raisin	Virginia Capers
	Seesaw	Tommy Tune
MOVIE	*The Sting*	Paul Newman, Robert Redford, Robert Shaw, Eileen Brennan
	Save the Tiger	Jack Lemmon, Jack Gilford
	A Touch of Class	Glenda Jackson, George Segal
	The Paper Chase	John Houseman, Lindsay Wagner
	Paper Moon	Ryan O'Neal, Tatum O'Neal, Madeline Kahn
	The Way We Were	Barbra Streisand, Robert Redford
	Magnum Force	Clint Eastwood, Hal Holbrook, David Soul
	Three Musketeers	Oliver Reed, Raquel Welch, Michael York
	American Graffiti	Richard Dreyfuss, Ron Howard, Cindy Williams
TV	*Barnaby Jones*	Buddy Ebsen, Lee Meriwether
	Kojak	Telly Savalas
	The Jeffersons	Sherman Helmsley, Isabel Sanford
BOOK	*Serpico*	Peter Maas
	Breakfast of Champions	Kurt Vonnegut
	The Onion Field	Joseph Wambaugh
	The Best and the Brightest	David Halberstam
	Fear of Flying	Erica Jong
	Burr	Gore Vidal

MUSIC

Send in the Clowns
Rocky Mountain High
Bad, Bad Leroy Brown
You're So Vain
You Are the Sunshine of My Life
Superstition
Killing Me Softly With His Song

Live and Let Die
Crocodile Rock
Amanda
Why Me?
Everybody's Had the Blues
Tie a Yellow Ribbon Round the Old Oak Tree

QUOTES

"To make oneself hated is more difficult than to make oneself loved."
Pablo Picasso (1881-1973)

INCIDENTALS AND TRIVIA

Yellow Ribbons Tied to Trees and Fences Signify, "Come Home Safe" After Beatles Hit, "Tie a Yellow...Round the Old Oak Tree."
Valerie Perrine Bares Her Breasts on American TV in the PBS Broadcast of *Steambath*

1974 *The Nightmare is Over*

WORLD

The US and Communist China Establish Diplomatic Relations
The Arab Oil Embargo Is Lifted as Kissinger Mediates Terms with Israel and Egypt
Somalia Is the First Black African Country to Become a Soviet Satellite

NATION

Faced with Impeachment, Richard Nixon Resigns the Presidency on August 9
VP Gerald R. Ford Is Sworn in as the 38th US President
Nelson A. Rockefeller, Former NY Governor Becomes Vice President
Henry Kissinger Agrees to Stay on as Secretary of State
Pres. Ford Pardons Richard Nixon for any Crimes He May Have Committed or May Have
        Participated in While in Office
Ella Grasso Wins Connecticut Governorship—First Woman to Do So
President Ford Offers a Conditional Amnesty for Vietnam War Deserters and Draft-Evaders
President Ford Offers WIN (Whip Inflation Now)
Congress Passes the Freedom of Information Act Assuring Broader Public Access

ENVIRONMENT, SAFETY AND HEALTH

Tornadoes from Georgia North to Canada Kill 350 and Cause a Billion in Damages
CFCs from Spray Cans and Air Conditioners May Be Destroying the Earth's Ozone Layer
Federal Legislation Reduces the Highway Speed Limit to 55 mph to Conserve Gasoline and
        Reduce Highway Fatalities (see 1995)

LIFESTYLE

Is a Depression Ahead? Inflation Is at 10.3%, Unemployment Soars to 7.2%
The Federal Minimum Hourly Wage Is $2.00
The Dow Jones Industrial Average Drops to 570
There Are 120 Million Television Sets in American Homes

SCIENCE AND TECHNOLOGY

Scientists Discover "Lucy" Skeleton in Ethiopia, an Early Human Relative
Mariner 10 Spacecraft Flies Within 500 Miles of Mercury

BUSINESS AND INDUSTRY

Volkswagen Becomes the Best Selling Automobile of the Century
Bill Gates (19) and Paul Allen Form Microsoft Corporation
NCR Corp. Demonstrates a Supermarket Checkout Scanner in Ohio

CONSUMER PRODUCTS AND SERVICES

Hey Good Buddy! Everyone Wants a Citizen's Band (CB) Radio
The Bricklin SV-1 Plastic Body Sports Car Is Introduced. They Will Sell Only 2,897 Cars
        Before Ending Production in 1975
People Magazine Begins Publication

PRICES

Average New US Manufactured Automobile $4,000
First Class Postage Climbs to $.10 (see 1971, 1975)

It Is a Time for Healing 1974

SPORTS

Hank Aaron Beats Babe Ruth's Home Run Record as He Hits Number 715
Frank Robinson Becomes Baseball's First Black Manager as He Leads the Cleveland Indians

ARTS AND MEDIA

STAGE   *A Moon for the Misbegotten*   Colleen Dewhurst, Ed Flanders, Jason Robards Jr.

MOVIE   *The Godfather II*   Frances Ford Coppola, Robert DeNiro
         The Towering Inferno   Paul Newman, Steve McQueen
         The Exorcist   Ellyn Burstyn, Max von Sydow, Linda Blair, Lee J. Cobb
         Chinatown   Jack Nicholson, Faye Dunaway, John Huston

TV   *Happy Days*   Ron Howard, Henry Winkler, Tom Bosley, Marion Ross
         Police Woman   Angie Dickenson, Earl Holliman
         Kolchak: The Night Stalker   Darren McGavin
         Rhoda   Valerie Harper, Nancy Walker
         Six Million Dollar Man   Lee Majors, Richard Anderson
         Little House on the Prairie   Michael Landon, Melissa Gilbert, Merlin Olsen

BOOK   *Watership Down*   Richard Adams
         All the President's Men   Carl Bernstein & Robert Woodward
         Jaws   Peter Benchley

MUSIC

Sunshine on My Shoulders
Hooked on a Feeling
The Way We Were
I'll Have to Say I Love You in a Song
Haven't Got Time for the Pain

Rikki Don't Lose That Number
You and Me Against the World
Feel Like Making Love
Stop and Smell the Roses
Another Lonely Song

PEOPLE

Jim Bakker (34) Founds the PTL (Praise The Lord Ministry)

QUOTES

"I don't think any novelist should be concerned with literature."
Jacqueline Suzanne (1918-1974)

INCIDENTALS AND TRIVIA

Gerald Ford Is the Only Vice President and President Never
    Elected to Either Office
"Trucker" Talk Is All the Rage: *Handle, 10-4, Smokey* and *Bear*
US Convertible Automobile Sales Plummet to 28,000 (see 1965)
Streaking Naked Is a Rage That Will Last only a Few Months

COMMENTARY

"The nation is shaken once again. President Nixon has resigned—the first president to ever do so. As he takes off for California, Gerald Ford is sworn in. Ford urges a time of 'healing.' We pray that will happen, and soon!"

Hank Hawthorne

1975 *South Vietnam Is Lost After All*

WORLD

South Vietnam Unconditionally Surrenders to the Vietcong
Americans and South Vietnamese Rush to Leave Saigon Before the City Falls
Terrorists Kill Hundreds Worldwide
US Imposes Sanctions on South Africa Because of Apartheid
United Nations Declares 1975 The International Year of the Woman

NATION

Sara Jane Moore Attempts to Shoot President Ford in San Francisco, But Misses
The National Debt Is $533 Billion
High Cost Loans and Low Market Prices Create a Severe Credit Crunch for Farmers

DISASTER

7,000 Die in Two Devastating Mexico City Earthquakes

LIFESTYLE

The Federal Minimum Hourly Wage Is $2.10
Average Hourly Production Wage Is $6.22 (see 1965)
Soft Drink Consumption Passes Coffee for the First Time (see 1976)

SCIENCE AND TECHNOLOGY

Soviet Space Probe Transmits Pictures from the Surface of Venus
Apollo and Soyuz Space Capsules Link in Space Orbit for Two Days
Lyme Disease, from the Bite of a Tick, Is Identified in Lyme, Connecticut

BUSINESS AND INDUSTRY

The Cray-1 Supercomputer Performs 100 Million Operations Per Second
The Three TV Networks Agree to Family Time Shows Between 7-9 p.m. This Idea Fails as
    Most Family Time Shows Are Low Rated

CONSUMER PRODUCTS AND SERVICES

The VISA Credit Card Replaces BankAmericard, Available Since 1958
Phillip Morris Markets Miller Lite Beer
IBM Introduces the First Laser Printer
MITS Altair 8800 Computer Is Marketed in Kit Form (256 byte memory)
Cadillac Offers the Seville. Downsized Luxury at a Higher $12,500 Price
The Bulbous AMC Pacer Is the "Glassiest" Car on the Road
Digital Watches, LED Types (red) and LCD Types (black) with Tiny Buttons Are Impractical
    But Wildly Popular
Water Beds Are Considered Very Sexy
Sony Introduces the One-Hour Betamax Videotape Recorder/Player
Pop Rocks Candy Crackles and Fizzes in the Mouth to the Delight of Children

PRICES

First Class Postage Climbs to $.13 (see 1974)

SPORTS

Pete Rose Passes Ty Cobb's Record of 4,141 Base Hits
Arthur Ashe Becomes the First Black Man to Win Tennis' Wimbeldon Singles Title by
Defeating Jimmy Conners
Pele's Three-Year, Seven Million Dollar Contract Makes Him the Highest Paid Team Player

ARTS AND MEDIA

STAGE		
	Death of a Salesman	George C. Scott
	A Chorus Line	
	The Wiz	
	Chicago	Gwen Verdon
	Same Time Next Year	Ellyn Burstyn
	Travesties	Tom Stoppard

MOVIE		
	One Flew...Cuckoo's Nest	Milos Forman Jack Nicholson, Louise Fletcher
	The Sunshine Boys	George Burns , Walter Matthau
	Shampoo	Lee Grant, Julie Christie, Warren Beatty
	Jaws	Robert Shaw, Roy Scheider, Lorraine Gary
	Rocky Horror Picture Show	Tim Curry, Susan Sarandon, Barry Bostwick
	Dog Day Afternoon	Al Pacino, Charles Durning, Chris Saranden
	Nashville	Robert Altman, Keith Carradine

TV		
	Welcome Back, Kotter	Gabe Kaplan, Marcia Strassman, John Travolta
	Starsky and Hutch	Paul Michael Glaser, David Soul
	Barney Miller	Hal Linden, Abe Vigoda, Maxwell Gail, Jack Soo
	Switch	Eddie Albert, Robert Wagner
	The Invisible Man	David McCallum, Craig Stevens
	Saturday Night Live	Chevy Chase, Gilda Radner, John Belushi, Bill Murray, Dan Ackroyd

BOOK		
	Ragtime	E.L. Doctorow
	Shogun	James Clavell
	Humboldt's Gift	Saul Bellow
	Looking for Mr. Goodbar	Judith Rossner

MUSIC

Love Will Keep Us Together
Lucy in the Sky with Diamonds
Please Mr. Postman
Rhinestone Cowboy
Feelings
Midnight Blue

The Entertainer
Fame
Listen to What the Man Said
Don't Take Your Love
I'm Easy

PEOPLE

Japanese Climber, Junko Tabei, Is First Woman to Reach Everest Summit
Beverly Sills Joins the Metropolitan Opera After 20 Years with the NY City Opera
William O. Douglas (77) Retires from the US Supreme Court
Teamster Boss, Jimmy Hoffa, Disappears and Is Believed to Have Been Murdered

INCIDENTALS AND TRIVIA

Mood Rings and Pet Rocks Are All the Rage

1976 *Happy Birthday, America!*

WORLD

Lebanon's 19-Month Civil War Ends with Troops in Control. Beirut Is in Ruins
Violence Continues in Northern Ireland as It Has Since 1969
The US and USSR Agree on Limited Underground Nuclear Tests and Mutual Inspection
Israel Agrees to Withdraw from Most of the Sinai That It Previously Captured
The Episcopal Church Begins to Ordain Women

NATION

The US Celebrates the Bicentennial of Its Founding
Democrats Select James Carter as Their Candidate and Walter Mondale for VP
In a Tight Convention, the GOP Selects Gerald Ford over Ronald Reagan
Robert Dole of Kansas Is Selected as Ford's Running Mate
Democrat James E. Carter Defeats Gerald R. Ford for President
NASA. Accepts Women for Astronaut Training
Supreme Court Rules that the Death Penalty Is <u>Not</u> Cruel or Unusual Punishment (see 1972)
Atlantic City, New Jersey, Legalizes Gambling

LIFESTYLE

The Federal Minimum Hourly Wage Is $2.30
Soft Drink Consumption Passes Milk for the First Time (see 1975)
Aerobics, Originally Developed for the Military, Go Mainstream
Finding Yourself: e.s.t. (Erhardt Seminar Training) Is an "IN" Thing
Long Haul Truckers Become Popular Icons in Song and Film

SCIENCE AND TECHNOLOGY

US Viking Space Probe Transmits Pictures from the Surface of Mars
NASA Unveils the Space Shuttle Enterprise at Palmdale, California
The Supersonic Concorde Jet Enters Trans-Atlantic Service

BUSINESS AND INDUSTRY

Britain and France Open Trans-Atlantic Concorde Air Service
Steve Jobs (21) and Stephen Wozniak (26) Form Apple Computer
Ted Turner Founds WTBS, an Atlanta Superstation
Wang Laboratories Produces Word Processors as Work Stations Using a Central Computer
Fax (facsimile transmission) Machines Gain Greater Business Interest as the Speed Drops
      to 3 Minutes Per Page from 6 Minutes Per Page. Quality Is Still Poor

CONSUMER PRODUCTS AND SERVICES

US Manufactured Convertible Production Stops with the Last Two Cadillac Eldorados
Apple I Personal Computer. It's Cute, But What Can You Do with This Thing?
LED Watch Interest Fades. Texas Instruments Sells One at $9.95 (see 1972)
Several Japanese Electronics Firms Counter the Sony Betamax with a Two-Hour
      Videocassette Recorder in a Competing VHS Format
The Radar Detector, an Early Warning Device of Police Radar Traps, Is Sold

PRICES

A Median Single Family US Home Is Now $38,400

"Jimmy" and "Rocky" Both Win   1976

SPORTS

Chris Evert Lloyd and Jimmy Conners Take the Women's and Men's US Open Tennis Singles
Reggie Jackson of the Yankees Signs for a Record 2.9 Million over 5 Years
Skateboarding Is Now Being Taken Seriously

ARTS AND MEDIA

STAGE   The Year Includes Several Black Productions Including, *For Colored Girls Who Have Considered Suicide When the Rainbow Is Enuf* and Revivals of *Guys and Dolls*, *Bubbling Brown Sugar* and *Porgy and Bess*

California Suite	Neil Simon
No Man's Land	John Gielgud, Ralph Richardson
Pacific Overtures	Hal Prince

MOVIE

Rocky	Sylvester Stallone, Talia Shire, Carl Weathers, Burgess Meredith
Network	Peter Finch, Faye Dunaway , Bernice Straight
All the President's Men	Jason Robards, Robert Redford, Dustin Hoffman
The Shootist	John Wayne, Lauren Bacall, James Stewart
Taxi Driver	Robert De Niro, Jodie Foster
Murder By Death	Peter Sellers, Peter Falk, Maggie Smith, James Coco, Eileen Brennan, David Niven

TV

Mary Hartman, Mary Hartman	Louise Lasser, Greg Mullavey
Laverne and Shirley	Penny Marshall, Cindy Williams
Charley's Angels	Kate Jackson, Jaclyn Smith, Farrah Fawcett
The Bionic Woman	Lindsay Wagner, Richard Anderson
Donnie and Marie	Donnie Osmond, Marie Osmond
MacNeil-Lehrer Report	Robert MacNeil, James Lehrer
The Muppet Show	Jim Henson, Frank Oz

BOOK

Roots	Alex Haley
Trinity	Leo Uris
Sleeping Murder	Agatha Christie

MUSIC

50 Ways to Leave Your Lover	*This One's for You*
I Write the Songs	*Still Crazy After All These Years*
Tonight's the Night	*Inseparable*
Good Hearted Woman	*Silly Love Songs*
Don't Pull Your Love	*Dream Weaver*

QUOTES

"I have committed adultery in my heart many times."
"Jimmy" Carter (as reported by *Playboy*)

INCIDENTALS AND TRIVIA

Good Humor Succumbs to the Times (home freezers) and Sells Off Its Fleet of 1,500 Trucks to Independent Ice Cream Sellers
"Punk" or "New Wave" Rock Begins to Spread in Major Cities

1977 New Leadership in China, USSR

WORLD

Leonid Brezhnev Assumes Control of Both Party and State in the USSR
Former Purged Chinese Leader, Deng Xiaoping, Returns to Power after Mao's Death
Yielding to Public Pressure, the South African Government Finally Allows TV Broadcasts

NATION

President Carter Pardons Almost All Vietnam War Draft Evaders
The US Department of Energy Is Created
Legislation Passes to Return the Panama Canal to Panama by the Year 2000

ENVIRONMENT, HEALTH AND SAFETY

The 760 Mile Trans-Alaska Oil Pipeline from Prudhoe Bay to Valdez Is Completed
California Has Its Worst Drought Year in History
US Bans Most Aerosol Products That Contain Fluorocarbons
911 Emergency Phone Systems Are Now Implemented in Most Urban Areas

LIFESTYLE

A Videotape Movie Rental Store Opens in Los Angeles
New York Power Failure in July Traps Thousands in Subways
Levi's Jeans Are Still the Most Popular, But High-Priced Designer Jeans Are in Demand
The Top 1% (2.4 Million) of Americans Have as Many after Tax Dollars to Spend as the
 Bottom 49 Million (see 1998)

LIFESTYLE

Worst Plane Crash in History! KLM 747 Collides with Pan Am 747 on a Foggy Runway in the
 Canary Islands. All 247 on KLM and 333 of 354 on Pan Am Are Killed

SCIENCE AND TECHNOLOGY

The Rings of Uranus Are Discovered
US Launches Voyager 2 Spacecraft to Travel Beyond the Solar System. It Carries Messages
 from Earth in Music, Sounds and Languages
Experimental Space Shuttle Enterprise Makes a Successful Flight and Bumpy Landing
 at Edwards Air Force Base in California

BUSINESS AND INDUSTRY

The Improved Apple II Personal Computer Connects to a TV Monitor and Uses
 Audiocassette Tapes for Data Storage
Kohlberg, Kravis and Roberts Pioneers the Use of Bank Loans to Do a Leveraged Buyout

CONSUMER PRODUCTS AND SERVICES

Apple Computer Offers Apple II, First PC Readily Accepted by Consumers
Commodore and Tandy (Radio Shack TRS 80) Also Offer Personal Computers
VHS Format Videotape Recorder/Players Under Many Manufacturer's Names Flood the Market

PRICES

Apple II Computer	$1,298.00	No Monitor
Tandy TRS-80 Computer	2,500.00	One Unit with Monitor and Keyboard
Gasoline	$.70	

The "King" Is Gone

SPORTS

Seattle Slew Wins Racing's Triple Crown
Bjorn Borg Takes the Men's Singles at Wimbledon; Virginia Wade the Women's

ARTS AND MEDIA

STAGE	*Anna Christie*	Liv Ullman
	Golda	Anne Bancroft
	Dracula	Frank Langella
	Chapter Two	Neil Simon, Judd Hirsch
	The Gin Game	Hume Cronyn, Jessica Tandy
	Annie	Andrea McCardle, Dorothy Loudon
MOVIE	*Annie Hall*	Woody Allen, Diane Keaton, Tony Roberts, Carol Kane
	Star Wars	Carrie Fisher, Harrison Ford, Mark Hamill, Alec Guinness
	Close Encounters 3rd. Kind	Richard Dreyfuss, Teri Garr
	Saturday Night Fever	John Travolta, Karen Lynn Gorney
	Smokey and the Bandit	Burt Reynolds, Sally Field, Jackie Gleason
TV	*Roots (miniseries)*	Ben Vereen, Cicily Tyson, Lavarr Burton
	Three's Company	John Ritter, Joyce DeWitt, Suzanne Somers
	The Love Boat	Gavin MacLeod, Ted Lange, Lauren Tewes
	Soap	Katherine Helmond, Diane Canova, Robert Guillamine, Robert Mandan, Billy Crystal
	Eight Is Enough	Dick Van Patten, Diana Hyland
BOOK	*Overcoming Procrastination*	Albert Ellis
	The Thorn Birds	Colleen McCullough

MUSIC

I Just Want to Be Your Everything
Evergreen
Nobody Does It Better
Signed, Sealed and Delivered
Hard Rock Cafe
How Deep Is Your Love
Heard It in a Love Song

Hotel California
Blue Bayou
Star Wars Theme
Anne
Easy Street
Tomorrow

QUOTES

"Don't step on my blue suede shoes."
Elvis Presley (1935-1977)

COMMENTARY

"The idea of 'new' diseases seems strange, but we are about to learn that deadly unknown ailments can come from seemingly nowhere to plague the human race. Variants of herpes, sexually transmitted, are already rampant. We've faced the mysterious Legionnaires Disease and the debilitating Lyme Disease. Now there are increasing reports of a 'Gay Cancer' that leads to certain death."

Kate Hawthorne

1978 *Camp David Accords Signed*

WORLD

US and Panama Exchange Instruments for Ratification of the Panama Canal Treaty
OPEC Oil Producing Nations Agree to Increase Oil Prices by 15% in a Year
The US Officially Recognizes the People's Republic of China
"Boat People" Pour out of Vietnam in Search of Asylum

NATION

Ongoing Petroleum Shortages Cause Severe Inflationary Pressure on the Economy
The Camp David Peace Conference Achieves an Agreement Between Egypt and Israel
US Students Can Now Get Federally Insured, Subsidized Loans
The Mandatory Retirement Age Is Raised to 70 Years
The Airline Deregulation Act Will Reduce Most Federal Regulatory Control

ENVIRONMENT, SAFETY AND HEALTH

Love Canal Community in New York Is Evacuated After a Toxic Dump Is Uncovered
The US Adds Five More Nuclear Reactors to Its Energy Base

DISASTER

A Private Cessna and a PSA Airlines Boeing 727 Crash over San Diego; 144 Deaths
Minister, Jim Jones, Leads 911 of His Followers, Mostly Americans, to Their Poisoning Death
     in Guyana

LIFESTYLE

The Federal Minimum Hourly Wage Is $2.65
Running Becomes a National Addiction
More Women Enter College Than Men for the First Time
Harvest Gold Color Kitchen and Laundry Appliances Replace Avocado (see 1964, 1972)
Atlantic City Begins Legal Gambling as the First Casino Opens

SCIENCE AND TECHNOLOGY

The Smallpox Disease Is Finally Declared to Be Eliminated World-Wide
First "Test Tube" Baby Born in Britain
Pioneer Venus II Sends Back Photos and Information About the Surface of Venus

BUSINESS AND INDUSTRY

Renault of France Buys American Motors Corporation
Coca Cola Gets Exclusive Rights to Market Their Cola in China; Pepsi Gets the USSR

CONSUMER PRODUCTS AND SERVICES

Sony's Betamax Duels with the VHS Format in Video Tape Recording Sales
Garfield, the Cat Cartoon Appears in Newspaper Syndication
Kimberly Clark Markets *Huggies,* Disposable Diapers with an Hourglass Shape

PRICES

First Class Postage $.15
Gasoline   .66 per gallon (see 1980)

OPEC Raises the Price of Energy 1978

SPORTS

Gary Player Takes Golf's US Masters Tournament
Nancy Lopez Wins the LPGA Golf Tournament

ARTS AND MEDIA

STAGE   *Ain't Misbehavin'*

MOVIE

The Deer Hunter	Christopher Walken, Meryl Streep
California Suite	Maggie Smith, Alan Alda, Jane Fonda
Midnight Express	Brad Davis, John Hurt, Randy Quaid
Grease	John Travolta, Olivia Newton-John
An Unmarried Woman	Jill Clayburgh, Alan Bates, Michael Murphy
Superman	Christopher Reeve, Margot Kidder, Marlon Brando, Glenn Ford, Susannah York, Ned Beatty

TV

Dallas	Larry Hagman, Linda Gray, Mary Crosby, Patrick Duffy, Victoria Principal, Barbara Bel Geddes
20/20	Barbara Walters, Hugh Downs
Different Strokes	Gary Coleman, Dody Goodman, Conrad Bain
Mork and Mindy	Robin Williams, Pam Dawber
Fantasy Island	Ricardo Montalban, Herve Villechaize
Battlestar Gallactica	Lorne Greene, Richard Hatch, Dirk Benedict
The Incredible Hulk	Bill Bixby, Lou Ferrigno

BOOK

The Complete Book of Running	Jim Fixx
The World According to Garp	John Irving
Chesapeake	James Michener
War and Remembrance	Herman Wouk
Scruples	Judith Krantz

MUSIC

Stayin' Alive
You Don't Bring Me Flowers
Mammas, Don't Let Your Babies Grow Up to Be Cowboys
Just the Way You Are
Love Will Find a Way

Ease on Down the Road
Three Times a Lady
Ready to Take a Chance Again
Macho Man
Close Encounters Theme

PEOPLE

Cardinal Karol Wojtyla Is Chosen as Pope of the Catholic Church; Takes the Name, John Paul II
TV Evangelists Jim and Tammy Faye Bakker Form the PTL Club (see 1974)

QUOTES

"I was brought up to believe that the only thing worth doing was to add to the sum of accurate information in the world."

Margaret Mead (1901-1978)

INCIDENTALS AND TRIVIA

Jimmy Carter Grew Up on a Farm with No Plumbing or Electricity

1979 *Troubles Abroad and at Home*

WORLD

Soviet Troops Invade Neighboring Afganistan (see 1988)
An Egyptian-Israeli Peace Treaty Ends a 30 Year State of War Between the Two Countries
Civil War in Iran. Shah Reza Pahlevi Flees the Country.
Ayatollah Khomeini Seizes Power after 15 Years in Exile
Iranian Militants Take Over the US Embassy and Hold 90 Hostages, Including 65 Americans
Militants Demand Return of Deposed Shah. The US Refuses. Militants Keep 50 Hostages
Saddam Hussein Becomes President of Iraq
Margaret Thatcher Becomes Prime Minister of England; First Woman to Head a European Country

NATION

The US Continues to Experience High Interest Rates, Inflation and a Large Foreign Trade Deficit
The Senate Blocks a Strategic Arms Limitation Agreement Signed Earlier by Carter and Brezhnev
Carter "Reorganizes" His Cabinet to Get the Nation Moving
Paul Volker Is Named Chairman of the Federal Reserve Board
The Susan B. Anthony Dollar Coin Flounders in Weak Public Acceptance

ENVIRONMENT, SAFETY AND HEALTH

The Nuclear Reactor at Three Mile Island in New Jersey Has a Partial Meltdown
The Abandoned US Space Station, Skylab, Burns up upon Earth Atmosphere Re-entry,
    Scattering Debris over Australia and the Indian Ocean

DISASTER

Hurricane David Ravages the Caribbean and US Eastern Seaboard, Killing 1,100
An American Airlines DC-10 Crash at Chicago's O'Hare Airport, Kills All 272 on Board, 3 on Ground

LIFESTYLE

The Federal Minimum Hourly Wage Is $2.90

SCIENCE AND TECHNOLOGY

Voyager 1 Space Probe Shows That the Planet Jupiter Has Rings
Oceanographers Find Hot Vents in Ocean Floor Surrounded by Exotic Life Forms Based on
    Sulfur, Not Oxygen
Even Low Levels of Lead in Children Is Found to Reduce Intelligence

BUSINESS AND INDUSTRY

The Federal Chrysler Loan Guarantee Bill Saves the Company from Bankruptcy
Gold Soars Above $400 Per Ounce as Financial Markets React to US Inflation Problems
OPEC Has Raised Oil Prices to $24 Per Barrel, with Some Producers Selling at $28-$40

CONSUMER PRODUCTS AND SERVICES

WORDSTAR Becomes a Popular Word Processing Program
Mass Produced Hot Tubs and Spas Now Number 300,000 Nationwide
The *Master Charge* Card Is Renamed *MasterCard*
CompuServe Offers E-mail and Computer Discussion Groups Via Modem
Sony Introduces the Walkman Cassette Player

What's Wrong, America?

SPORTS

Linda Fratianne Takes the Women's Singles World Figure Skating Championship
Tai Babilonia and Randy Gardner Take the Pairs Title
Hale Irwin Wins the US Open Golf Tournament

ARTS AND MEDIA

STAGE	*Evita*	Patti Lupone, Bob Gunton
	Sweeney Todd	Angela Lansbury, Len Cariou
MOVIE	*Kramar vs Kramar*	Dustin Hoffman, Meryl Streep
	Norma Rae	Sally Field, Ron Leibman, Beau Bridges
	Being There	Melvyn Douglas, Peter Sellers, Shirley MacLaine
	Apocalypse Now	Marlon Brando, Martin Sheen, Robert Duvall
	All That Jazz	Bob Fosse, Roy Scheider, Jessica Lange, Ben Vereen
	Star Trek	William Shatner, Leonard Nimoy, DeForrest Kelly
	Manhattan	Woody Allen, Diane Keaton, Mariel Hemingway
	Alien	Sigourney Weaver, Tom Skerritt, John Hurt
RADIO	*Prairie Home Companion (PBS)*	Garrison Keillor
TV	*Sunday Morning*	Charles Kuralt
	Hart To Hart	Robert Wagner, Stephanie Powers, Lionel Stander
	Knott's Landing	Ted Shackelford, Joan Van Ark, Michelle Lee
BOOK	*The Pritikin Diet Program*	Nathan Pritikin
	Sophie's Choice	William Styron
	The Executioner's Song	Norman Mailer

MUSIC

We Are Family
The Pina Colada Song
She Believes in Me
I Want You to Want Me
Mama Can't Buy You Love

The Gambler
Love Is the Answer
Soul Man
Shadows in the Moonlight
This Moment in Time

PEOPLE

Mother Teresa Wins the Nobel Peace Prize for Her Lifelong Giving to the Poor
Jimmy Carter's "Malaise" Speech, Laments a "Crisis of Confidence" in America
A Graphical User Interface (GUI) at Xerox Research Impresses Steve Jobs
Pope John Paul II (Karol Wojtyla) Visits His Native Poland
Boris Godunov of the Moscow Bolshoi Ballet Defects to the US
Jerry Falwell Founds the *Moral Majority*

COMMENTARY

"Our president says that there is a 'malaise over the land' and, frankly, we're a bit confused. If he means frustrated to the point of not seeming to care, that may be true. At home we're facing higher prices every day, particularly at the gas pumps. Abroad, our citizens are held captive and we are beset by terrorists. As a people we ask, 'Why can't America be strong and proud?'"

"Miss Picky"
Irene English

1980 *Ronald Reagan Wins Big*

WORLD

The Death of Long-Time Leader, Josip Broz Tito, Leaves a Power Vacuum in Yugoslavia
Poland's Solidarity Labor Movement Is Born After a 17 Day Strike
The Persian Gulf Conflict Between Iran and Iraq Escalates into Full Scale War
The Iranian Hostage Crisis Continues as a US Commando Rescue Attempt Fails

NATION

US Population Now 226.5 Million; the National Debt Is $908 Billion
Inflation Is 12.4%, the Second Year of Double-Digit Inflation
Unemployment Climbs to 7.1% as the Nation Slips into a Recession
Race Riots in Miami Leave 14 Dead and 300 Injured
The GOP Nominates Ronald Reagan for President; George Bush for Vice President
Democrats Re-nominate President Carter and Vice President Walter Mondale
Ronald Reagan Easily Defeats Incumbent Jimmy Carter for President
The Department of Health and Human Services Is Created

ENVIRONMENT, SAFETY AND HEALTH

Mount St. Helens in Washington State Explodes; 57 Die
The "Superfund" Act Provides Funds to Clean Up Hazardous Waste Sites

LIFESTYLE

The Federal Minimum Hourly Wage Is $3.10
2.44 Million Now Live on US Farms, Down to 2.7% of the Population (see 1901, 1970)
"Normal" Clothes Are Back in Style with the Preppie Look.
The "Official" Preppie Handbook Introduces Buffy, Muffy, Biff and Skip

DISASTER

A Fire at the MGM Grand Hotel in Las Vegas Leaves 84 Dead

SCIENCE AND TECHNOLOGY

Demise of Dinosaurs Theorized as Caused by a Comet Impacting the Earth
Successful Transfer of a Functioning Gene from One Mouse to Another
Voyager I Flies by Saturn; Finds More Rings and Three More Moons

BUSINESS AND INDUSTRY

Ted Turner's Cable News Network (CNN) Begins 24 Hour Programming
IBM Decides to Manufacture and Market a Personal Computer.
H&R Block Buys CompuServe and Expands Its Services

CONSUMER PRODUCTS AND SERVICES

Rollerblades, In-Line Roller Skates, Are Born
Toxic Shock Syndrome Has Killed 25 Women; P&G Recalls and Discontinues the Tampon
The 900 Pay-Per-Minute Phone Prefix Is Marketed

PRICES

Gasoline $1.20 per gallon (see 1978)

Will Reaganomics Be a Winner? 1980

ARTS AND MEDIA

STAGE

Amadeus	Tim Curry, Ian McKellan
42nd Street	Gower Champion
The Elephant Man	Phillip Anglim, Carole Shelley, Kevin Conway
Barnum	Jim Dale

MOVIE

Ordinary People	Robert Redford, Timothy Hutton, Mary Tyler Moore, Elizabeth McGovern
Nine to Five	Jane Fonda, Dolly Parton, Lily Tomlin, Dabney Coleman, Sterling Hayden
Coal Miner's Daughter	Sissy Spacek, Tommy Lee Jones
Raging Bull	Robert DeNiro, Cathy Moriarty, Joe Pesci
Melvin and Howard	Mary Steenburgen, Jason Robards
The Empire Strikes Back	Mark Hamill, Carrie Fisher, Harrison Ford, B. D. Williams
Atlantic City	Burt Lancaster, Susan Sarandon
The Stunt Man	Peter O'Toole, Steve Railsback, Barbara Hershey
The Big Red One	Lee Marvin, Mark Hammill, Robert Carradine

TV

Shogun	Richard Chamberlain, Toshiro Mifume
That's Incredible	John Davidson, Cathy Lee Crosby, Fran Tarkington
Magnum, P.I.	Tom Sellick, John Hillerman
Nightline	Ted Koppel

BOOK

White House Years	Henry Kissinger
The Covenant	James Michener
The Joy of Sex	Alex Comfort
A Woman of Substance	Barbara Taylor Bradford

MUSIC

It's Still Rock and Roll to Me
Don't Fall in Love with a Dreamer
Fame
And the Beat Goes On
New York, New York

On the Road Again
Don't Ask Me Why
Never Knew Love Like This Before
Don't Say Goodnight
Upside Down

PEOPLE

John Williams Succeeds the Late Arthur Fiedler as Boston Pops Conductor
John Lennon (40) Is Fatally Shot Outside His New York Apartment
TV Evangelist Pat Robertson Forms the 700 Club

COMMENTARY

"Our incoming president is warm and charming. He speaks to us as a friend who is here to help, rather than a Washington bureaucrat. Well, the country certainly needs help; in particular, it needs a big boost of self confidence—that we haven't had since before Vietnam."

"Miss Picky"
Irene English

INCIDENTALS AND TRIVIA

Ronald Reagan, at 69, Is the Oldest Elected US President
"Who Shot J.R.?" This *Dallas* Episode Is the Highest Ever Watched Regular TV Program

163

1981 Reagan Assassination Attempt

WORLD

The Iranian Crisis Ends When the Hostages Are Released, Minutes after Ronald Reagan Is Sworn in as President.

An Attempted Assassination of Pope John Paul in the Vatican, Fails

Egyptian President Anwar Sadat Is Killed By Extremists

Israeli Planes Raid and Destroy a Nuclear Power Plant in Iraq

A Seven-Month Hunger Strike by Irish Nationalists at Maze Prison in Belfast, Northern Ireland, Gains World Attention but Claims 10 Lives

Lech Walesa, Solidarity Leader, Negotiates for Greater Rights in Poland

NATION

Inflation Rises to 14% and Unemployment Rises to 7.4%

President Reagan Is Wounded in an Assassination Attempt by John Hinkley

Press Secretary, James Brady, Is Shot and Paralyzed in the Same Attack

Reagan Fires the Air Traffic Controllers for Striking

Sandra Day O'Conner of Arizona Becomes First Female Justice on the Supreme Court

The US Supreme Court Holds That the Male-Only Draft Is Constitutional

DISASTER

Fire in Las Vegas Hilton Hotel Casino Kills 8 and Injures 198

LIFESTYLE

The Federal Minimum Hourly Wage Is $3.25

The Spread of Genital Herpes Is Alarming. 20 Million Americans May Be Infected

SCIENCE AND TECHNOLOGY

The Reusable Space Shuttle Columbia Blasts into Orbit for the First Time

Mysterious "Gay Cancer" Is Formally Defined as Acquired Immune Deficiency Syndrome (AIDS)

Surgeons Perform the First Successful Operation on a Fetus

Cyclosporin, a New Anti-Rejection Drug, Dramatically Improves Survival of Heart Transplant Operations

BUSINESS AND INDUSTRY

Microsoft Buys an Operating System for $50,000 and Modifies It for IBM PC Requirements

IBM Legitimatizes the PC by Advertising Its Logical Use by Professionals and Freeing Them From the Mainframe

Boeing's Twin-Engine 767 Makes Its Maiden Flight

CONSUMER PRODUCTS AND SERVICES

IBM Corporation Introduces the Personal Computer (PC) Using Microsoft's PC-DOS (Disk Operating System).

The Osborne 1 Portable Computer Appears

Videocassette Recorders (VCR) Sales Hit One Million

Video Rental Stores Appear in Most Every Neighborhood

MTV Is Introduced and Recording Artists Become Video Stars

Aspertane, 200 Times Sweeter Than Sugar, Is Marketed as *Nutrasweet*

Peacemaker, Sadat, Assassinated 1981

SPORTS

One Third of the Season Is Lost as Baseball Players Strike

ARTS AND MEDIA

STAGE	*Dreamgirls*	Sheryl Ralph, Jennifer Holliday, Loretta Devine
MOVIE	*Chariots of Fire*	Ben Cross, Ian Charleson
	Reds	Warren Beatty, Maureen Stapleton, Diane Keaton, Edward Hermann
	On Golden Pond	Henry Fonda, Katherine Hepburn, Jane Fonda
	Arthur	John Gielgud, Dudley Moore, Lisa Minelli
	Raiders of the Lost Ark	Harrison Ford, Karen Allen
	French Lieutenant's Woman	Meryl Streep, Jeremy Irons
	The Four Seasons	Alan Alda, Carol Burnett, Sandy Dennis, Jack Weston, Rita Moreno
TV	*Dynasty*	Joan Collins, John Forsythe, Linda Evans
	Falcon Crest	Jane Wyman, Robert Foxworth, John Saxon, Abby Dalton
	Hill Street Blues	Daniel J. Travanti, Veronica Hamel, James Sikking
	People's Court	Joseph A. Wopner
	This Week With...	David Brinkley
BOOK	*Cosmos*	Carl Sagan
	Noble House	James Clavell

MUSIC

Endless Love	*Fire and Ice*
9 to 5	*Fool That I Am*
Queen of Hearts	*Elvira*
Hill Street Blues	*For Your Eyes Only*
The Old Songs	*Really Wanna Know You*

PEOPLE

Prince Charles (32) of England Marries Diana Spencer (19)
Paul Simon and Art Garfunkel Reunite and Give a Free Concert for 400,000 in NY

QUOTES

"Civilization is a stream with banks. Historians are pessimists because they ignore the banks (ordinary life) with the river (the stealing and killing).

Will Durant (1885-1981)

COMMENTARY

"Although they will recover, Ford, Chrysler and General Motors lost billions this and last year as they retooled for smaller models to meet Japanese competition and US government mandatory fuel economy requirements. Unfortunately, consumers are hesitant to buy the smaller, gutless models, that cost more but offer less."

Bill Goodpage

1982   *Britain Wins a Little War*

WORLD

Various Factions Turn Lebanon into an Ongoing War Zone
Israeli Forces Invade South Lebanon
Argentine Troops Seize the Disputed Falkland Islands from Britain
Argentina Surrenders in the Ten-Week War with Britain over the Falkland Islands
Solidarity Trade Union Members and Police Clash in Poland
Leonid Brezhnev, Soviet Premier for 18 Years, Dies. Yuri Andropov Is His Successor
US Orders Economic Sanctions on Libya for Its Support of Terrorist Groups
US Marines Land in Beirut to Oversee the Withdrawal of PLO Forces

NATION

Inflation Slows to 6% and the Recession Appears to Be Over
Vietnam Veterans War Memorial Commemorated in Washington, D.C.
The Equal Rights Amendment Goes Down to Defeat

DISASTER

Air Florida 737 Crashes into the Potomac River After Takeoff in a Winter Ice Storm, Killing 78
A Pan Am Jet Crashes on Takeoff in New Orleans, Killing 154

LIFESTYLE

Tanning Salons and Gyms for Working Out Are Much in Fashion
"Lite" Foods Are Suddenly Very Popular, but Labels Are Unclear as to What That Means
Estimates Say That 25 Million Americans Smoke Marijuana

SCIENCE AND TECHNOLOGY

First Artificial Heart Transplant Operation. Barney Clark, Retired Dentist, Lives 112 Days
AIDS Now Believed to be Spread by Blood and Sexual Contact
The National Science Foundations Creates NSFnet, Which Will Evolve into the Internet (see 1990)

BUSINESS AND INDUSTRY

Dow Jones Stock Index Passes 1,000 for the First Time
Other Manufacturers Begin to "Clone" the IBM PC
Tylenol Cyanide Poisoning Scare Brings About Industry-Wide Tamper-Proof Packaging
Honda Opens a Manufacturing Plant in Marysville, Ohio.
Japanese Automobiles Take Nearly 23% of All Auto Sales
AT&T Is Forced to Shed Its 22 Regional Telephone Companies. Now We <u>Buy</u> Telephones
Businesses Readily Accept the Newest Generation Fax Machines at 20 Seconds Per Page
Boeing Introduces the 767 Model Jetliner

CONSUMER PRODUCTS AND SERVICES

Today, A National Newspaper, Begins Publication
Every GM Division Gets a Small "J" Car Model, Including Cadillac's Cimarron
Compact Audio Disks Are Marketed
Compac Markets a Portable IBM Compatible Computer
Jane Fonda's Workout Videotape
Smurf Dolls and Characters Are Marketed
Sony Markets Its "Watchman," Pocket-Sized TV
Pillsbury Introduces the Frozen Pie Crust

The US Economy Is Recovering   1982

SPORTS

Jimmy Conners Takes Both the Wimbledon and US Open Titles
Chris Evert-Lloyd Wins the Women's US Open
Martina Navratilova Wins at Wimbledon
The National Football League Season Is Shortened by a Players' Strike

ARTS AND MEDIA

STAGE	*CATS*	Andrew Lloyd Webber
MOVIE	*Ghandi*	Richard Attenborough, Ben Kingsley
	Sophie's Choice	Meryl Streep, Kevin Kline
	Tootsie	Jessica Lange, Dustin Hoffman
	An Officer...Gentleman	Lou Gosset Jr, Richard Gere, Debra Winger
	Deathtrap	Michael Caine, Christopher Reeve, Dyan Cannon
	E.T.—The Extra-Terrestrial	Peter Coyote, Drew Barrymore
	Victor/Victoria	Julie Andrews, James Garner, Robert Preston
	Poltergeist	Craig T. Nelson, JoBeth Williams
TV	*Cheers*	Ted Dansen, Shelly Long, Rhea Perlman, Kelsey Grammer
	Knight Rider	David Hasselhoff, Edward Mulhare
	St. Elsewhere	Ed Flanders, David Birney, Ed Begley, Jr., Cynthia Sikes
	T.J. Hooker	William Shatner, Heather Locklear
	Cagney & Lacey	Tyne Daly, Sharon Gless
	Family Ties	Meredith Baxter, Michael Gross, Michael J. Fox
	Late Night With...	David Letterman
BOOK	*The Cardinal Sins*	Andrew M. Greeley
	Gorky Park	Martin C. Smith
	The Color Purple	Alice Walker

MUSIC

Eye of the Tiger
Chariots of Fire
Oh Pretty Woman
Always on My Mind

What's Forever For
Making Love
One Hundred Ways
Turn Your Love Around

PEOPLE

Princess Grace (Kelly) of Monaco Dies After an Automobile Accident
Marcos Opponent, Benigno Acquino, Is Shot and Killed Upon His Return to the Philippines

REFLECTION

Surgeon General, C. Everett Koop, Calls Cigarette Smoking the Chief Preventable Cause of
Death in the US. Over 110,000 Americans Succumb to Lung Cancer Each Year and More
Suffer from Other Smoking Ailments. The Good News Is That Over 30 Million Americans
Have Quit Smoking Since 1964.

INCIDENTALS AND TRIVIA

E.T. Memorabilia Are Very Popular
"Valspeak" as in Valley Girls Language Is a Hit with the Teens
Pac Man Is Heralded as *Time* Magazine's, Man of the Year

1983 *Terrorism in Lebanon*

WORLD

US Troops Land on the Island of Grenada to Protect US Citizens There
Thousands of Europeans Protest the Deployment of US Nuclear Weapons on Their Continent
Lebanon Remains a Powder Keg

NATION

The US Supreme Court Rules That Many Local Abortion Restrictions Are Unconstitutional
The President Declares a War on Drugs

ENVIRONMENT, SAFETY AND HEALTH

Scientists Predict a Nuclear War Could Produce a "Nuclear Winter" That Might Destroy Most
    Living Creatures
Soft Drink Manufacturers Begin Switching from Saccharin to NutraSweet

LIFESTYLE

The Term "Yuppies" Is Coined to Describe Young Urban Professionals
A Crystallized Form of Cocaine Called "Crack" Is Being Introduced into the US

DISASTER

Terrorists Blow Up the US Embassy in Beirut; 64 Are Killed
A Soviet Fighter Shoots Down a Korean Airlines 747 That Strayed over Soviet Air Space. 269 Die
A Terrorist Bomb Kills 161 US Marines Stationed in Beirut

SCIENCE AND TECHNOLOGY

Pioneer 10 Spacecraft Crosses Pluto's Orbit into the Milky Way
The President Proposes a Strategic Defense Initiative (SDI) to Create a High-Tech Shield
    Against Nuclear Missiles

BUSINESS AND INDUSTRY

The IBM PC Is a Phenomenal Success. Two Million Units Sold Since Its Introduction
    Two Years Ago
Compac Computer Offers a "Portable" Clone Version of the IBM PC
Apple II Is Fading and the Lisa Replacement Is Too Expensive. Apple Spurs Development of
    the Macintosh with a User Friendly Interface
General Motors and Toyota Establish a Joint Manufacturing Plant in Fremont, California

CONSUMER PRODUCTS AND SERVICES

Apple Introduces the Lisa Computer and IBM, the PC Junior. Neither Sells Well
Lotus 1-2-3 for Spreadsheets Makes Its Appearance
Parents Go Wild over Cabbage Patch Dolls, Even Buying Up Counterfeit Copies
McDonalds Introduces Chicken McNuggets
Wireless Cellular Telephone Service Is Now Available in Limited Areas (see 1998)

PRICES

Cellular Telephone	$3,000
Monthly Service Fee	$ 150

Build a Nuclear Shield? 1983

SPORTS

John McEnroe Wins the Men's Tennis Singles at Wimbledon
Richard Noble Sets New Land Speed Record of 633 mph in the Nevada Desert

ARTS AND MEDIA

STAGE	*La Cage aux Folles*	Stephen Sondheim
	My One and Only	Tommy Tune
MOVIE	*Terms of Endearment*	Shirley MacLaine, Jack Nicholson
	Tender Mercies	Robert Duvall, Tess Harper, Ellen Barkin
	The Right Stuff	Scott Glenn, Ed Harris, Fred Ward
	Flashdance	Jennifer Beals, Michael Nouri
	Year of Living Dangerously	Linda Hunt, Mel Gibson, Sigourney Weaver
	Yentl	Barbra Streisand, Mandy Pitinkin, Amy Irving
TV	*The A-Team*	George Peppard, Mr.T, Dirk Benedict
	Webster	Emmanuel Lewis, Alex Karras, Susan Clark
	Hotel	James Brolin, Connie Sellica, Anne Baxter
	Hardcastle & McCormick	Brian Keith, Daniel Hugh-Kelley
	Remington Steele	Stephanie Zimbalist, Pierce Brosnan
	Scarecrow and Mrs. King	Bruce Boxleitner, Kate Jackson, Beverly Garland
BOOK	*Megatrends*	John Naisbitt
	In Search of Excellence	Thomas Peters, Robert Waterman, Jr.

MUSIC

Puttin' on the Ritz
You Can't Hurry Love
What a Feeling
Up Where We Belong
The Girl Is Mine

Don't Let It End
I've Got a Rock and Roll Heart
Billie Jean
Maneater
Let's Dance

PEOPLE

Doctor Sally Ride Becomes the First Female US Astronaut
Guion S. Bluford Jr. Becomes the First Black US Astronaut

QUOTES

"Just Say No."
Nancy Reagan (Opening the War on Drugs)

COMMENTARY

"Vietnam is now ten years behind us and Americans are beginning to take a new look at our military. Its negative post Vietnam image is being restored by volunteer forces that are far better equipped and trained. Grenada showed us how fast and effectively the military could react. Beirut pained us but we retained public resolve to support our troops wherever they might be needed in this troubled world."

Hank Hawthorne

1984   *It's Reagan and Bush Again!*

WORLD

US Is Helping the Government in El Salvador and the Contras in Nicaragua
Britain and China Agree to Transfer Hong Kong to Chinese Sovereignty in 1997
Major Clashes Continue Between Sikhs and Hindus in India.
Prime Minister, Indira Ghandi, Is Assassinated
Soviet Premier, Yuri Andropov, Dies. He Is Succeeded by Konstantin Chernenko

NATION

US Supreme Court Rules That Home Video Recording Does Not Infringe on Copyrights
The Junior Chamber of Commerce, Jaycees, Now Allows Full Membership to Women
It's Reagan and Bush Again for the Republicans
Democrats Select Walter Mondale and Geraldine Ferraro as His Running Mate
Ferraro Is the First Woman to Run for Vice President on a Major Presidential Ticket
Ronald Reagan Wins a Landslide Second Term over Walter F. Mondale

DISASTER

Toxic Gas from a Union Carbide Plant in Bophal, India, Kills Over 2,000

LIFESTYLE

The Word, Cholesterol, Is Added to Our Vocabulary
Infomercials Begin on TV after FTC Lifts Local Station Restrictions

SCIENCE AND TECHNOLOGY

A Baby Produced From a Frozen Embryo Is Born in Australia
Cosmonaut, Svetlana Savitskaya, Is First Woman to Walk in Space
Astronaut, Kathryn Sullivan, Is the First American Woman to Walk in Space

BUSINESS AND INDUSTRY

Texaco Outbids Getty Oil to Buy the Pennzoil Corporation
Standard Oil (California) Buys Gulf Oil and Changes Its Name to Chevron
IBM, Sears & CBS' Partnership Is *Trintex*, a Computer Banking and News Service

CONSUMER PRODUCTS AND SERVICES

Financially Ailing Chrysler Introduces the Minivan as an Alternative to the Station Wagon
Apple Introduces the Macintosh with First MAC Software Programs
IBM Counters with the PC-AT Computer
PG-13 Is Added to the Movie Rating System
Everyone Wants a Taco Salad
The Trivial Pursuit Board Game Gains Instant Acceptance
Mousse Is Perfect for the New Hairdos of Both Men and Women

PRICES

Average New Single Family Home	$101,000
Apple Macintosh Computer	2,495
IBM PC	1,500

SPORTS

The Olympic Games in Los Angeles Attract a Record 7,800 Athletes from 140 Countries,
Despite a Boycott by 14 Soviet Bloc Countries

ARTS AND MEDIA

STAGE	*The Real Thing*	Glenn Close, Jeremy Irons
	Starlight Express	Andrew Lloyd Weber
	Sunday in the Park with George	Mandy Pitinkin
MOVIE	*Amadeus*	F. Murray Abraham, Tom Hulce
	Places in the Heart	Sally Field, Ed Harris, Amy Madigan
	A Passage to India	Peggy Ashcroft, Judy Davis, Alec Guinness
	The Killing Fields	Haing S. Ngor, Sam Waterston
	Ghostbusters	Bill Murray, Dan Aykroyd, Sigourney Weaver
	Splash	Darryl Hannah, Tom Hanks, John Candy
	Terms of Endearment,	Shirley MacLaine, Jack Nicholson, Debra Winger
	Purple Rain	Prince
TV	*The Cosby Show*	Bill Cosby, Felicia Rashad
	Murder, She Wrote	Angela Lansbury, Tom Bosley, William Windom
	Highway to Heaven	Michael Landon, Victor French
	Hunter	Fred Dryer, Stepfanie Kramer
	Miami Vice	Don Johnson, Edward James Olmos
	Night Court	Harry Anderson, John Larroquette, Markie Post
BOOK	*Motherhood:*	
	The Second Oldest Profession	Irma Bombeck
	The One Minute Manager	Kenneth Blanchard, Spencer Johnson

MUSIC

I'm So Excited
What's Love Got to Do with It?
Girls Just Want to Have Fun
Time After Time
Joanna
Sad Songs

I Guess That's Why They Call It the Blues
I Just Called to Say I Love You
Islands in the Stream
Love Somebody

COMMENTARY

"I finally decided to give up my old trusty IBM Selectric and make an investment in an electronic computer with word processing technology. That Apple Macintosh is really exciting. It uses little pictures—they call them icons—on the screen that control tasks by clicking on them with a visual pointer controlled by a "mouse." It's a little hard to explain.

"The IBM PC isn't nearly as clever but it gets the job done for almost a thousand dollars less. It's going to be a tough choice between these two.

"Either way, once I select my computer, it's comforting to know that I will have state-of-the-art equipment for at least five years—maybe more."

Kate Hawthorne

1985 A Younger Soviet Leader Emerges

WORLD

Vietnamese Forces Drive the Last of the Khmer Rouge Army Out of Cambodia

Mikhail S. Gorbachev Succeeds Konstantin U. Chernenko as Soviet Premier upon Chernenko's Death

World-Wide Terrorism Continues—Achille Laurel Ship Highjacking and Attacks at Vienna and Rome Airports

US Imposes Economic Sanctions on South Africa over Apartheid Policy

In Geneva, Reagan and Gorbachev Agree to Work Toward Strategic Arms Reductions

Saudi Arabia Starts an Oil Price War That Results in a World-Wide Glut. Many Higher Cost US Wells Shut Down

NATION

The Federal Budget Deficit Is 172 Billion, Largely Due to Military Expenditures

Many Farmers Are Pushed into Bankruptcy Due to Inflation, High Mortgage Rates and Low Market Commodity Prices

Congress Votes to Stop the President from Sending Anything But Non-Lethal Aid to the Nicaraguan Contras (Rebels)

ENVIRONMENT, SAFETY AND HEALTH

US Program Removes Environmentally Sensitive Farm Land from Use

Legendary Route 66 from Chicago to Santa Monica Is Decertified

DISASTER

7,000 Dead and 30,000 Homeless in Tragic Mexico City Earthquakes

Violent Thunderstorms (Wind Shear) Down a Delta L-1011 in Dallas, Killing 141

SCIENCE AND TECHNOLOGY

Remains of the Sunken Liner, Titanic, Discovered near Newfoundland

Scientists Report That a "Hole" Is Opening Each Spring in the Ozone Layer Above Antarctica

BUSINESS AND INDUSTRY

The Cray 2 Supercomputer Performs 1.2 Billion Operations Per Second

General Electric Acquires RCA and Its NBC Broadcasting Operations

Phillip Morris Acquires General Foods; It Is Now the Largest US Consumer Products Company

Corporate Mergers Increase Through the Increased Use of High-Yield "Junk" Bonds

CONSUMER PRODUCTS AND SERVICES

Coca Cola Company Changes Its Syrup Formula But Due to Public Outcry Returns to the Old Syrup as "Classic" Coke After Three Months

Toshiba Markets a Laptop Computer that Consumers Like

Tartar Control Toothpaste Is Marketed

Montgomery Ward Ends Catalog Sales That Had Lasted over a Hundred Years

Long Play (LP) Records Are Rapidly Giving Way to Compact Disk Audio Technology

PRICES

First Class Postage $.22

But, Can We Trust Him?

SPORTS

Pete Rose Sets a New Baseball Career Record of 4,192 Hits
Willie Shoemaker Breaks $100,000,000 in Career Purse Money
Brian Boitano Wins the US Figure Skating Championship

ARTS AND MEDIA

STAGE

Joe Egg	Stockard Channing, Jim Dale
Biloxi Blues	Neil Simon
I'm Not Rappaport	Judd Hirsch, Cleavon Little
Big River	Roger Miller

MOVIE

Out of Africa	Meryl Streep, Robert Redford
Kiss of the Spider Woman	William Hurt, Raul Julia
The Trip to Bountiful	Geraldine Page, Rebecca De Mornay
Cocoon	Don Ameche, Jessica Tandy, Hume Cronyn
Prizzi's Honor	Angelica Huston, Jack Nicholson, Kathleen Turner
The Color Purple	Danny Glover, Whoopee Goldberg, Oprah Winfrey
Back to the Future	Michael J. Fox, Christopher Lloyd

TV

The Golden Girls	Bea Arthur, Betty White, Estelle Getty, Rue McClanahan
Spenser: For Hire	Robert Urich, Avery Brooks
Growing Pains	Alan Thicke, Joanna Kearns
Lady Blue	Jamie Rose, Danny Aiello

BOOK

The Hunt for Red October	Tom Clancy
If Tomorrow Comes	Sidney Sheldon
Full Circle	Danielle Steel

MUSIC

We Are the World	Material Girl
Like a Virgin	The Power of Love
I Want to Know What Love Is	St. Elmo's Fire
Saving All My Love for You	Born in the USA
If You Love Somebody Set Them Free	Private Dancer

PEOPLE

Outrageous Madonna Becomes an Instant Superstar
Christa McAuliffe of New Hampshire Is Chosen to be the First School Teacher in Space
Oprah Winfrey Makes Her Television Debut
Leontine Price Sings Her Final Performance with the Metropolitan Opera
Lionel Ritchie's We Are the World, Strikes a Universal Chord

REFLECTION

Live Aid, a Rock Concert, Raises 70 Million for Starving Africans. Stars Include Joan Baez,
    Phil Collins, Mick Jagger, Madonna, Paul McCartney and Tina Turner

QUOTES

**"After one look at this planet any visitor from outer space would say,
'I WANT TO SEE THE MANAGER.'"**

William Burroughs

1986   *The Space Shuttle Explodes*

WORLD

US Launches Air Strikes Against Libya for Its Support of Terrorist Groups
Iran and Iraq Continue Their Long, Mostly Stalemated War
Contras Battle Sandinistas in Nicaragua
Philippines' President Marcos Concedes Defeat to Aquino Corazon and Flees the Country

NATION

US National Debt Climbs Above 2 Trillion Dollars, Up from 1 Trillion in 1981
Martin Luther King Jr. Birthday Is Established as a Federal Holiday
President Reagan Declares Economic Sanctions on Libya for Supporting Recent Wave of
    World-Wide Terrorism. US Warplanes Bomb Libya
The Rebuilt Statue of Liberty Is Rededicated. It First Opened 100 Years Ago
A Yearlong Amnesty Program Starts, Offering Citizenship to Illegal Immigrants Meeting
    Specific Conditions
William Rehnquist Replaces Chief Justice Warren E. Burger, Who Has Retired

ENVIRONMENT, SAFETY AND HEALTH

A Massive Meltdown Occurs in the Chernobyl Nuclear Reactor in the USSR
A Worldwide Ban on Whaling Begins
Kerr-McGee Corporation Agrees to Pay 1.38 Million to Karen Silkwood's Estate to Settle a
    10 Year Old Nuclear Contamination Lawsuit

DISASTER

Space Shuttle Challenger Explodes after Takeoff, Killing All 7 Astronauts.
Soviet Passenger Ship Admiral Nakhimov and a Merchant Vessel Collide and Sink in the
    Black Sea. 448 Perish
An Aeromexico Jetliner Collides with a Small Private Plane over Cerritos,
    California, Killing 82 People

LIFESTYLE

The Number of Deaths from AIDS Is Mounting and Is Expected to Climb Higher

SCIENCE AND TECHNOLOGY

Gordon Gould Finally Gets Patent for the Laser After Long Struggle
The Muscular Dystrophy Gene Is Discovered
Richard Rutan and Jeana Yeager Pilot the Fragile Plastic and Stiffened Paper Airplane,
    Voyager, Around the World without Refueling

BUSINESS AND INDUSTRY

Rupert Murdock Forms the TV Fox Network
Computer Giants Burroughs and Sperry Merge to Form Unisys Corporation
Insider Trading Scandals Rock Wall Street

CONSUMER PRODUCTS AND SERVICES

Nintendo Games Are Marketed
Korea Enters the US Auto Market with the Hyundai Excel Sedan at Less Than $5,000

SPORTS

The NCAA Approves a Three Point Field Goal Rule in Men's Basketball
Willie Shoemaker (54) Caps a 37 Year Career by Winning the Kentucky Derby

ARTS AND MEDIA

STAGE	*Phantom of the Opera*	Michael Crawford, Sara Brightman
MOVIE	*Platoon*	Oliver Stone, Tom Berenger, Willem Dafoe
	The Color of Money	Paul Newman, Tom Cruise
	Children of a Lesser God	Marlee Matlin, William Hurt, Piper Laurie
	Hannah and Her Sisters	Woody Allen, Mia Farrow Dianne Wiest, Michael Caine
	Top Gun	Tom Cruise, Kelly McGillis
	Peggy Sue Got Married	Kathleen Turner, Nicholas Cage
	A Room with a View	Maggie Smith, Denholm Elliot
	Crocodile Dundee	Paul Hogan, Linda Koslowski
TV	*Matlock*	Andy Griffith, Linda Purl
	L.A. Law	Richard Dysart, Alan Rachins, Harry Hamlin, Susan Dey, Jill Eikenberry, Corbin Bernsen
	Designing Women	Delta Burke, Dixie Carter, Jean Smart, Annie Potts
	MacGiver	Richard Dean Anderson, Dana Elcar
	Moonlighting	Cybill Shepherd, Bruce Willis
	My Sister Sam	Pam Dawber, Rebecca Schaeffer
BOOK	*Fatherhood*	Bill Cosby
	Red Storm Rising	Tom Clancy

MUSIC

Sarah   *That's What Friends Are For*
Rock Me Amadeus   *On My Own*

PEOPLE

Robert Penn Warren Becomes the First Official Poet Laureate of the United States
Desmond Tutu Is Elected the Anglican Bishop of South Africa
Donald Pelotte of New Mexico Is the First American Indian Ordained as a Catholic Bishop

COMMENTARY

"We are saddened beyond comprehension by the unexpected explosion of the shuttle Challenger and the instant deaths of her crew of seven. Yes, the public had grown complacent with our space program. Quite unlike the days of Shepard and Glenn on the end of a roman candle, it was becoming routine. Now, this terrible, terrible tragedy!

"We must continue to remind ourselves that machines are not perfect and that our astronauts are, indeed, very brave and risk their lives each and every time they explore the heavens."

Bill Goodpage

1987 *Iran-Contra Scheme Exposed*

WORLD

US and USSR Agree to Reduce Intermediate Nuclear Weapons
Mikhail Gorbachev Demands Perestroika (reform) for USSR Economic Progress
Kuwait Asks for US Protection of Tankers as the Iran-Iraq War Continues
The US Frigate Stark Is Attacked by an Iraqi Warplane, Killing 37. Iraq Apologizes
US and Canada Agree to Eliminate All Tariffs Between the Two Largest Trading Partners

NATION

The Stock Market Plunges 508 Points on October 19, "Black Monday," Although the Nation Is
        Enjoying a Relatively Strong Economic Year
A Massive AIDS Quilt Is Unfurled in Washington to Draw Attention To the Growing Epidemic
Lt. Col. Oliver North Testifies That Money from Arms Sales to Iran Was Used to Fund
        Secret Central American Military Operations
Iran-Contra Report Says the President Bears "Ultimate Responsibility" for Actions of Aides
Supreme Court Rules That Rotary Clubs Must Admit Women. Lion's Club and Kiwanis Follow

ENVIRONMENT, SAFETY AND HEALTH

President Reagan Declares AIDS as Public Health Enemy Number One
The Last Known Wild California Condor Is Trapped and Taken to a Zoo in an
        Attempt to Save the Species
Worst Forest Fire Ever Burns 18 Million Timber Acres in China and USSR
The Montreal Protocol, a Treaty Designed to Save the Earth's Ozone Layer,
        Is Signed by 24 Nations
Considered Dangerous, 3-Wheel All Terrain Vehicles (ATV), Are Withdrawn

DISASTER

A Northwest Airlines Jet Crashes on Takeoff in Detroit, Killing 156 of 157 on Board. One
        Four-Year Old Girl Survives

LIFESTYLE

Oat Bran Is the Latest Craze for Dieting and Cholesterol Reduction

SCIENCE AND TECHNOLOGY

The Drug, Azidothymidine (AZT) Is Approved to Treat AIDS Victims

BUSINESS AND INDUSTRY

Texaco Files for the Largest Bankruptcy Ever
Chrysler Corporation Acquires American Motors Corporation
The Teamsters Union Is Voted Back into the AFL-CIO after 30 Years
The Dow Jones Industrial Average Breaks 2,000

CONSUMER PRODUCTS AND SERVICES

Microwave Ovens Are Hot Sellers. Companies Rush to Produce New Microwavable Food Products
Cherry 7UP
Kellogg's *Just Right* Cereal Has Raisins, Nuts and Dates for Health Conscious Appeal

"*Black Monday*" *on Wall Street* 1987

SPORTS

Tom Watson Wins a record $3,000,000 at Golf's Nabisco Championship in San Antonio
Don Mattingly Hits a Record Six Grand Slam Home Runs in One Season

ARTS AND MEDIA

STAGE	*Les Miserables*	
	Into the Woods	Stephen Sondheim, Joanna Gleason, Bernadette Peters
	Fences	James Earl Jones, Mary Alice
	Driving Miss Daisy	Dana Ivey, Morgan Freeman
MOVIE	*The Last Emperor*	John Lone, Joan Chen
	Wall Street	Michael Douglas, Charlie Sheen, Darryl Hannah, Hal Holbrook, Martin Sheen
	Moonstruck	Cher, Olympia Dukakis, Nicholas Cage
	The Untouchables	Sean Connery, Kevin Costner
	Dirty Dancing	Jennifer Grey, Patrick Swaze
	Fatal Attraction	Michael Douglas, Glenn Close, Ann Archer
	The Big Chill	Meg Tilly, Jo Beth Williams, Mary Kay Place
	The Right Stuff	Sam Shepard, Scott Glenn, Ed Harris, Fred Ward, Dennis Quaid, Barbara Hershey
TV	*The Geraldo Rivera Show*	
	Jake and the Fat Man	William Conrad, Joe Penny
	Beauty and the Beast	Linda Hamilton, Ron Perlman
	Thirtysomething	Ken Olin, Mel Harris
	Married...With Children	Ed O' Neill, Katey Sagal
	Wiseguy	Ken Wahl, Steven Baur, Jonathan Banks
	Star Trek: Next Generation	Patrick Stewart, Jonathan Frakkes, LaVar Burton
BOOK	*Beloved*	Toni Morrison
	Bonfire of the Vanities	Tom Wolfe
	Trump: The Art of the Deal	Donald Trump

MUSIC

Somewhere Out There
Tunnel of Love
A Momentary Lapse of Reason
Tango in the Night

QUOTES

**"I've never yet met a man who could look after me. I don't
need a husband. What I need is a wife."**
Joan Collins

COMMENTARY

"We have just survived the largest single day stock market
drop in history. Of course many individuals have been hurt, but most
will recover financially. What is fascinating is that our economy is
now so strong and healthy, that even a stock correction of that
magnitude has little day-to-day effect"

"Miss Picky"
Irene English

1988   *Two Foreign Wars Finally End*

WORLD

Terrorist Bomb Explodes in Pan Am Flight 103 over Lockerbie, Scotland, Killing All 259
     on Board and 11 on the Ground
Soviet Troops Begin to Pull Out of Afghanistan, a War That Has Been Termed,
     the USSR's "Vietnam." (see 1979)
Polish Workers Strike, Demanding Return of the Outlawed Solidarity Organization
The Eight-Year Iran-Iraq War Ends in a Cease Fire Stalemate. Over a Million Are Dead

NATION

GOP Nominates George Bush for President and Dan Quayle for Vice President
Democrats Nominate Michael Dukakis; Lloyd Bentsen Jr. Is His Running Mate
George H. Bush Defeats Michael Dukakis for President

ENVIRONMENT, SAFETY AND HEALTH

US Ocean Dumping Ban Aimed at Industrial Waste and Sewage Sludge
Severe Drought Hurts US Crops and We Import Grain for the First Time

LIFESTYLE

US Surgeon General Reports that Nicotine Is an Addictive Drug
Network Television Viewing Drops Off from Traditional Levels; 53% of US Homes
     Now Have Cable Service and 56% Have a VCR
Smoking Is Now Prohibited on US Domestic Flights of Two Hours or Less

DISASTER

In the Tense Persian Gulf, an Iranian Passenger Jet Is Mistakenly Shot Down by the Cruiser
     Vincennes, which Was Battling Iranian Gunboats at the Time

SCIENCE AND TECHNOLOGY

NASA Scientists Warn That Global Warming Is Threatening Mankind
The B-2 Stealth Bomber Is Shown to Members of Congress and the Media

BUSINESS AND INDUSTRY

Savings and Loan Associations Across the Nation Collectively Lose Billions of Dollars
     Due to Poor Oversight, Bad Loans, Mismanagement and Outright Fraud
Businesses Must Now Inform Workers 60 Days in Advance of a Plant Closing
Phillip Morris Buys Kraft Foods for 13 Billion
Ted Turner Buys Most Old MGM Films and Starts Turner Network Television (TNT)

CONSUMER PRODUCTS AND SERVICES

IBM and Sears Launch *Prodigy*, an Online Service
Fanny Packs For Men and Women Are Very Popular with Casual Wear
The Last Playboy Club Closes (see 1960, 1972)

PRICES

First Class Postage $.25

Savings & Loans Go Belly Up   1988

SPORTS

Jack Nicklaus Is the First Professional Golfer to Win More Than 5 Million in Tournament Play
Chicago's Wrigley Field Is the Last Baseball Park to Install Lights for Night Games (see 1935)
Largest Sports Trade to Date: Ice Hockey Superstar, Wayne Gretzky, Goes to the Los
        Angeles Kings for 15 Million
Stefan Edberg (22) Takes Men's Singles at Wimbledon; Steffi Graf (19) Wins Tennis' Grand Slam

ARTS AND MEDIA

STAGE	*M. Butterfly*	John Lithgow, B.D. Wong, John Getz
	The Heidi Chronicles	John Allen, Peter Friedman, Boyd Gaines
	Rumors	Joyce Van Patten, Ken Howard
MOVIE	*Rain Man*	Dustin Hoffman, Tom Cruise
	The Accused	Jodie Foster, Kelly McGillis
	A Fish Called Wanda	Kevin Kline, Jamie Lee Curtis, John Cleese
	The Accidental Tourist	Geena Davis, William Hurt, Ed Begley Jr
	Mississippi Burning	Gene Hackman, Willem Dafoe
	Bull Durham	Susan Sarandon, Kevin Costner
	Who Framed Roger Rabbit?	Bob Hoskins, Christopher Lloyd, Joanna Cassiday
TV	*China Beach*	Dana Delaney, Nan Woods, Chloe Webb
	Empty Nest	Richard Mulligan, Kristy McNichol, Dinah Manoff
	Murphy Brown	Candace Bergen, Charles Kimbrough, Joe Regalbuto
	Roseanne	Rosanne Arnold, John Goodman, Ned Beatty
	The Wonder Years	Fred Savage, Jason Hervey, Olivia d'Abo
BOOK	*A Brief History of Time*	Stephen Hawking
	The Prince of Tides	Pat Conroy
	Presumed Innocent	Scott Turow
	The Satanic Verses	Salman Rushdie

MUSIC

Don't Worry, Be Happy
So Emotional
Sweet Child O' Mine
Roll With It

PEOPLE

Gen. Manuel Noriega Is Indicted in US Court for Bribery and Drug Trafficking. He Remains
        Safely Protected in Panama
Evangelist, Jimmie Swaggert, Is Defrocked by the Assembly of God Church for Immoral
        Behavior. He Will Return to Preaching within Months

QUOTES

"Read My Lips."
        Candidate George Bush Promising Not to Raise Taxes

INCIDENTALS AND TRIVIA

George Bush Is the First Sitting Vice President Elected President Since 1836

1989 *The "Evil Empire" Crumbles*

WORLD

Major Student Protests in China's Tiananmen Square Are Crushed by Government Troops
Reactions in Eastern European Countries Are Strong. Ethic Minorities Urge Freedom
Hungary Proclaims Itself a Democratic Republic and Plans Multi-Party Elections
Hungary Permits East German "Visitors" to Cross Freely into Austria. The Rush to the
      West Begins to Escalate
Lithuania, Estonia and Latvia Demand Autonomy. Poland Elects Non-Communists
The Berlin Wall Is Breached in November
At a December Summit, Bush and Gorbachev Agree That the Cold War Is Over

NATION

A Savings and Loan Bail Out Bill Is Approved
Legislation Passes to Compensate Interned Japanese Americans from WWII

ENVIRONMENT

The Exxon Valdez Grounding in Prince William Sound, Alaska, Spills 260,000 Barrels of Oil,
      Causing Major Environmental Damage
Industrial Nations Agree to Stop CFC Production by the Year 2000

DISASTER

San Francisco Earthquake (7.1 Richter) Kills 62 People and Causes Six Billion in Damages.

LIFESTYLE

Rap Music, Born From Earlier Hip Hop, Begins to Go Mainstream
Smoking Is Now Banned on Almost All US Domestic Flights Regardless of Length
US Worker's Minimum Wage Is $3.35

SCIENCE AND TECHNOLOGY

Voyager 2 Space Probe Flies Past Uranus; Discovers Ten Moons
Voyager 2 Space Probe Flies Past Neptune, Finding Rings and Moons
US Launches the First Satellite in the Global Positioning System (GPS)
The Text-Only Internet or World Wide Web (www) Is Created
The First US Liver Transplant Operation Using a Live Donor

BUSINESS AND INDUSTRY

America Online (AOL) Is Born
Sony Corporation Buys Columbia Pictures
Ford Acquires Jaguar Motors for 2.5 Billion
General Motors Gains Half Interest in Sweden's Saab Motors
Donald Trump Acquires Eastern Airlines' Shuttle and Names It, Trump Shuttle

CONSUMER PRODUCTS AND SERVICES

Importer Malcolm Bricklin Sells the East European YUGO for $3,995, But Not for Long
After Several Years of Relatively Cheap Gasoline, Larger Cars Have Made a Comeback, But
      The Smaller Japanese Hondas, Toyotas and Nissans Are Much in Demand
Consumers Agree That American Auto Assembly Quality Is Much Poorer Than Equivalent
      Japanese Models

Valdez Oil Spill Creates Havoc

1989

SPORTS

Pete Rose Is Banned from Baseball for Gambling

ARTS AND MEDIA

STAGE   *Miss Saigon*
            Grand Hotel
            City of Angels
            Love Letters   Jason Robards, Colleen Dewhurst, Swoozie Kurtz
            A Few Good Men   Tom Hulce, Roxanne Hart

MOVIE   *Driving Miss Daisy*   Jessica Tandy, Morgan Freeman, Dan Ackroyd
            Born on the Fourth of July   Oliver Stone, Tom Cruise, Willem Dafoe
            My Left Foot   Daniel Day-Lewis, Brenda Frickler
            Glory   Denzel Washington, Matthew Broderick
            Field of Dreams   Kevin Costner, Amy Madigan James Earl Jones
            Parenthood   Steve Martin, Mary Steenburgen
            Batman   Michael Keaton, Kim Basinger, Jack Nicholson,
                                        Pat Hingle, Billie Dee Williams

TV   *Baywatch*   David Hasselhoff, Pamela Anderson, Susan Anton
            Alien Nation   Gary Graham, Eric Pierpoint, Michelle Scarabelli
            Doogie Howser, M.D.   Neil Harris, James B. Sikking, Belinda Montgomery
            Major Dad   Gerald McRaney, Shanna Reed
            Quantum Leap   Scott Bakula, Dean Stockwell
            Rescue:911   Host: William Shatner

BOOK   *The Joy Luck Club*   Amy Tan
            All I Really Need to Know, I
                  Learned in Kindergarten   Robert Fulghum

MUSIC

Don't Be Cruel
Girl You Know It's True
Fool Hearted
Hangin' Tough

PEOPLE

Television Evangelist, Pat Robertson, Founds the Activist Christian Coalition
Architect, I.M. Pei, Designed the New Glass and Metal Pyramid Entrance to Paris' Louvre Museum

COMMENTARY

"'Will the Cold War ever end?' we had asked ourselves countless times over the years. It had gone on for so long that many younger Americans could not remember a time without it. Surely it would end, but maybe not in our lifetime, and certainly not in this century.

"Suddenly, Communism as a political system began to crumble before our very eyes—in what just seemed like a few months! The Soviet Union, in deep economic trouble at home was encouraging its satellite states to go off on their own."

Kate Hawthorne

1990 *The Two Germanys Reunite*

WORLD

Lithuania Votes to Break Away from the USSR and Establish a Republic

Iraq Invades Kuwait, Taking Control of the Oil-Rich Emirate

Iraqi Pipelines Are Shut Down in Turkey and Saudi Arabia as the World Boycotts Iraqi Oil

The Two Germanys Reunite After 45 Years of Political Separation

Gorbachev Comes Under Heavy Political Attack as Soviet Citizens Cope with Shortages

The Fifteen Year Old Civil War in Lebanon Ends

NATION

US Population Now 248.7 Million

National Debt Is $3,233 Billion

An Eight-Year Boom Economy Ends as the US Goes into a Recession

The President Reverses His Stand and a Tax Increase Bill Passes

The Americans with Disabilities Act Is Passed

Dr. Antonia Novello Becomes Surgeon General; First Woman and Hispanic

ENVIRONMENT, SAFETY AND HEALTH

Forty Five Nations Agree to Prohibit Dumping Industrial Waste at Sea

Ellis Island Reopens as a Museum, Rebuilt with Private Funds

LIFESTYLE

2.1 Million US Farms (1.9%) of Population

US Population Is Now 249 Million. 12.5% Over Age 65

Fourteen Million Americans Attend College, 80% at Public Universities Where Tuition
Averages $2,000 Per Year. Top Universities Such as Stanford Charge $14,000

One in Five Americans Now Has a College Degree (see 1940, 1947, 1956)

SCIENCE AND TECHNOLOGY

The Hubble Space Telescope Is Launched But Has Technical Problems

Magellen Space Probe Orbits Venus on a Mapping Mission

BUSINESS AND INDUSTRY

McDonalds Opens Its First Restaurant in Russia

Boeing 747 (VC-25A), Modified as Air Force One, Is a Flying White House Command Center;
Carries 70 Passengers and a Crew of 26

Trintex (see 1984) becomes Prodigy Services

General Motors Introduces the Saturn, Plastic Bodied Automobile, with a No-Haggle Sales Price

Wal-Mart Stores Now Number Over 1,500 (see 1962, 1991)

CONSUMER PRODUCTS AND SERVICES

Microsoft Introduces Windows 3, a Graphical Interface Operating System Designed to
Compete with Macintosh. It Sells 30 Million Copies This Year, But Is Berated by the
Public for Its Frequent "Crashes"

Iraq Invades Kuwait 1990

SPORTS

Jose Canseco of Oakland Is Baseball's Best Paid Player at 23.5 Million over Five Years
23 Baseball Players Now Make over $3,000,000 Per Year
Hale Irwin Takes Golf's US Open Tournament
Gabriella Sabatini and Pete Sampras (19) Win US Open Women's and Men's Tennis Singles

ARTS AND MEDIA

STAGE	*Six Degrees of Separation*	James McDaniel, Stockard Channing
	Prelude to a Kiss	Tim Hutton, Marion Parker, Barnard Hughes
MOVIE	*Dances With Wolves*	Kevin Costner, Mary McDonnell
	Reversal of Fortune	Jeremy Irons, Glenn Close, Ron Silver
	Misery	Kathy Bates, James Caan
	Goodfellas	Joe Pesci, Robert De Niro, Lorraine Bracco
	Ghost	Whoopi Goldberg, Demi Moore, Patrick Swayze
	Dick Tracy	Warren Beatty, Madonna, Glenne Headly
	Pretty Woman	Richard Gere, Julia Roberts, Ralph Bellamy
TV	*Twin Peaks*	Kyle MacLachlan, Michael Ontkean, Joan Chen, Piper Laurie
	Wings	Timothy Daly, Steven Weber, Crystal Bernard
	The Flash	John Wesley Shipp, Amanda Pays, Alex Desert
	Get a Life	Chris Elliot, Bob Elliot, Elinor Donihue
	Fresh Prince of Bel Air	Will Smith, James Avery, Janet Hubert-Whitten
	Seinfeld	Jerry Seinfeld, Julia Lewis-Dreyfuss, Jason Alexander, Michael Richards
BOOK	*Burden of Proof*	Scott Turow
	Rabbit at Rest	John Updike
	Hollywood	Gore Vidal
	Life on the Road	Charles Kuralt

MUSIC

Time's Up
World Clique
Listen Without Prejudice
Sooner or Later

PEOPLE

Manuel Noriega Gives Himself Up and Is Flown to the US to Face Drug Charges
South African Activist, Nelson Mandella, Is Freed After 27 Years in Captivity
Soviet Premier Mikhail S. Gorbachev Is Awarded the Nobel Peace Prize
David Dinkins Is Elected as New York City's First Black Mayor
Imelda Marcos Is Acquitted of Four Counts of Racketeering and Fraud. Husband Ferdinand
      Did Not Stand Trial and Died in 1989

QUOTES

"Sometimes you can tell a large story with a tiny subject."
      Eliot Porter, US Photographer (1901-1990)

1991 *The USSR Ceases to Exist*

WORLD

US and Allies Begin Intensified Air War on Iraq In January
Desert Storm: 100-Hour Offensive Against Iraq Ends on February 28 with Kuwait Freed
With the Active Support of Boris Yeltsin, USSR President Mikhail Gorbachev Overcomes a
    Hard-Line Coup Attempt
The Soviet Union Ends as Russia and Two Republics Form a New Commonwealth
Mikhail Gorbachev Resigns as the Last Soviet Leader
US Recognizes Independent Republics of the Old USSR
Armed Conflicts Break Out Among Serbs, Croats and Bosnians in the Old Yugoslavia
Boris Yeltsin Becomes First Elected President of the Russian Republic

NATION

President Bush Lifts South Africa Economic Sanctions, Citing Its "Profound Transformation"
    Toward Racial Equality
Thurgood Marshall Resigns from the US Supreme Court
Clarence Thomas Is Narrowly Confirmed to the Supreme Court After Bitter Hearings in
    Which Thomas Is Accused of Sexual Harassment by Anita Hill

ENVIRONMENT, SAFETY AND HEALTH

Iraq Dumps a Million Gallons of Oil from Occupied Kuwait into Persian Gulf
Hundreds of Oil Well Fires Are Set by Retreating Iraqis

LIFESTYLE

The Federal Minimum Hourly Wage Is $4.25
Red Cross Announces Measures Aimed at Better Screening of Blood for the AIDS Virus
Registration of Domestic Partnerships Begins in San Francisco. The Law Has No Legal Rights
National Poll Says 61% of Women Claim Sexual Harassment at Work, But Only 4% Complain

DISASTER

The Death Toll from AIDS in the US Is over 100,000 and Expected to Double
The Worst Fire in California History near Oakland Takes 23 Lives and Consumes 2,777 Homes

SCIENCE AND TECHNOLOGY

Prototype Digital High-Definition Television Is Demonstrated
Biosphere 2 in Oracle, AZ, Is Sealed With Eight People for a Planned Two Year Stay

BUSINESS AND INDUSTRY

The Dow Jones Industrial Average Breaks 3,000
AT&T Acquires NCR Corporation for 7.4 Billion to Solidify Its Position in Computers
Eastern Airlines and Pan America Airways Cease Operations
Wal-Mart Replaces Sears as the Nation's Largest Retailer in Gross Sales (see 1962, 1990)

CONSUMER PRODUCTS AND SERVICES

Home Shopping Network Begins Broadcasting 24 Hour Shopping Programs
Microwave Cake Mixes Appear
McDonalds Introduces the McLean Deluxe, a Low Fat Hamburger. The Public Doesn't Bite
Starbucks, Started in Seattle, Is Creating a New Coffee Culture

Desert Storm: Short & Successful   1991

PRICES

First Class Postage	$.29
Bread	.70 Per Pound
Dozen Eggs	1.10
Ground Beef	1.65 Per Pound

SPORTS

Earven "Magic" Johnson Retires from the NBA Los Angeles Lakers Because He Is Infected with the HIV Virus.

Bobby Bonilla of the NY Mets Signs for $29 Million over 5 Years

Six Baseball Players Are Now Paid over $5,000,000 Per Year

Payne Stewart Wins Golf's US Open Championship

Baseball Hall of Fame Directors Vote to Exclude Anyone Who Has Been Banned from the Game

ARTS AND MEDIA

STAGE	Lost in Yonkers	Neil Simon
	The Will Rogers Follies	Keith Carradine
	The Secret Garden	Daisy Eagen, Mandy Patinkin

MOVIE	The Silence of the Lambs	Jodie Foster, Anthony Hopkins
	JFK	Kevin Costner, Sissy Spacek
	City Slickers	Jack Palance, Billy Crystal, Helen Slater
	The Fisher King	Mercedes Ruehl, Robin Williams
	Bugsy	Warren Beatty, Annette Bening
	Thelma and Louise	Geena Davis, Susan Sarandan
	Beauty and the Beast	(animated)

TV	Evening Shade	Burt Reynolds, Marilou Henner
	Home Improvement	Tim Allen, Patricia Richardson
	The Commish	Michael Chiklis, Theresa Saldana
	Sisters	Swoozie Kurtz, Sela Ward, Patricia Kalember
	Beverly Hills 90210	Shannen Doherty, Jason Priestley, Tori Spelling
	Nurses	Stephanie Hodge, Mary Jo Keenen

BOOK	The Work of Nations	Robert Reich
	The Promised Land	Nicholas Lemann
	St. Maybe	Anne Tyler
	Brotherly Love	Peter Dexter

PEOPLE

Reagan Library Dedication Features a Record Gathering of Five Chief Executives (Nixon, Ford, Carter, Reagan, Bush)

Queen Elizabeth II Becomes First English Monarch to Address US Congress

Sharon Pratt Dixon Is the First Black Female Mayor of Washington, D.C.

REFLECTION

The Cost of Operation Desert Storm in US Service Personnel:

Died	293
Injured	467

1992 *Bill Clinton Is Elected*

WORLD

Communist Control Collapses in Afghanistan. Islamic Forces Take Kabul
President Bush and Russia's Boris Yeltsin Agree to Slash Long Range Nuclear Arsenals
     by Two Thirds
F.W. de Klerk and Nelson Mandella Agree to Establish an Interim Government in South Africa
Representatives of Canada, Mexico and the US Approve the Basics of the North American
     Free Trade Agreement (NAFTA)
US Maintains Sanctions on Iraq, Including Limited Oil Sales and No-Fly Areas
Price Controls Are Eliminated in Russia, Resulting in Huge Price Increases for Food

NATION

Democrats Nominate Gov. Bill Clinton of Arkansas and Sen. Albert Gore of Tennessee for VP
Republicans Nominate Pres. George Bush and Vice President Dan Quayle to Run Again
Democrat William Clinton Defeats Presidential Incumbent George Bush
303 Present and Former Lawmakers Are Overdrawn on Their House Banking Accounts

ENVIRONMENT, SAFETY AND HEALTH

Earth Summit Treaties Pledge to Increase the Diversity of Animal and Plant Species and to
     Halt Global Warming
The FDA Sharply Restricts the Use of Silicone Gel Breast Implants

DISASTER

Hurricane Andrew Lashes Florida, Louisiana and the Bahamas Causing 55 Deaths and
     Record Property Damage
Los Angeles Riots Claim 54 Lives and a Billion in Damages after Acquittal of Police
     Officers in the Rodney King Beating

LIFESTYLE

Smoking Among Adults Has Dropped Dramatically to About 26 Percent
Drab Colors and "Washed Out" Fabric Looks Are All in Vogue

SCIENCE AND TECHNOLOGY

Remains of a Whale That Walked on Land Are Discovered in Pakistan
Space Shuttle Endeavour Completes Its Maiden Voyage
A 5,700 Pound Mars Observer Is Launched to Map the Planet and Study Its History
Mosaic, a Graphical Browser System, Improves the Text-Only Internet

BUSINESS AND INDUSTRY

The Mall of America, Largest Mall Ever, Opens in Bloomington, Minnesota
Lloyds of London Announces Losses of Millions of Dollars

CONSUMER PRODUCTS AND SERVICES

Chrysler Offers a Limited Production High Performance Sports Car, the VIPER
"Clear" and "Additive Free" Products Are Much in Demand
Nicotinell, Is a Patch You Wear to Reduce the Craving for Cigarettes

Hurricane Andrew Takes Its Toll   1992

SPORTS

Toronto A.L. Defeats Atlanta N.L. in World Series, First Non-US Team to Win
US Basketball "Dream Team" Gets the Gold at the Barcelona Summer Olympics
George Brett of Kansas City Passes 3,000 Career Hits
Fred Couples Wins Golf's Masters Tournament

ARTS AND MEDIA

STAGE	*Crazy For You*	Glenn Close, Judd Hirsch
	Oleanna	David Mamet
	Six Degrees of Separation	John Guare
MOVIE	*Unforgiven*	Clint Eastwood, Gene Hackman
	Scent of a Woman	Al Pacino, Chris O'Donnell
	Howards End	Emma Thompson, Anthony Hopkins, Vanessa Redgrave
	My Cousin Vinny	Marisa Tomei, Ralph Macchio, Joe Pesci
	A River Runs Through It	Robert Redford, Brad Pitt, Tom Skerritt
	Hoffa	Jack Nicholson, Danny DeVito
	Chaplin	Robert Downey Jr., Geraldine Chaplin
	Batman Returns	Michael Keaton, Michelle Pfeiffer, Danny DeVito
TV	*Love and War*	Jay Thomas, Susan Dey
	Mad About You	Paul Reiser, Helen Hunt
	Brooklyn Bridge	Danny Gerard, Marion Ross
	Delta	Delta Burke, Gigi Rice, Earl Holliman
	Civil Wars	Mariel Hemingway, Peter Onorati, Debi Mazar
	Picket Fences	Tom Skerritt, Kathy Baker, Ray Walston
	The Larry Sanders Show	Gary Shandling, Rip Torn
	Melrose Place	Grant Show, Courtney Thorne-Smith
BOOK	*Earth in the Balance*	Al Gore
	United We Stand	H. Ross Perot
	Rising Sun	Michael Crichton
	Jazz	Toni Morrison
	Black Water	Joyce Carol Oates
	The Volcano Lover	Susan Sontag
	The English Patient	Michael Ondaatje

MUSIC

Tears in Heaven	Eric Clampton

PEOPLE

Manuel Noriega, Is Convicted in Miami of Drug and Racketeering Charges
Space Shuttle Endeavour Carries Mae Jemison, First Black Woman in Space; Mamoru
    Mohri, First Japanese National, and Married Couple Mark Lee and Jan Davis
Carol Moseley-Braun of Illinois Is the First Black Woman Elected to the Senate
Arthur Ashe, Black Tennis Champion, Announces That He Has Contracted AIDS

QUOTES

**"...the memories and the mouths of the ancient elders was the only way that early
histories of mankind got passed along...for all of us today to know who we are."**
Alex Haley (1921-1992)

1993 *The Economy Begins to Improve*

WORLD

The European Economic Community (EEC) Is Born. With Some Restrictions, Goods and
Services Can Move Freely Across Country Borders
Czechoslovakia Divides into the Czech Republic and the Republic of Slovakia
Israel and the Palestinians Come to Terms on an Accord for Limited
Palestinian Autonomy (see People)
Israel and the Vatican Agree to Recognize One Another
North Korea Withdraws from the Nuclear Non-Proliferation Treaty
The Warsaw Pact Ends. Russian Troops Withdraw from Poland and Cuba (see 1955)

NATION

Janet Reno Is Sworn in as First Female US Attorney General
Ruth Bader Ginsburg Is Sworn in as an Associate Justice of the US Supreme Court
The EPA Concludes That "Second Hand Smoke" Causes Serious Respiratory Problems for
Infants and Small Children
The US Holocaust Memorial Museum Is Dedicated in Washington DC
Hawaii Supreme Court Rules That the Refusal to Allow Same Sex Marriages Is Unconstitutional

ENVIRONMENT, SAFETY AND HEALTH

AIDS Is the Leading Cause of Death for Men 25-44 in the United States

DISASTER

A Terrorist Bomb Blasts the World Trade Center in Lower Manhattan, Killing 5 and
Injuring Hundreds
A 51 Day Standoff Between the FBI and the Branch Davidian Cult Compound in Waco,
Texas, Ends in Fire and Mass Suicide

LIFESTYLE

Almost Half of US Workers Now Use a Computer at Work, Primarily for Word Processing
A New Wave of Grunge Music Pours Out. Torn Jeans and Combat Boots Are a Must

SCIENCE AND TECHNOLOGY

Crew of Space Shuttle Endeavor Repairs the Hubble Telescope Main Lens
French Geneticists Develop a Map of Human Chromosomes
Patricia Bianconi Produces a Diamond from a Polyacetylene Plastic
Huntington's Disease Gene Is Discovered
Alzheimer's Disease Gene Is Discovered; One in Thirty May Carry the Mutation
The US Global Positioning System Is Completed, Using 24 Navstar Satellites. Can Locate
Anyone, Anywhere in the World within 300 Feet

BUSINESS AND INDUSTRY

Intel Corporation Begins Shipping the Pentium Chip
Microsoft Introduces Windows 3.1, to Fix the Many "Bugs" in Version 3.0

CONSUMER PRODUCTS AND SERVICES

Theme Restaurants Like *Planet Hollywood* and the *Hard Rock Café* Are Very Popular
The Apple Newton MessagePad Converts Your Handwriting to Text, But Not Very Well

SPORTS

The National Baseball League Adds the Denver Rockies and the Florida Marlins
With 325 Wins, Miami Dolphins Coach Don Shula Becomes Football's Winningest Coach,
Exceeding the Legendary George Halas

ARTS AND MEDIA

STAGE	*Moonlight*	Harold Pinter
	Arcadia	Tom Stoppard
MOVIE	*Schlindler's List*	Steven Speilberg, Liam Neeson, Ben Kingsley, Ralph Fiennes
	Philadelphia	Tom Hanks, Denzel Washington
	The Piano	Holly Hunter , Anna Paquin
	The Fugitive	Tommy Lee Jones , Harrison Ford
	Dave	Kevin Kline, Sigourney Weaver, Frank Langella
	Jurrasic Park	Sam Neill, Laura Dern, Jeff Goldblum, Richard Attenborough
	Shadowlands	Debra Winger, Anthony Hopkins
	Indecent Proposal	Robert Redford, Woody Harrelson, Demi Moore
TV	*Lois and Clark*	Dean Cain, Teri Hatcher
	SeaQuest DSV	Roy Scheider, Stephanie Beacham, Don Franklin
	Dave's World	Harry Anderson, DeLane Matthews
	The Nanny	Fran Drescher, Charles Shaughnessey, Daniel Davis
	Dr. Quinn, Medicine Woman	Jane Seymour, Joe Lando, Orson Bean
	The X-Files	David Duchovney, Gilian Anderson
	Diagnosis Murder	Dick Van Dyke, Scott Baio, Victoria Powell
	Frazier	Kelsey Grammer, David Hyde Pierce, John Mahoney
	Day One (ABC News)	Forrest Whittaker
BOOK	*Beloved*	Toni Morrison
	The Pelican Brief	John Grisham
	Lincoln at Gettysberg	Garry Willis
	7 Habits of Very Effective People	Steven R. Covey
	The Bridges of Madison County	Robert Waller

PEOPLE

Israeli Prime Minister, Yitzhak Rabin, and PLO Chairman, Yasser Arafat, Shake Hands in
an Historic White House Scene (see World)
Michael Jackson Appears on the Oprah Winfrey Show, His First Interview in 14 Years

QUOTES

**"Palestinians—we say to you today, in a loud and a clear voice:
enough of blood and tears. Enough."**
Yitzhak Rabin (1922-1995)

COMMENTARY

"This just may be a good decade, maybe a memorable one.
The Cold War is over and the US stands unchallenged as the leading
world power. We built a coalition in 1990 to stop a regional despot
with little loss of American life. The recession is rapidly waning and it
looks like good times are ahead. Is this the good life we're always
talking about. I certainly hope so, but knock on wood!"

Hank Hawthorne

WORLD

Israeli Prime Minister Yitzhak Rabin and Jordan's King Hussein Sign a Declaration Ending
   Their 46 Year-Old State of War
Unable to Verify the Status of North Korea's Nuclear Program, US Seeks Economic Sanctions
The North American Free Trade Agreement (NAFTA) Is Now Effective
NATO Develops a "Partnership for Peace" Program to Involve Former Members of the Warsaw Pact
Russian Troops Finally Withdraw from Latvia and Estonia
The Last Russian Troops Leave Poland as US, British and French Troops Quit Berlin
US Troops Landing in Haiti to Overthrow the Military Junta There Find No Resistance
AIDS Cases World-Wide Now Exceed One Million

NATION

The National Debt Is $4,644 Billion
Former President Reagan Writes a Letter Disclosing That He Has Alzheimer's Disease
Bill and Hillary Clinton Testify under Oath About Their Involvement in the Whitewater Scandal
The President's Health Care Reform Plan Collapses from Congressional Resistance
Estimates Say 4 Million Undocumented Aliens Are Now Entering the US Each Year, with Half
   of the Total in California

ENVIRONMENT, SAFETY AND HEALTH

American Bald Eagle Status Is Upgraded from "Endangered" to "Threatened"

DISASTER

A Major Earthquake in Southern California Kills 57 People

LIFESTYLE

Piercing Noses, Tongues, Lips, Navels and Even Nipples Is "Hot" with the Younger Set
Backpacks Are Now Commonplace for Almost All Occasions. "Fanny Packs" Are Popular Too
Median Household Income Is $32,200

SCIENCE AND TECHNOLOGY

Fragments of Comet Shoemaker-Levy 9 Bombard Jupiter Creating Fireballs and Storms
   the Size of Earth
The Hubble Telescope Sends Back Photos of Galaxies in Their Infancy
The Oldest Yet Discovered Ancestor of Man, 4.4 Million Years, Is Found in Ethiopia
S.R. Woodard Extracts DNA from 80 Million Year Old Dinosaur Bones
Artificial Blood Transfusions Are Tested Using Genetically Engineered Hemoglobin
The Eurotunnel (Chunnel) Beneath the English Channel Opens

BUSINESS AND INDUSTRY

The Boeing 777 Makes Its First Flight

CONSUMER PRODUCTS AND SERVICES

Beanie Babies Appear
Fast Food Promotional Toy-Movie Tie-Ins Drive Parents Crazy

Reagan Discloses an Illness 1994

SPORTS

No Baseball World Series. 232 Day Work Stoppage Over Pay Forces Cancellation. Fans Are Irate and Say They'll Boycott the Ballparks Next Year

Tiger Woods (18) Is the Youngest Player to Win Golf's Amateur Championship

ARTS AND MEDIA

STAGE	*Three Tall Women*	Edward Albee
MOVIE	*Forest Gump*	Tom Hanks, Sally Field, Gary Sinese
	Blue Sky	Jessica Lange, Powers Boothe
	Ed Wood	Martin Landau, Johnny Depp
	Bullets Over Broadway	Dianne Wiest, John Cusack, Jennifer Tilly
	Legends of the Fall	Brad Pitt, Anthony Hopkins, Aidan Quinn
	Braveheart	Mel Gibson, Sophie Marceau, Patrick McGoohan
	Speed	Sandra Bullock, Keanu Reeves, Dennis Hopper
	Pulp Fiction	John Travolta, Samuel L. Jackson, Uma Thurman
	The Lion King (animated)	Disney Studios
TV	*Ellen*	Ellen DeGeneres, Holly Fulger, Maggie Wheeler
	Grace Under Fire	Brett Butler, Dave Thomas
	M.A.N.T.I.S.	Carl Lumbly, Roger Rees
	N.Y.P.D. Blue	David Caruso, Dennis Franz
	Party of Five	Matthew Fox, Scott Wolf
	Me and the Boys	Steve Harvey, Madge Sinclair
	My So-Called Life	Bess Armstrong, Tom Irwin
	Turning Point	Barbara Walters, Diane Sawyer
BOOK	*Theory of War*	Joan Brady
	Remember Babylon	David Malouf
	The Downing Street Years	Margaret Thatcher
	Truman	David McCullough

PEOPLE

Heather Whitestone of Atlanta Becomes the First Deaf Woman to Be Crowned "Miss America"

Paula Jones Files a Sexual Abuse Case Against Bill Clinton—While He Was Governor of Arkansas

CRIME AND PUNISHMENT

O. J. Simpson Is Accused of the Stabbing Murders of His Former Wife, Nicole Brown Simpson, and Her Friend Ronald Goldman

Lorena Bobbitt of Virginia Is Cleared of Maliciously Wounding Her Husband When She Cut Off His Penis Last Year. The Court Accepted Her Plea of Temporary Insanity

QUOTES

"The children have been a wonderful gift to me, and I'm thankful to have once again seen our world through their eyes. They restore my faith in the family's future."

Jacqueline Kennedy Onassis (1929-1994)

"The one sure thing about politics is that what goes up comes down and what goes down often comes up."

Richard M. Nixon (1913-1994)

1995 *GOP Takes Control of Congress*

WORLD

The Japanese Parliament Offers a Resolution of Regret over World War II Atrocities, But
    Many Around the World Criticize It as Falling Short of an Apology
Tutsi and Hutu's Continue Tribal Massacres in Burundi
Fighting Continues in Bosnia. Cease Fires Are Agreed upon and Broken within Days
Irish Sinn Fein Party Leader, Gerry Adams, Is Allowed to Raise Funds in the US
Russian Troops Battle the Breakaway Chechnyan Forces

NATION

US Authorizes a $40 Billion Loan to Mexico to Stabilize the Falling Peso
US Announces Intent to Resume Full Diplomatic Relations with Vietnam
Newt Gingrich, First Republican House Speaker Since 1955, Proposes a 100 Day Legislation
    Drive Called, *Contract with America*. Most Legislation Passes
Federal Highway Speed Limits Are Abolished (see 1974)
A Senate Panel Begins Hearings on the Whitewater Corporation Financial Dealings
President Clinton Announces That the FDA Plans to Regulate Tobacco Sales
The "Million Man March" of Black Men Led by Louis Farrakhan Gathers in Washington, DC
Many Government Offices Are Temporarily Closed as Republicans and Democrats Clash
    over Budget Issues

LIFESTYLE

One Quarter of U.S. Households Now Own a Personal Computer (See 1999)
11% of US Households Have Internet Access
46.1 Million Americans Belong to HMO's Compared to 9.1 Million in 1980
23% of Americans over Age 25 Now Have a College Degree

DISASTER

A Terrorist Bomb Explodes at a Federal Building in Oklahoma City, Killing 169
    (including 19 children) and Injuring over 400

SCIENCE AND TECHNOLOGY

30 Million Year Old Bacteria Spores in Bees Trapped in Amber Are Revived
Astronomers Discover Comet Hale-Bopp
Olestra Tastes and Acts Like Fat in Foods, But Has No Calories and Passes Through the
    Body Unabsorbed
Disney's *Toy Story* Is the First Full Length Movie That Is Entirely Computer Generated

BUSINESS AND INDUSTRY

The Walt Disney Company Acquires Capital Cities-ABC Inc.
The Dow Jones Industrial Average Breaks 4,000, Then 5,000

CONSUMER PRODUCTS AND SERVICES

Microsoft Introduces the Windows 95 Operating System
Microsoft Adds the Microsoft Network (MSN) to Windows 95
The Netscape Graphical Browser Is Introduced for Easy Web Surfing

Ripkin Is the New Iron Man 1995

SPORTS

Baltimore's Cal Ripkin Breaks Lou Gehrig's Record 2,130 Consecutive Baseball Game Record
Picabo Street Is the First US Skier to Win a World Cup Downhill Title
Dan Marino of the Dolphis Breaks Fran Tarkington's Passing Records in Attempts,
    Completions, Yardage and Touchdowns This Season

ARTS AND MEDIA

STAGE	*Break of Day*	Timberlake Wertenbaker
MOVIE	*The Bridges of Madison County*	Clint Eastwood, Meryl Streep
	Nixon	Anthony Hopkins, Joan Allen, Powers Boothe
	Waterworld	Kevin Costner, Jeanne Tripplehorn, Dennis Hopper
	Batman Forever	Val Kilmer, Nicole Kidman, Chris O'Donnell
	Goldeneye	Pierce Brosnan, Judi Dench
	The American President	Michael Douglas, Annette Bening
	Apollo 13	Ron Howard, Bill Paxton, Tom Hanks, Kevin Bacon
	Pocahontas (animated)	Disney Studios
TV	*Touched by an Angel*	Della Reese, Roma Downey
	Unhappily Ever After	Geoff Pierson, Stephanie Hodge
	Due South	Paul Gross, David Marciano
	Star Trek: Voyager	Kate Mulgrew, Robert Beltran
	Hercules	Kevin Sorbo, Michael Hurst, Elizabeth Hawthorne
BOOK	*Making the Connection*	Oprah Winfrey and Bob Green
	The Rainmaker	John Grisham
	Men Are From Mars, *Women Are From Venus*	John Gray
	Executive Orders	Tom Clancy

MUSIC

The Ghost of Tom Joad	Bruce Springsteen
Think Twice	Celine Dion
These Days	Bon Jovi

PEOPLE

Israeli Prime Minister, Yitzhak Rabin, Is Assassinated
Martha Stewart and Her Helpful Hints Seem to Be Everywhere
Michael Jackson Releases an Album, *HIStory—Past, Present and Future Book 1*
John F. Kennedy Jr. Starts Publishing *George* Magazine

CRIME AND PUNISHMENT

O. J. Simpson Is Found Not Guilty of Criminal Charges in the Stabbing Deaths of His
    Former Wife, Nicole Brown Simpson, and Her Friend Ronald Goldman

QUOTES

**"Celebrity distorts democracy by giving the rich, beautiful and famous, more
authority than they deserve."**
    Maureen Dowd (*New York Times* 1995)

1996 *Clinton Wins a Second Term*

WORLD

The PLO Annuls Clauses Calling for the Destruction of Israel
Yasser Arafat Is Elected President in the First General Palestinian Elections
Israel's Labor Party Abandons Its Opposition to a Palestinian State
Boris Yeltsin Receives a Vote of Confidence in Russian Elections
Japan Compensates 20,000 "Comfort Women" from WWII Occupied Countries Who Were
        Forced to be Concubines for Soldiers

NATION

Republicans Nominate Robert Dole of Kansas for President; Jack Kemp for Vice President
Robert Dole Gives Up His Senate Responsibilities to Devote Full Time to His Campaign
Democrats Re-nominate President Bill Clinton and Vice President Albert "Al" Gore
William Clinton Is Easily Re-elected President over Republican Robert Dole
Congress Passes a Sweeping Welfare Reform Bill
Clinton Signs Bill Ensuring Two Day Hospital Stays for New Mothers
Madeline Albright Is Named the First Female Secretary of State

DISASTER

ValuJet Flight 592 Crashes in Florida Swampland, Killing 110
TWA Flight 800 Explodes in Flight Minutes after Takeoff at JFK International Airport,
        Killing All 230 Aboard

LIFESTYLE

The Minimum Wage Is $4.75/Hour
"Soccer Moms," Suburban Women With Children Are Now a Major Political Voting Bloc

SCIENCE AND TECHNOLOGY

Triple Therapy Drug Cocktails Now Used in Treating AIDS
NASA Scientists Find Microscopic Life Forms in Mars Rocks

BUSINESS AND INDUSTRY

Boeing Corporation Buys the Defense Divisions of Rockwell International
The Dow Jones Industrial Average Breaks 6,000
Apple Computer Buys Next Software, Inc., and Next Owner Steve Jobs Returns as a
        Consultant to the Company He Founded (see 1976)

CONSUMER PRODUCTS AND SERVICES

Stretch Diapers for Babies
Baked Potato Chips
Self Rising Pizza Crust
Nicorette Gum Finds New Popularity as More Americans Try To Quit Smoking
MSNBC, a 24 Hour All-News Network Debuts on Cable and Internet
McDonald's Adult Taste, Arch Deluxe Hamburger, Flops in the Marketplace

PRICES

Average New Car	$21,750
McDonalds Big Mac Sandwich	$1. 95

Good Night, George.

SPORTS

Dan Marino of the Miami Dolphins Achieves a Career Record 50,000 Passing Yards
NFL Cleveland Browns Move to Baltimore Where They Are Renamed, the Ravens
After Winning the US Amateur Golf Championship for Three Consecutive Years,
    Tiger Woods Turns Professional

ARTS AND MEDIA

STAGE	*Rent*	Jonathan Larson
	Passion	Stephen Sondheim

MOVIE	*The English Patient*	Ralph Fiennes, Juliette Binoche
	Fargo	Frances MacDormand William H. Macy
	Shine	Geoffrey Rush, Lynn Redgrave
	Sling Blade	Billie Bob Thornton, J.T. Walsh
	Jerry Maguire	Tom Cruise, Cuba Gooding Jr., Renee Zellweger
	Independence Day	Will Smith, Bill Pullman, Jeff Goldblum, Mary McDonnell
	Dead Man Walking	Sean Penn, Susan Sarandon
	Mission Impossible	Tom Cruise, Kirsten Scott-Thomas, John Voight
	101 Dalmations	Glenn Close, Jeff Bridges
	Evita	Madonna, Antonio Bandaras, Jonathan Pryce
	Star Trek: First Contact	Patrick Stewart, Jonathon Frakkes, James Cromwell, A. Krige

TV	*3rd. Rock From the Sun*	John Lithgow, Jane Curtin, Kirsten Johnson
	Buffy, The Vampire Slayer	Sarah Michelle Geller

BOOK	*The Tailor of Panama*	John Le Carre
	Hitler's Willing Executioners	Daniel Goldhagen

MUSIC

Spice	The Spice Girls
Falling Into You	Celine Dion
Road Tested	Bonnie Raitt
Children	Robert Miles

PEOPLE

Female Astronaut Shannon Lucid Begins a Five Month Stay on the MIR Spacecraft
Russian Chess Master, Gary Kasparov, Beats IBM's Deep Blue Computer, the First
    Computer to Challenge a Chess Champion (see 1997)
Angela Lansbury Does the Last, *Murder, She Wrote* TV Show. Started in 1984, It Is the
    Longest Running Detective Show at 264 Episodes

CRIME AND PUNISHMENT

Dr. Jack Kervorkian Is Acquitted of Assisted-Suicide Charges
Theodore Kaczynski, the Alleged "Unabomber" Is Found and Arrested in a One Room
    Cabin in Remote Montana

QUOTES

**"Too bad that all the people who know how to run the country are busy driving
taxicabs and cutting hair."**
    George Burns (1896-1996)

1997 Hong Kong Reverts to Chinese Rule

WORLD

Long Negotiations Transfer Control of Hebron from Israel to Palestine
China Regains Sovereignty over Hong Kong after 156 Years of British Colonial Rule

NATION

A Memorial to Franklin D. Roosevelt Is Dedicated in Washington D.C.
Congress Passes a Historic Budget Balancing and Tax Cut Bill
President Clinton Makes Use of the New Line Item Veto Provision
The Virginia Military Institute Goes Coed
The Million Woman March in Philadelphia Draws 1.5 Million, Protesting Blacks as Victims

DISASTER

Mass Suicide of 39 Heaven's Gate Cult Members North of San Diego Is Tied to the Proximity
of the Hale Bopp Comet and Afterlife

LIFESTYLE

The Fen/Phen Fad Diet Ends. Doctors Find That This Combo Can Cause Heart Damage
The Government Can Now Regulate Tobacco as a Drug
40 States Reach Agreement with Tobacco Companies on Advertising and Sale of Cigarettes
Alternative Medicine Such as Acupuncture and Herbal Treatments Have Gone Mainstream
Personal Computers Are Now in 40% of US Homes
Health Maintenance Organizations (HMOs) Now Cover 75% of Privately Insured Americans
US Worker's Minimum Wage Is $5.15

SCIENCE AND TECHNOLOGY

Dolly, a Sheep, Is Cloned from a Single Cell
The Hale-Bopp Comet Is Visible to the Naked Eye Longer Than Any Other Comet
The FDA Approves a Virtually Painless Dental Laser to Treat Tooth Decay
An IBM Deep Blue Computer Beats World Chess Champion, Garry Kasparov (see 1996)
Pathfinder Spacecraft Lands on Mars and Returns Detailed Photos from Its Rover Module
Andy Greene in Jet Powered Thrust SSC Breaks the Sound Barrier on Land and Sets a
Speed Record of 763 mph on the Nevada Desert (see 1947)

BUSINESS AND INDUSTRY

Boeing Corporation Buys Rival McDonnell Douglas
Lockheed Martin Corporation Buys Aerospace Rival, Northrop Grumman
The Dow Jones Industrial Average Breaks 7,000, Then 8,000
Toyota's Corolla Passes the Volkswagon Beetle as the Best Selling Auto of All Time
America On Line Acquires Rival Compuserve
Woolworth's Five-and-Dime Stores Close
Television Networks Agree to Voluntary Content-Based Program Ratings

CONSUMER PRODUCTS AND SERVICES

R.J Reynolds Drops the Joe Camel Cigarette Ad Campaign after 9 Years
Flat Panel LCD Computer Monitors Debut
Pocket Sized Electronic (virtual) Pets Require Daily Attention to Function
Digital Cameras That Shoot Pixels Instead of Film Compete Strongly with 35mm Cameras
Amazon.com Sells Books on the Internet

If It's Electronic, I Want It! 1997

SPORTS

Tiger Woods (21) Wins Masters Golf Tournament with Record 18 Under 270
Jackie Robinson's #42 Is Retired from the Majors in a 50 Year Tribute to First Black Player
Susie Maroney Becomes the First Woman to Swim 118 Miles from Cuba to the Florida Keys
Evander Holyfield Retains the Heavyweight Boxing Crown as Mike Tyson Is Disqualified for Biting
      Him Twice, Once on Each Ear
Robert Parrish (44) Retires After Playing a Record 1,611 Pro Basketball Games Over 21 Years

ARTS AND MEDIA

| STAGE | *The Lion King* | |
| | *Lord of the Dance* | Michael Flatley |

MOVIE	*Titanic*	James Cameron, Leonardo diCaprio, Kate Winslett
	As Good As It Gets	Jack Nicholson, Helen Hunt, Greg Kinnear, Cuba Gooding Jr.
	The Lost World	Jeff Goldblum, Julianne Moore, Richard Attenborough
	Air Force One	Harrison Ford, Gary Oldman, Glenn Close
	Contact	Jodie Foster, Matthew McConaughey, Tom Skerritt
	My Best Friend's Wedding	Julia Roberts, Cameron Diaz, Dermot Mulroney

MUSIC

Diana, Princess of Wales—Tribute	(Various Artists)
Candle in the Wind '97	Elton John
Time Out of Mind	Bob Dylan

PEOPLE

Princess Diana of Wales (36) the "People's Princess," Is Killed in a Paris Auto Accident
Paul McCartney of Beatles Fame Is Knighted for His Services to Music
Linda Finch Completes the Amelia Earhart Journey of 1937 in a Similar Lockheed Electra 10-E
Actor, Gary Sinese, Portrays Harry Truman and George Wallace in Separate TV Productions
Bobbi McCaughey of Des Moines Gives Birth to Septuplets
Lee P. Brown Becomes the First Black Mayor of Houston
Ellen DeGeneres "Comes Out" in an April Episode of Her TV Sitcom, *Ellen*

QUOTES

"(F.D.R.) electrified the farms and hollows, but even more important, he electrified
the nation, instilling confidence with every tilt of his head and boom of his laugh."
      Bill Clinton at Roosevelt Memorial Dedication

"Wishing to escape hawks, doves, gurus and rock acid, I took to the road."
      On the Road CBS Television
      Charles Kuralt (1934-1997)

"I see God in every human being. When I wash the leper's wounds I feel I am
nursing the Lord himself. Is it not a beautiful experience?"
      Mother Teresa (Agnes Gonxha Bojaxhiu 1910-1997)

INCIDENTALS AND TRIVIA

Spanish Marijuana Growers Stage Best Cannabis Crop Contest But Judges End Up in No
      Condition to Pick a Winner

1998 *The President Is Impeached*

WORLD

Accord Is Reached in Ireland between Catholics and Protestants
India and Pakistan Test Below-Ground Nuclear Weapons
Israel and the PLO Reach an Understanding in Land for Peace
US Embassies in Kenya and Tanzania Are Bombed
US Strikes at Iraqi Military Targets for Their Lack of Cooperation in On-Site Inspections

NATION

The Nation Has a Budget Surplus of 70 Billion. First Since 1969
46 States Accept 206 Billion Settlement with Tobacco Companies
The Explicit Clinton-Lewinsky Scandal Shocks the Nation
US House of Representatives Votes for Two Articles of Impeachment

DISASTER

Hurricane Mitch Kills over 7,000 in Honduras and Guatemala
A Swissair MD-11 Jetliner Crashes off Nova Scotia, Killing All 229 People Aboard

LIFESTYLE

Nearly 60 Million Americans Have Cell Phones (see 1983)
New Words in the Everyday Vocabulary Include: *Internet, Website, Modem* and *Websurfing*
The New Twenty Dollar Bill Looks Funny, But It Should Deter Counterfeiters
The Top 1% (2.7 Million) of Americans Have as Many After Tax Dollars to Spend as the
    Bottom 100 Million, Double That of Just 20 Years Ago (see 1977)

SCIENCE AND TECHNOLOGY

Nineteen European Nations Sign Treaty Banning Human Cloning
The First Pieces of the International Space Station Are Assembled in Orbit
AIDS Deaths Are Down 47% in One Year Due Largely to Improved Treatment Methods

BUSINESS AND INDUSTRY

Bank of America and Nationsbank Merge
Citicorp and Travelers Group Merge to Form Citigroup
Daimler Benz and Chrysler Merge to Form Daimler Chrysler
Volkswagen Buys Rolls Royce from England's Vickers
Compac Computer Buys Digital Equipment Corporation (DEC)
The Dow Jones Industrial Average Breaks 9,000
The Standard and Poor's 500 Stock Index Breaks the 1,000 Level for the First Time

CONSUMER PRODUCTS AND SERVICES

The Viagra Impotence Pill Receives Overwhelming Acceptance
Microsoft Introduces the Windows 98 Operating System
Volkswagen Sells a Retro Looking "New Beetle." It's a Hit with Younger Drivers
Excedrin Is Approved by the FDA as an Over-the-Counter Treatment for Migraine Headaches
Hand-Held Computers and Personal Digital Assistants (PDAs) Are Much in Demand

PRICES

Movie Ticket	$7.00
Personal Computer	Below $1,000 for Entry Level Models

SPORTS

Cal Ripkin Jr. Ends His Consecutive Game Streak After 2,632 Games
Mark McGuire (70) and Sammy Sosa (66) Both Top Roger Maris' Season 61 Home Run
     Record (see 1961)

ARTS AND MEDIA

MOVIE

Beloved	Oprah Winfrey, Danny Glover
Saving Private Ryan	Tom Hanks, Matt Damon, Tom Sizemore
The Mask of Zorro	Antonio Bandaras, Catherine Zeta-Jones
Shakespeare in Love	Joseph Fiennes, Ben Affleck, Judi Dench, Gwyneth Paltrow
Star Trek: Insurrection	Patrick Stewart, Jonathan Frakkes, Brent Spiner
There's Something About Mary	Cameron Diaz, Ben Stiller, Matt Dillon
The Truman Show	Jim Carrey, Laura Linney, Ed Harris

TV

Felicity	Kerl Russell

BOOK

A Man in Full	Thomas Wolfe
Charming Billy	Alice McDermott
Personal History	Katherine Graham
Angela's Ashes	Frank McCourt

MUSIC

Ray of Light	Madonna
Taming the Tiger	Joni Mitchell
Theatro	Willie Nelson
Pilgrim	Eric Clampton
When You Believe	Whitney Houston, Mariah Carey
Blues on the Bayou	B.B. King

PEOPLE

Elton John Is Knighted for His Services to Music
John Glenn at 77, Returns to <u>Space</u> Aboard the Space Shuttle Discovery

QUOTES

"May you live to be 100 and may the last voice you hear be mine."
     Frank Sinatra (1915-1998)

"I'm back in the saddle again. Out where a friend is a friend."
     Gene Autrey (1907-1998)

COMMENTARY

"My, my, how far we have come in this century! The advances in science, technology and medicine have been particularly striking and 1900 now seems quaint, almost unreal. For most Americans we close out the century, blessed with a lifestyle that could not have even been imagined when the century started.

"Yet, there is much inequality and a growing, dangerous gap between rich and poor. We have accomplished much and for that we can be rightly proud. But the bounty of progress must extend into all of American life and the entire world as well."

Bill Goodpage

1999 *As the Millennium Approaches*

WORLD

NATO Bombs Yugoslavia for 58 Days to Stop Albanian Ethnic Cleansing in Kosovo
Serbs Agree to Withdraw 40,000 Troops from Kosovo to Stop NATO Bombing
The Kosovo Liberation Army Is Demilitarized as Ethnic Albanians Return Home
Ehud Barak Soundly Defeats Benjamin Netanyahu in Israeli Elections
India and Pakistan Continue Their War of Words and Sporadic Air Battles
The International Criminal Tribunal Charges Yugoslav President Slobodon Milosevic and
      Four Other Serbs of Crimes against Humanity
Protests Break Out in Iran for Greater Democracy
The Euro Becomes the Common European Currency

NATION

Senate Acquits Clinton of Both the Perjury and Obstruction of Justice Impeachment Articles
Congressional Probe Accuses China of Stealing US Nuclear Secrets
The Senate Passes but House Rejects Gun Control Measures in Wake of High School Shootings
Clinton Calls to Keep Guns from Kids and to Curb Media Violence Marketed to Children

ENVIRONMENT

The American Bald Eagle, Now Up to 5,800 Breeding Pairs, Will Be Removed from the
      Government's Endangered Species List (see 1963)

LIFESTYLE

Life Expectancy in the US Is Now 78 Years—74 for Men, 83 Women (see 1900)
One Half of US Households Now Own a Personal Computer (see 1995)
Public Accepts Electronic Internet Shopping (E-commerce) as Safe and Reliable
Wireless Personal Communication Like Cellular Phones and Pagers Are the Norm

DISASTER

Turkish Earthquake Kills Over 15,000 People
Colombian Earthquake Kills Over 1,000 People

SCIENCE AND TECHNOLOGY

Bertrand Piccard and Brian Jones Make the First Nonstop Balloon Trip Around the World
US Astronauts Repair and Leave Supplies at the Space Station for a Permanent Crew in 2000
DNA Matching Now Being Used to Identify Unknown Soldiers from Earlier Wars
Mars Global Surveyor Probe Yields Stunning Three Dimensional Photos of the Red Planet

BUSINESS AND INDUSTRY

Ford Buys Volvo's Automotive Operations
General Motors Acquires the Hummer Vehicle Rights from AM General
The Dow Jones Industrial Average Breaks 10,000, then 11,000

CONSUMER PRODUCTS AND SERVICES

Ford Sells Excursion, which at 19 Feet and Four Tons, Is the Biggest SUV Built to Date
Palm Corders with Wireless Internet Access Are Now Available for the Very Mobile
Get a Free Computer by Signing Up for a Two-Year Internet Access Contract
With Added Taxes to Discourage Smoking, Cigarettes Are Up to $3.00 a Pack (see 1968)

We Have Not Eradicated Hate   1999

SPORTS

Michael Jordan Retires from Professional Basketball
US Women's Soccer Team Beats China to Capture the World Cup
Baseball Salaries of 5 Million Are Common. Top Players Make 12-15 Million

ARTS AND MEDIA

MOVIE	*Star Wars Episode I*	Liam Neeson
	Notting Hill	Julia Roberts, Hugh Grant
	The Muse	Albert Brooks, Andie MacDowell, Sharon Stone
	The Thomas Crown Affair	Pierce Brosnan, Rene Russo
	Runaway Bride	Julia Roberts, Richard Gere
	American Beauty	Kevin Spacey, Annette Bening
	Breakfast of Champions	Nick Nolte, Bruce Willis
	Double Jeopardy	Ashley Judd, Tommy Lee Jones
	Random Hearts	Harrison Ford, Kristen Scott-Thomas
	Anywhere But Here	Susan Sarandan, Rachel Portman
	Bicentennial Man	Robin Williams, Sam Neill
	The Straight Story	Richard Farnsworth, Sissy Spacek
TV	*Who Wants to Be a Millionaire?*	Regis Philbin
	The Sopranos	James Gandolfini
	Action	Jay Mohr, Illeana Douglas
	The West Wing	Rob Lowe, Bradley Whitford, Moira Kelly
BOOK	*'Tis*	Frank McCourt
	Children Are From Heaven	John Gray
	The Gifts of the Jews	Thomas Cahill

PEOPLE

At $90 Billion, Bill Gates Is the Richest Man in the World (see 1901,1909)
Sergei Krushchev, Son of Former Soviet Premier, Nikita Kruschev, Becomes a US Citizen
Col. Eileen Collins Is the First Woman to Command a US Shuttle Space Mission
John F. Kennedy Jr., His Wife and Sister-in-Law, Die in a Plane Crash near Martha's Vineyard
Janet Reno Calls for an Independent Investigation of the 1993 Branch Davidian Disaster
George W. Bush Jr. Collects a Record $60 Million for His 2000 Presidential Bid
Bill and Hillary Clinton Buy a 1.7 Million Home in Chappaqua, New York, Fueling Evidence
    That Hillary Will Run for the Senate From That State in 2000

REFLECTION

The number of new cases of measles in the US is so small, that the Center for
Disease Control (CDC) considers the disease eradicated. New cases are
believed to be imported. Measles then, has joined the ranks of smallpox,
diphtheria and other diseases that are gone from the American scene as the
century comes to an end.

COMMENTARY

"At every World's Fair this century, the pundits have offered
views of future life. Other than predicting that things will be better,
they have generally been wrong. I certainly don't know what the next
century will bring but it will certainly be exciting, and challenging,
probably even more so than this *Astonishing Century!*"

"Miss Picky"
Irene English

Person Index

219

References

Allen, Frederick Lewis *The Big Change - America Transforms Itself 1900-1950,* Harper & Row 1952

Benford, Timothy B. *The World War II Quiz and Fact Book,* Harper and Row 1982

Binney, Ruth (editor) *The Origins of Everyday Things*, Reader's Digest Association, 1999

Brooks, Tim and Marsh, Earl, *The Complete Directory to Prime Time Network and Cable TV Shows 1946-Present,* Ballantine Books, New York, 1995

Buxton, Frank & Owen, Bill *The Big Broadcast 1920-1950*, Viking Press 1972

Campling, Elizabeth *Portrait of a Decade 1900-1909*, B.T. Batsford, Ltd., London 1990

Carruth, Gorton *The Encyclopedia of American Facts and Dates*, Harper Collins 1993

Corey, Melinda and Ochoa, George *American History: The New York Public Library Book of Answers,* Simon & Shuster 1993

Csida, Joseph and June, *American Entertainment,* Billboard Publications 1978

Edelstein, Andrew and McDonough, Kevin *The Seventies From Hot Pants to Hot Tubs,* Dutton, New York 1990

Ellis, Edward Robb, *A Nation In Torment The Great Depression 1929-1939*, Coward-McCann, New York 1970

Everson, William K., *American Silent Film,* Oxford University Press 1978

Grant, Neil *Chronicle of 20th Century Conflict,* Smithmark Publishers, Inc. 1993

Gwinn, Alison (editor) *The 100 Greatest Stars of All Time,* Time, Inc. 1997

Klein, Reinhard, *Family History Logbook*, Betterway Books, Cincinnati, Ohio, 1996

Langley, Veronica B. *The Nobel Prize*, Barnes & Noble Books, New York, 1999

Maltin, Leonard (editor) *1997 Movie and Video Guide,* Penguin Books 1997

Marshall, Richard (editor) *Great Events of the 20th Century,* The Reader's Digest Association, 1977

McCutcheon, Mark **Everyday Life from Prohibition through World War II**, Writer's Digest Books 1995

O'Conner, John (editor) *American History American Television,* Frederick Ungar Publishing Company 1983

Saturday Evening Post, *Reflections of a Decade 1901-1910,* Curtis Publishing Company, Indianapolis 1980

Schlesinger Jr., Arthur M. (editor) *The Almanac of American History,* G.P. Putman's Sons, 1983

(Staff) *The 1990 Information Please Almanac,* Houghton Mifflin Company, 1990

(Staff) *Life: The First Fifty Years 1936-1986* Little, Brown & Company 1986

(Staff) *The Literary Almanac 1900-to the Present* MJF Books, New York, 1997

(Staff) *The New York Times Page One*, Galahad Books, New York, 1998

(Staff) ***Our Glorious Century,*** The Reader's Digest Association 1994

(Staff) ***Statistical Abstract of the United States,*** The Reference Press 1995

Stern, Jane & Michael ***Encyclopedia of Pop Culture,*** Harper Collins 1992

Van Tune, C., ***Motor Trend 50th Anniversary Collector's Edition***, Petersen
     Publishing, 1999

Walker, John, ***Halliwell's Film and Video Guide 1999***, Harper Collins Publishers,
     N.Y. 1999

Wilk, Max ***The Golden Age of Television,*** Delacorte Press 1976

Wright, John W. (editor) ***The Universal Almanac 1996,*** Andrews and McMeel,
     1996